THE HEATHEN CHINEE

*A Study of American Attitudes
toward China, 1890–1905*

Ohio State University Press

THE
HEATHEN
CHINEE

A Study of American Attitudes

toward China, 1890–1905

Robert McClellan

For Sara, Mary, Karen,
Sara, and Martha

Acknowledgments

The fashioning of this study has created an indebtedness to friends and colleagues beyond my ability to repay. Without the continuing encouragement of Professor Paul A. Varg, whatever there is of value in these pages would never have reached its present form. I should also like to thank the anonymous readers who reviewed the manuscript for the Ohio State University Press for their helpful criticisms and suggestions, and Weldon A. Kefauver and Robert S. Demorest, director and editor of the Press, for their thoughtful assistance. Mrs. Phyllis Pennell produced the final typewritten manuscript with such dispatch and accuracy that it relieved the author of much of the strain usually associated with that task. The staff in the manuscript room of the Library of Congress was very helpful, particularly in making suggestions for locating letters which were uncatalogued. I am also indebted to the director of the Massachusetts Historical Society and the fine people there for granting access to the papers of Henry Cabot Lodge, and to the staff at the Houghton Library, Harvard University, for help with the Rockhill Papers. My own family have contributed their support in many ways, not the least of which was their patience and understanding toward the many separations caused by the preparation of the manuscript. I am particularly indebted to my wife for her support and encouragement, the absence of which would have made the whole project a joyless and even impossible task.

R. McC.

June, 1970

Contents

Introduction

It is the purpose of this study to explore the background of American orientation to China and to illuminate the image which was shaped at the turn of the century as a result of the confrontation between this nation and an emerging China. The impression of the Oriental acquired during those formative years became a part of the American attitude of later decades and still influences our understanding of the Chinese.

Prior to 1894 the major point of encounter between Americans and Chinese was that of immigration. American ships and goods made their appearance in the East during the nineteenth century, and American missionaries and diplomats collected converts and defended the national interest; but it was not until Chinese laborers appeared in California that Americans really became aware of China. The arrival of the Chinese was welcomed at first because a railroad needed building and the Chinese were willing to accept the difficult and dangerous tasks which that job required. But later as they entered into the labor market and into American life, their presence provoked resentment, antagonism, and finally legislation to prevent any more from coming. This was the nation's first real experience with the Chinese.

The second major encounter took shape after the nationwide agitation for exclusion legislation had diminished. It was in essence a three-dimensioned experience, in which the missionary played a prominent role. These were the years when ministers spoke enthusiastically to their congregations of the responsibility of Christians to carry the gospel to all corners of the globe. It was a time when laymen and professionals alike made decisions of commitment which resulted in years of toil in a strange land under severe hardship. Students left college campuses following the tune of the evangelist and went to China to work. The stories which filtered back, the impressions gained, the reasons given to justify the cost, all had a formative impact on American concepts of the Chinese.

The second dimension of the experience with the Chinese after the immigration imbroglio concerned commercial contacts with China. Though far less active than their religious counterparts, the evangelists of American business were equally as vocal. They bore loud and public testimony to the need for new markets and the opportunity presented by the unsophisticated wants of the Chinese. If China was an opportunity to win converts for Christ, it was also an opportunity to apply the tenets of the American gospel of commercial enterprise. God and commerce had become partners, and the good life had become inseparable from material success; therefore, increased trade with China would serve a doubly constructive purpose. Consequently it was out of the needs of business as well as religion that the image of China emerged.

The third dimension of the experience of these years was the awakening concern as to what China's modernization might mean to the family of nations and to the United States in particular. American statesmen were speaking increasingly of the nation's responsibility to provide leadership for the whole world, particularly for those oppressed peoples whose economic, political, and religious framework deprived them of the full fruits of the human experience. These years were a time for thinking again about first principles of national life and about the kinds of relationships which should be established as contact with the world expanded. The question raised by the giant stirring in the East was whether a new peril or a new opportunity for the Western world was rising on the horizon. The answer to this question, especially for the United States, rested to a large degree on the nature of the interpretation of the Chinese.

During the years preceding and following 1894, at the time of the immigration controversy and in the years when religious and national interest ran high, a single attitude stood forth. Those Americans who had direct contact with the Chinese, as well as those whose interests required an assessment of them, based their evaluation upon private needs and not upon the realities of Chinese life. Interpretations of the Chinese—by politicians interested in office, by labor leaders, businessmen, missionaries, diplomats and statesmen —derived almost without exception from individual and immediate concerns rather than from an understanding of the Chinese. Many of the things said about the Chinese were true, but in isolation they presented a false picture. Consequently the response of Americans to the Chinese during these years can be best understood in terms of making "their China" fit their biases.

THE HEATHEN CHINEE

A Study of American Attitudes
toward China, 1890–1905

1

Chinese Immigration
and the Rationale
for Exclusion

". . . For ways that are dark / And for tricks that are vain, / The Heathen Chinee is peculiar . . ."—Bret Harte

Ah Fe was his name, and he was a pagan just like all the rest of his brother Mongolians. He talked in a shrill voice, babbling heathenish jargon which no one except another slant-eyed, pig-tailed Celestial could understand. The people in the town might bring their laundry to him, but in their view he was good for little else than to wash their dirty clothes. One sunny California day, Ah Fe was sent on an errand to San Francisco via Sacramento. Traveling was rugged even for a native son of the west, but for a "Chinaman" it was downright dangerous. According to the story told about his journey, Ah Fe was twice playfully thrown from the top of the stagecoach by an "intelligent but deeply intoxicated caucasian whose moral nature was shocked at riding with one addicted to opium smoking." At Hangtown, where he changed to another stage, he was thoughtfully beaten by a passing stranger, "purely as an act of Christian supererogation." At Dutch Flat he was robbed by "well-known hands from unknown motives," and in Sacramento he was arrested on suspicion of "being something or other" but was later released when no charge was brought against him. When he arrived at last in San Francisco, he was freely stoned by the children of the public schools. There is no record of how he fared on his return trip, at least not as Bret Harte tells the story.[1]

Ah Fe may be slightly fictional, but the Chinese who swung off the stage at Great Falls, Montana, on March 23, 1893, was a living member of the American west. The *Tribune* was on top of the story in a flash, and the lead that evening described how "the news spread like a prairie fire that a pig-tailed Celestial had planted his wooden-soled shoes upon the sacred soil of Great Falls —a city where the people of his race are excluded." That same evening a meeting of the local labor leaders gave vigorous and unanimous assent that there would be no Chinese laundry in Great Falls because, as everyone knew, to allow one of his race to enter was to open the gates to all. The bewildered visitor was arrested amidst a howling mob and carried to the edge of town, where he was sent on his way with appropriate ceremonies. The *Tribune* concluded the next day that "there is no room for the almond-eyed sons of China in this city . . . no pig-tailed saffron will be allowed to call this city his home." The incident in Great Falls was typical of town after town in the west and also in the east, where violent prejudices often produced violent action similar to the beating of a Chinese laundryman in Washington, D. C.[2]

The arrival of the Chinese came about in a precipitous

manner; only forty-two were residing in San Francisco in 1853, but two years later there were between three and four thousand.[3] Immigration rocketed in succeeding years: nearly 40,000 Chinese entered in 1882 just prior to the enactment of the exclusion legislation of that year. Estimates of the total Chinese population in the country varied widely and usually reflected the point of view of the analyst. Dennis Kearny, leader of the anti-Chinese movement in California, estimated the Chinese population in his state at 200,000 in 1876, with 75,000 in San Francisco alone.[4] However, in October of the same year a joint committee of Congress placed the figure at 117,331 for the entire state; yet four years later the U. S. census indicated a Chinese population for the whole nation of 105,448.[5] It is not possible to adjust these figures satisfactorily, nor is it really necessary to do so; the point is that the Chinese did come in sufficient numbers to arouse the concern, rightly or wrongly, of a large number of Americans.

In the 1850s Americans on the West Coast did not view the Chinese as heathens, but by the time the stage carrying the first Chinese had arrived in Great Falls, their opinion had changed. Originally the Chinese came as laborers to take advantage of the high wages and plentiful supply of work stimulated by railroad construction, farming, and mining. But when the demand for labor in California slackened in the 1870s, the qualities which had made the Chinese desirable as laborers in the first place made them feared and hated by other workers. The uneasiness of California workmen at the presence of Chinese cheap labor was exploited by politicians both in California and Washington. Anti-Chinese agitation showed a marked increase immediately preceding every presidential election in the 1870s and 1880s. California was usually a doubtful state, and the closeness of the political contests during those years magnified the issue of the Chinese into one of national importance.[6]

The anti-Chinese attitude of the West Coast soon spread to the rest of the nation. Because the Chinese laborers were from the coolie class in China, it was easy to emphasize their undesirable characteristics. Most of what was said about the crowded, filthy conditions in Chinatown was probably true. Opium-smoking was fairly widespread among Chinese laborers, and a strong criminal element was also present. But the important fact about these unfavorable descriptions is that the many attractive qualities of the Chinese were almost completely ignored. What Americans said about the Chinese was true, but it was only one part of the truth. The undesirable aspects of Chinese life were emphasized because of the widespread antagonism toward the Chinese in the United States.

It was not just the laborer in California who resented and feared the presence of the Chinese. The anti-Chinese feeling was spread across the nation and influenced every level of American society. Literary magazines such as *Scribner's, Century,* and the *Atlantic Monthly* carried articles describing the low character of the Chinese. Journals with a reputation for honest reporting and unbiased comment on the contemporary scene, such as the *Outlook* and the *Independent,* shared in the anti-Chinese sentiment. The *Arena,* a liberal reform magazine in the 1890s and usually in the lead on progressive issues, also supported Chinese exclusion. Professional journals such as the *Engineering Magazine, American Architect,* and *Political Science Quarterly* carried articles written from an anti-Chinese viewpoint. Religious magazines (including missionary publications), popular weeklies, and monthly reviews such as the *Review of Reviews* and *Forum,* all spoke from an attitude hostile to the Chinese. The anti-Chinese feeling was shared by writers across the nation and was essentially a national attitude.

The presence of the Chinese in the country in increasing numbers stimulated a growing concern over the effect which they might have on economic and social institutions. The result was that exclusion legislation was suggested as a means of curbing the threat which they were thought to represent. It was through the debates over exclusion that the rest of the country outside of the West Coast became aware of the Chinese. The question of excluding the Chinese expanded into a consideration of all things Chinese, and in the process Americans were exposed to some rather narrow interpretations of oriental institutions. A book by a missionary in China, Arthur Smith, contained one of the most influential and at the same time most distorted descriptions of Chinese life and culture ever to appear in the United States.[7] The author's conclusion that the Chinese could endure greater amounts of pain because of a less highly developed nervous system was commonly accepted at the turn of the century.

First contacts of Americans in San Francisco with the Chinese were typical. Fresh from the Far East with its consignment of freight and coolies, a ship from the Orient would tie up at a San Francisco wharf to disgorge its human cargo. Herded down the gangplank into the frantic melee on the dock, the Chinese were identified and gathered into groups around the wagons which would carry them to the waiting flatcars and boxcars. They had been invited to come by the railroads because they were needed as construction workers to help accomplish the vast project of connecting the West Coast with Chicago and points east. Railroad agents had gone to China to describe the need for laborers, the high wages, and plentiful work, and to arrange for passage, sometimes with the assistance of a United States consul.[8] Other agents met them in San Francisco and hurried them to the construction sites where the shortage of white laborers made their presence so desirable. Some Chinese also came to work in the mines, to help develop the barren regions of the west, and to pick the fruit.

The Chinese had been told that they were needed; they came; and then in a few years they were told to leave. For twenty years the Chinese worked alongside European immigrants and native Americans. They marched in the Fourth of July parades, and the Chinese display was often the most elaborate and vigorously applauded. In 1868 the Chinese merchants of San Francisco were present at a banquet honoring their contributions to the life and well-being of that city.[9] Occasionally instances of persecution of the Chinese by members of other minorities occurred, but they were of a minor nature. In the same year that the Chinese merchants were banqueted in San Francisco, the Burlingame Treaty was applauded in that city as the keystone of a new era of prosperity based on Chinese immigration. In 1869 the Central Pacific met the Union Pacific in Utah. Nine years later the Nevada mines collapsed. In between these dates the presence of the Chinese had changed from a blessing to a curse in the minds of most Californians.

Hostility toward the Chinese was increased by agitators like Dennis Kearny. When the overflow crowd from an anti-Chinese mass meeting gathered on the large sandy lot adjacent to San Francisco's city hall, he exhorted them in excited tones to defend their jobs and homes from the Chinese peril.

These "sandlotters" became the nucleus for the agitation which culminated in the first exclusion act of 1882. In the presidential campaign of 1879–80 California and Oregon were doubtful states. The Republicans were the first to seek the support of the anti-Chinese sentiment in those areas by sending a commission to China to "investigate" the immigration problem and discuss changes in the treaty of 1868.[10] The instructions to the commissioners were vague, but the mission accomplished its main purpose when California and Oregon voted Republican in the election. In 1881 the terms of the Burlingame Treaty were modified with the consent of China, and the following year a restrictive act suspended immigration from China for ten years. In 1888 a new treaty strengthening the restrictions on immigration was drawn up and presented to China; but she debated "too slowly," and Congress rushed through a new exclusion act, with the Scott Act, which, with the exceptions of merchants and diplomats, even barred Chinese then on leave from the country.[11]

The people who lived on the West Coast, particularly in California, were the first to come into contact with the Chinese in America, and their attitude had a formative influence on the rest of the nation. "John Chinaman" (or even just "John") soon became the derisive epithet for the Chinese immigrant, indicating the facelessness and anonymity attributed to him by his American hosts. "Only John!" warned one author on the West Coast in 1896, "yet in a few years he has overrun the coast."[12] Many Californians were hardly aware of the presence of the Chinese at first because they were employed in mining and railroad construction, occupations which took them away from the centers of population. But by the 1870s a sizable number had congregated in San Francisco, and almost every California town had at least one or two Chinese inhabitants.

Although the most vocal opponents of the Chinese were the labor unions, newspapers also routinely printed anti-Chinese articles and editorials. The San Francisco *Call* remarked in 1892 that "it ought to be understood at Washington by Republicans that a failure upon the part of the Senate to assist in the passage of an effective restriction law will deeply affect the future prospects of that party upon this coast. Our citizens are so deeply imbued with the idea that the Chinese are injurious to our civilization that they will sacrifice party obligations to get rid of them."[13]

In Seattle the Chinese were described as "opium-sodden," in Walla Walla as barbarians, and in Los Angeles their "fatuous ignorance," "treacherous mendacity, and "heathenish ways" were thought to separate them from the civilized world.[14] The *Times* also revealed its indebtedness to Arthur Smith's descriptions of the Chinese in his *Chinese Characteristics* by noting that "the Chinaman is never moved by the suffering of others" because "he is callous, cowardly, treacherous, a puzzle to the western mind."[15] In Denver at the time of the Boxer Rebellion the *Rocky Mountain News* announced that the actions of the Chinese against Westerners represented "the most atrocious crime against humanity and civilization that has been committed since the barbarians sacked Rome in the fifth century."[16]

The rest of the country usually followed the lead of Californians in their attitudes toward the Chinese. The *Review of Reviews* concluded in 1892 that "the Pacific Coast understands the Chinese question better than the rest of the country."[17] The magazine felt that the Pacific Coast viewpoint had won acceptance in the east because it was the right view. Several years later, Francis G. Newlands, senator from Nevada and author of the Newlands Irrigation Bill, described the process in California whereby educated people who had at first thought that the anti-Chinese feeling was based on ignorant prejudice came to realize the validity of the charges against Chinese competition.[18] He reached the conclusion that thinking men in California and elsewhere had come to realize that the Chinese ought to be excluded. There were some editors of national magazines who found fault with the radical views expressed by the so-called sand-lot orators; but most of the vocal opinion in the country accepted the lead of California, particularly in the early 1890s, because it was felt that Californians had the most experience with the Chinese. Several years later Henry Cabot Lodge observed that 90 percent of the country supported the administration in a vigorous policy of restricting Chinese immigration.[19]

The open dislike manifested toward the Chinese in the 1870s and 1880s received a fresh stimulus in 1891 when Thomas J. Geary, representative from California, submitted a bill to the House reaffirming the provisions of the old Chinese Exclusion Act of 1882 and adding a few new ones. The Geary Act of 1892 provoked a debate which marked a high point for Chinese exclusion agitation in the 1890s. Briefly, the feature of the Geary Act which differed most from the Act of 1882 was the requirement that all Chinese in the country register and submit to identification procedures, including photographing, or suffer the penalty of imprisonment and deportation. It was the prospect of being able to photograph every Chinese in the United States which caused the San Francisco *Chronicle* to proclaim enthusiastic support for the bill. Without this provision and given the look-alike appearance of the Chinese, it would be impossible to ever fully control immigration, the editor concluded.[20]

In his defense of the bill Geary argued that the nation had a right as well as a duty to protect itself from the evils of "asiatic slavery."[21] American labor did not have to suffer the consequences of competition from "degrading" Chinese labor. Sentiment, or human rights, he said, had no application in government because the first duty of a government was to protect its citizens. He frankly described the Chinese as undesirable, accusing them of working for as little as five dollars a month and living on six cents a day. The Chinese would degrade our civilization because a Chinese laborer did not bring any wife or children with him. He did not set up a family but acted only in his own interest, and if the American laborer was forced to compete with the Chinese, then American labor would be reduced to the level of Chinese labor. Nothing should stand in the way of exclusion. "American interests in the far West, the maintenance of American civilization and the just protection of American labor from Chinese competition is of more consequence than the profits of the Chinese trade, or the maintenance of missionary stations in China."[22]

There was significant public support for the position which Geary espoused. The San Francisco *Call* and the *Examiner,* understandably, were entirely in favor of the bill. These newspapers had been leaders in the exclusion agitation, and their chief concern seemed to be that the new provisions might not be strong enough. The *Bulletin* and the *Argonaut,* both San Francisco papers, also supported this view. The eastern magazines did not follow the lead of the California newspapers unreservedly, but there was a good measure of support. *Harper's Weekly* suggested in 1891 that the exclusion of the Chinese had been successful in ridding the country of an undesirable element and should be continued.[23] In fact, said the editor, the same methods used against the Chinese might be employed with profit in behalf of the criminal element among European immigrants. Terrence V. Powderly spoke for American laboring men when he warned that "the substitution of the Mongolian slave for the American freeman, the abandonment of home for the street and slum and the final overthrow of the republic" were likely consequences if a strong exclusion bill was not passed.[24]

In addition to strong public support one of the most interesting aspects of the controversy surrounding the Geary Act was the Chinese reaction. The Chinese in America had their own system for maintaining order within their communities. An organization called the "Six Companies," a compilation of six secret societies with headquarters in San Francisco, claimed the allegiance of most Chinese in America. When the Geary bill became law, the "Six Companies" organized a campaign to test its constitutionality. Every Chinese was encouraged to contribute two dollars to provide money for legal fees. The "Six Companies" announced that any Chinese who refused to register under the Geary Act would be provided with legal counsel. Pressure was applied to persuade Chinese not to register in order to make a massive protest against the law. The estimated two hundred thousand dollars which was collected was used to guide test cases through the courts. One of these finally reached the Supreme Court, which reversed a state court decision and pronounced the law constitutional.

This action of the "Six Companies" angered many Americans, who pointed out that such behavior was, in their view, characteristic of the debased and devious nature of the Chinese. The *Overland Monthly* in California published an article describing the attitude of the Chinese toward the law and the pressures placed upon them to prevent their compliance.[25] The author explained how notices were posted in San Francisco's Chinatown threatening violence to any Chinese who registered. Threats of torture and death were made against the few who did comply, so that over 90 percent of the Chinese failed to register. Those few who did register often produced "hired witnesses" who swore that the Chinese in question was a merchant and not a laborer and therefore entitled to leave the country and return if he wished. In the nation at large the opinion of West Coast writers received substantial support by editors and other commentators who thought it characteristic as well as despicable that the Chinese should be allowed to circumvent American laws.[26] The Geary Act was generally viewed as "one of the best of the late congress," and it was felt that the Chinese had been ill-advised not to obey it.[27]

The exclusion act of 1892 was limited to a duration of ten years; therefore, in 1901 the debate was reopened, though on a greatly reduced scale. A minister from Rockford, Illinois, summed up public opinion when he said, "There is little doubt that the Chinese exclusion law will be reenacted. Organized labor demands it almost to a man, legislators of both political parties favor it, and in doing so express the sentiment of their constituents."[28] James D. Phelan, mayor of San Francisco, reported that a convention of 3,000 delegates from county boards, municipal bodies, labor unions, and commercial and civic associations had voted unanimously to ask Congress to reenact the Geary exclusion law.[29] A writer in the *Arena*, a liberal reform magazine, thought that exclusion was a domestic concern only and ought to be decided strictly on the basis of American interests.[30] Several articles in 1904 summed up the whole problem of exclusion and concluded that the law had been effective as well as justified and might well be extended to other immigrants. Dr. Allen McLaughlin of the United States Public Health and Marine Hospital Service, with many years experience in immigration matters on the East Coast, said that the exclusion act had worked fairly well and had confined the problem to the West Coast.[31] "Mongolian trickery" had found many ways to evade the act, but without it the "mass of yellow coolies" would have swept into "Illinois, Pennsylvania and every other state in the Union."[32] Six months later Theodore Roosevelt wrote to William Rockhill from the White House that although it was desirable to secure better treatment for Chinese students, businessmen, and travelers legally present in the country, "Chinese laborers must be kept out."[33]

The Chinese themselves deeply resented the exclusion and objected in particular to the restrictions placed upon their right to seek employment and to the regulations controlling their entry into the country. They protested, insofar as they could, against the restrictions on travel within the country and against the wage scales which were applied to their type of employment. However, it appears that their resentment was stimulated more by the law's clear implications of cultural and racial inferiority than by any other cause. For example, the requirement of the Geary Act of 1892 that all Chinese must register and be photographed was particularly galling. As more Chinese acquired economic status and a degree of social respect, the resentment grew.

In 1905, when exclusion legislation had been on the books for more than twenty years and much of the emotionalism had passed, the United States consul in Amoy, China, George Anderson, supported this interpretation. "Most [Chinese] students going abroad . . . avoid the United States . . . because of the emigration restrictions and the constant and annoying espionage and questioning," he said, and in particular they objected to being singled out because of their race.[34]

Ho Yow, the Chinese consul-general at the port of San Francisco, a longtime and respected resident in the United States, carefully summarized the nature of Chinese resentment at the turn of the century.[35] The Chinese did not particularly resent the accusation that they competed with American workmen and sent much of their money back to China because most of them came to the United States in order to profit from better employment opportunities and in fact did send money home. But they resented deeply the implication that they were a threat to the American way of life because of the claim that they were an immoral people. A few years later Wong Kai Kah, vice-commissioner of the Louisiana Purchase Exposition, said that the Chinese objected most to the abuses of personal dignity which were inherent in the procedures of the exclusion law.[36] He cited several rules which restricted the rights of the Chinese immigrant to obtain witnesses in his behalf, to seek legal advice, and to appeal unfavorable decisions. The most influential aspect of the developing relationship between Americans and Chinese was not that pertaining to the real differences existing between the two peoples but rather the irrational attitude adopted by the former against the latter.

The primary result of the debates over the question of

Chinese exclusion was to create in the minds of those Americans who took an interest in such matters a well-defined image of the Chinese. Because these debates were usually highly charged with emotion, it was no surprise that the Chinese image fared poorly in the hands of the politicians, editors, and others who engaged in the controversy. In almost every instance the issue of the presence of the Chinese was raised because some special interest group sought to profit by stirring up feelings of animosity against the Chinese. On one occasion it might be a California politician seeking reelection or advancement to a higher office; another, the mayor of a West Coast city or a local union leader in the east who invoked the spectre of the "heathen Chinaman" in order to gather support. In almost every instance the real merits of the Chinese as individuals were not debated because the purpose was not to establish true understanding but to seek special advantage. Although such tactics are common in politics, it was nevertheless unfortunate that our image of a people with whom we needed to construct a working relationship was nurtured in a climate so hostile to an understanding of the true nature of the Chinese people.

From the perspective of today those who are willing to do so can see that much of what passed for fact about the Chinese was mere fancy. Unpleasant characteristics were magnified into distortion, and a great many imaginative stories were circulated under the guise of eye-witness accounts. Testimonials of strange and devious behavior observed by those who traveled among the Chinese or by those who met them only occasionally (and then often for the sole purpose of describing their unfavorable characteristics) were given wide credence by the American people. Some of the distortion which occurred was probably due to honest misunderstanding encouraged by the unfamiliarity of oriental ways in Western eyes, but much of it seems to have been caused by strong prejudices against the Chinese.

Even though the picture which emerged from the agitation over exclusion legislation was not an accurate description of the Chinese character, a rationale for the new point of view was not lacking. The rationale was based upon the assumption that the Chinese were an inferior, backward race; and from this point of reference three lines of reasoning developed establishing beyond doubt for most Americans that the Chinese were morally, economically, and socially undesirable. The reasons put forward in support of this view were not always consistent. Descriptions of the Chinese as possessing one or another character trait were sometimes in conflict. He was popularly described as being both honest and devious, clean in his personal habits yet prone to live in filth. Consequently, the rationale for the exclusion of the Chinese was often ambiguous in its particulars but always faithful to its main goal of displaying the Chinese in his most unfavorable light.

At the center of the antagonism toward the Chinese was the belief that the Chinese were willing to work for less than any other workman in the country. According to one story originating on the West Coast, a man living on the outskirts of San Francisco let it be known that he had some wood that needed cutting. In a few days an Irishman came to his place and offered to do the work for seventy-five cents. The agreement was made, and the Irishman then passed word that he needed a Chinese to cut some wood. A citizen from the flowery kingdom appeared and agreed to perform the task for fifty cents. The Irishman, while enjoying thoughts of his newfound status as an employer, spent his twenty-five cents in a place where his fellows often congregate. Perhaps the episode tells us as much about attitudes toward the Irish as the Chinese, but the moral which circulated with the story affirmed that the Chinese worked so cheaply that even an Irishman could make money by hiring them.[37]

Those who claimed that many Chinese were well paid were angrily rebutted by labor's spokesmen, who pointed to the manufacturing concerns in California where Chinese labor had supplanted white girls and women. The Chinese had spread widely in the field of agriculture, where they were employed as harvesters of many crops, particularly fruit, in preference to caucasian labor. The *Chautauquan* carried an article in 1897 by the author of several stories and a book on China describing the ruthless methods of the Chinese in driving out competition.[38] In San Francisco he said that two Chinese opened a factory for making women's and children's shoes in a narrow alley adjacent to the main street in Chinatown. By cutting prices they captured all the local business, whereupon they opened a fancy store on the main street. The same attitude was often expressed by American consuls in China, who were convinced that no white man could compete against a Chinese. The ability of the Oriental to work hard on one or two hours' sleep and to thrive under working conditions which would exhaust other workers was legendary.[39]

The Chinese were best known for their activities as laundrymen. The explanations offered for their monopoly of this work vary; in actuality it was probably due to the lack of women available for the work, particularly in California. Many observers felt, however, that it was the sort of work for which "John Chinaman" was best suited. The patrons of Chinese laundries usually evidenced a sort of paternal concern for the Chinese who ran them, and one of the topics of daily conversation was a discussion of the merits and mysteries of the Chinese laundry. The Chinese laundry was also the subject of innumerable cartoons which depicted the absurdity of the Chinese way of doing things. An illustration of a Chinese laundryman at work, captioned "His Sprinkler," portrayed a Chinese dampening clothes about to be ironed by expectorating water from his mouth.[40]

Labor's attitude toward the Chinese was devoid of all such humor, however. The Chinese crowded out white workers from cigar, clothing, shoe, and shirt factories, from agricultural work, and from surface mining. Terence V. Powderly, commissioner-general of immigration, said in 1901: "No graver danger has ever menaced the workingmen of America than that which faces them when the possibility of lowering the bars at our seaports and border-lines to the Chinese is presented."[41] This opinion from the noted labor leader received support four years later from President Theodore Roosevelt in a political speech in Atlanta aimed at the ears of labor. In his speech the president discussed our reponsibility toward the non-laboring Chinese in order to appease southern concern over the cotton boycott in China, which was organized to protest American treatment of Chinese immigrants. "It is our clear duty, in the interest of our own wage-workers, to forbid all Chinese of the coolie class . . . from coming here. I am convinced that the well-being of our wage-workers demands the exclusion of the Chinese. . . ."[42]

The complaint of the California wage-workers against the economics of Chinese competition was the initial reason given for Chinese exclusion. But a more emotional and imaginative explanation of the undesirability of the Chinese was based on their supposed defects. One common attitude held that it was unsafe for white people, particularly women, to come into contact with Chinese lest they be "corrupted." For a few years a minor controversy raged over whether or not white girls should be allowed to teach the Chinese in missionary Sunday schools organized in some American cities.[43] It was reported that in some instances these girls had married Chinese "students."[44] Many people felt that it was not worth the "corruption" of white girls in order to save the soul of a "heathen." There was considerable doubt expressed that the Chinese could be converted by anybody, so degraded was their moral condition. Frederick J. Masters, a missionary among the Chinese in California, commented that they were "irredeemably and irretrievably bad and vile, as a rule, and all efforts to Christianize them only makes them greater hypocrites than ever."[45] *Century* magazine in November, 1896, contained a carefully written article by a mission worker in New York comparing the qualities of various immigrant groups there. One conclusion was that "popular opinion, when considering our foreign immigrants, has given the lowest rank among them to the Chinese."[46] Even fertile imaginations sometimes failed to supply the necessary terms of approbation. One writer despaired of finding the appropriate term when he concluded that "morally and ethically they are in a fourth dimension."[47]

So lethal was the influence of oriental immorality that the presence of a single Chinese in any small town was thought sufficient to bring on a kind of religious dry rot. "The mere advent of a Chinaman in a community is an almost certain sign of impending moral degradation. He carries shame and ruin and unspeakable disease wherever he goes."[48] The author of these words wished to remain anonymous, possibly because he preferred not to appear in their defense, although he did appeal to one of the new social sciences for corroboration by saying, "Sociologists have observed with wonder that apparently the mere presence of the Chinaman seems to work for demoralization in a community. Children and women, when subjected to the influence of the Mongol, develop viciousness of striking intensity."[49]

Because of his supposedly demoralizing effect upon the community, the Chinese was considered a threat to American civilization. Lyman Abbott, who was a liberal clergyman and editor of the *Outlook,* in commenting upon the exclusion act in 1902, remarked that Chinese immigrants were "of a persistently servile and alien population, whose presence is injurious to the standards alike of American labor and American citizenship."[50] In the same year an article in *Forum* by Truxton Beale, the former United States minister to Persia and an extensive traveler in the Orient, suggested that the presence of the Chinese threatened the American way of life because they threatened American prosperity.[51] The difficulty of documenting such generalizations did not prevent them from being given wide circulation. An article by a Baptist minister in the *Baptist Quarterly Review* in 1890 concluded that the Chinese should be excluded for a number of reasons, but most of all because they represented a moral peril to our civilization.[52] It was not only his moral character that threatened American civilization, it was his unwillingness to assimilate. *Harper's Weekly* thought that the Chinese were the most "undesirable of immigrants, because, with all their useful qualities, they cannot assimilate socially or politically or morally with Americans."[53]

It was often pointed out that the tendency of the Chinese toward dishonest dealings was confirmation of their lack of moral character. Countless stories were told which centered around the theme of the Chinese who hoodwinked competitors by a great variety of means, all of which were either outrightly dishonest or so disreputable that supposedly no white man would attempt them. One Chinese was reputed to have bought a tract of land in Mexico and then to have sold stock in a fictitious company to pay for it. Another story was told of a Chinese landlord who crowded his Chinese tenants into worse quarters than the previous American owner had done. One Chinese took over the importation of coolies into San Francisco and controlled the female slave trade. It was admitted that much of his success was due to his industry and business acumen, but the implication was that no decent man would work as hard as the Chinese did. This point of view was summarized by a real estate broker in San Francisco who said, "By his industry, suavity, and apparent childlike innocence, seconded by unequaled patience and the keenest business ability, the Chinaman is always the winner. Let white men set over him whatever guards they may, he can surpass them in treading the by-ways of tortuousness."[54]

Interestingly enough, despite their industry and sharp business methods, the Chinese were described as a servile race. Their natural propensity for serving in menial capacities and outright slavery was attested by a large number of observers.[55] Most people were aware of the Chinese in America only in their capacity as "coolies," laundry workers, or house servants. They generalized upon this fact to prove that the Chinese as a race were fitted only for the lowest kind of labor. Those who were unaware of the resistance offered by the "Six Companies" viewed apparent Chinese submissiveness under the exclusion laws as proof that the Chinese had no backbone. Sometimes this view was contested by others who also attacked Chinese character but who wished to paint a picture of active rather than passive evil. Accordingly, the Chinatown visitor who came away with an impression of the "meek inoffensive, non-resistant Chinaman" was thought to have been misled.[56] Far from being meek, the Mongolian was a fatalist, with a ferocious fighting instinct and total lack of concern for human life. The inconsistency does not require explanation as long as we remember that, whether his evil ways were thought to be passive or active, the purpose of such descriptions was to discredit the Chinese as being a creature of immorality.

In addition to moral and economic explanations, the rationale for excluding the Chinese from the American scene included a strong distaste for many features of Chinese social life. For example, considerable emphasis was given to the health problem which the Chinese were thought to pose. In San Francisco the board of health published several reports in the years prior to 1900 which sought to advise the people of that city of the serious threat to their health created by the presence of the Chinese.[57] The report described with unusual vigor and clarity the crowded living conditions among the Chinese in San Francisco which established an environment where diseases of all sorts could flourish. James D. Phelan, who served as mayor of that city at the turn of the century, was fond of referring to the Chinese as "the greatest single threat to the health and welfare of our city."[58]

Not only were the crowded living conditions and primitive sanitation practices looked upon with alarm but the Chinese were thought to be peculiarly susceptible to leprosy. In 1893 Edward Shakespeare, who contributed frequently to national magazines in his capacity as writer, traveler, and observer of the American scene, appealed for the establishment of a nationwide quarantine against the entrance of infected Chinese immigrants.[59] At the time of the leprosy scare in New York City in 1897, E. C. Spitzka, a medical doctor who often volunteered his services to public health agencies, suggested that the only factor which prevented leprosy from reaching epidemic proportions was the effective restriction of Chinese immigrants.[60] In that year and the following it was pointed out in several newspaper and magazine articles that those Americans who were anxious to annex Hawaii should remember that such an act would expose Americans to leprosy, the indigenous disease of Chinese social life.[61]

The social life of the Chinese was scored not only for its supposed threat to community health but also for its threat to community solidarity. It was charged, with considerable truth, that the Chinese kept to themselves, lived in their own colonies, did not join into community activities, and thus became a divisive element in any city where they lived. The presence of the Chinese was feared because the part of the city or town where they congregated, even though it was an area of only a few square blocks, soon took on the character of Chinese life and thus was viewed as a foreign settlement in the midst of an otherwise homogeneous community. Because such areas were filled with strange sights, smells, and sounds which were incomprehensible to Western senses, it seemed to many inhabitants that they had actually forfeited their rights to what was legitimately theirs.

Their complaint was justified to an extent because oriental ways did contrast sharply with the life in most American cities. The oriental manner of dress, particularly of the male, was a source of bewilderment and disgust for the self-made

American man. Trousers that looked like pajamas topped by a loose fitting blouse, both of shiny, brightly colored silk, seemed to speak of a peculiar if not perverted way of life.[62] The absence of women and children from the Chinese communities, though perfectly understandable in view of the expense of transporting and maintaining a family, was viewed with suspicion. Many of the Chinese stayed in the country only long enough to acquire enough dollars to enable them to return to China and establish themselves in financial security for the rest of their lives. As a result of these characteristics, and many others which are perfectly understandable to those who know the Orient but mysterious to most Americans of those years, the Chinese were viewed as interlopers, as foreigners who could never be assimilated into American society.

The rationale for excluding the Chinese was not manufactured out of whole cloth. The Chinese were present in the United States to compete for the high wages that meant financial security back in China. Because most of them who came were of the coolie class, they often appeared no more desirable than native Americans of a similar class. Chinese society was represented to Americans in an imperfect way by men who had come for other reasons than to establish permanent settlements. Yet the truth that lies within these circumstances was woven into cloth of imaginative colors and fanciful design. As more and more Americans became aware of the Chinese, the truth about them was irretrievably lost in the midst of exaggeration. Fancy became fact until, fed by prejudice, an image of the Chinese evolved which bore little relationship to the actual circumstances of Chinese life. The rationale for exclusion had its origins in areas of legitimate concern, but by 1894 the real Chinese were no longer to be identified with the myths about them which circulated in American life.

1. Bret Harte, "An Episode of Fiddletown," *The Writings of Bret Harte,* 20 vols. (Boston, 1899–1914), VII, 139.

2. "Boys Beat Chinaman," Washington *Post,* July 17, 1900.

3. "Our Immigration during 1904," *National Geographic Magazine* XVI (January, 1905), 16.

4. Sunyowe Pang, "The Chinese in America," *Forum* XXXII (January, 1902), 598–607.

5. Ibid.

6. See, for further information on this point, Elmer Clarence Sandmeyer, *The Anti-Chinese Movement in California* (Urbana, Ill., 1939).

7. Arthur H. Smith, *Chinese Characteristics* (New York, 1894).

8. Edward Bedloe to Secretary of State John Hay, April 7, 1898, *Despatches from U. S. Consuls in Canton, 1790–1906,* National Archives (Washington: Government Printing Office, 1947).

9. John Bonner, "Labor Question on the Pacific Coast," *Current Literature* X (May, 1892), 50–54.

10. Chester Holcombe, "The Restriction of Chinese Immigration," *Outlook* LXXXCI (April 23, 1904), 971–77.

11. F. J. Masters, "Our Treaties with China," *Californian* IV (June, 1893), 24–32.

12. J. Torrey Connor, "Only John," *Land of Sunshine* IV (February, 1896), 111.

13. San Francisco *Call,* April 10, 1892, quoted in "Chinese Exclusion" (editorial), *Literary Digest* IV (April 23, 1892), 695.

14. Editorial, Seattle *Post-Intelligencer,* July 10, 1900; Walla Walla *Union,* July 23, 1900; Los Angeles *Times,* July 9, 1900.

15. "The Chinese Character," Los Angeles *Times,* July 11, 1900.

16. Editorial, *Rocky Mountain News,* July 8, 1900.

17. "The Chinese Question," *Review of Reviews* V (June, 1892), 526.

18. Francis G. Newlands, "How Japan Is Invading America," *Illustrated American* XXII (July 31, 1897), 138–41.

19. Henry Cabot Lodge to Henry White, June 29, 1900, Lodge Papers, Massachusetts Historical Society, Boston.

20. Editorial, San Francisco *Chronicle,* November 15, 1894.

21. Thomas J. Geary, "Should the Chinese Be Excluded?", *North American Review* CLVII (July, 1893), 52–67.

22. Thomas J. Geary, "The Law and the Chinaman," *Californian Illustrated* IV (July, 1893) , 313.

23. "Immigration" (editorial) , *Harper's Weekly* XXXV (May 16, 1891) , 358.

24. "The Chinese Evil, Master Workman Powderly Speaks Out, Urges Reenactment of the Exclusion Law by Congress," San Francisco *Chronicle,* January 8, 1892.

25. Elizabeth S. Bates, "The Chinese through an Official Window," *Overland Monthly* XXII (August, 1893) , 138–47.

26. Charles F. Holder, "The Chinaman in American Politics," *North American Review* CLXVI (February, 1898) , 226–33.

27. "The Chinese and the Geary Bill" (editorial) , *Review of Reviews* VII (April, 1893) , 265.

28. R. C. Bryant, "Chinese Exclusion," *Arena* XXVII (March, 1902) , 260.

29. James D. Phelan, "The Case against the Chinaman," *Saturday Evening Post* CLXXIV (December 21, 1901) , 4.

30. John Chetwood, "The Problem of Immigration," *Arena* XXVII (March, 1902) , 254–60.

31. Allen McLaughlin, "Chinese and Japanese Immigration," *Popular Science Monthly* LXVI (December, 1904) , 117.

32. Ibid.

33. Theodore Roosevelt to William Rockhill, May 18, 1905, Rockhill Papers, Houghton Library, Harvard University.

34. George E. Anderson to Assistant Secretary of State Robert Bacon, November 29, 1905, *Despatches from United States Consuls in Amoy, 1844–1906,* National Archives (Washington: Government Printing Office, 1947) .

35. Ho Yow, "The Chinese Question," *Overland Monthly* XXXVIII (October, 1901) , 228–31.

36. Wong Kai Kah, "A Menace to America's Oriental Trade," *North American Review* LXXVIII (March, 1904) , 369–78.

37. Yung Kiung Yen, "A Chinaman on Our Treatment of China," *Forum* XIV (September, 1892) , 85.

38. G. H. Fitch, "Races and the Labor Problem in California," *Chautauquan* XXIV (January, 1897) , 427–32.

39. E. H. Conger to Secretary of State John Hay, February 13, 1905, *Despatches from United States Ministers to China,* National Archives (Washington: Government Printing Office, 1946) .

40. "How It Is Done," *Land of Sunshine* VI (December, 1896) , 58.

41. Terence V. Powderly, "Exclude Anarchist and Chinaman," *Collier's Weekly* XXVIII (December 14, 1901) , 7. (This publication existed under two names during this period; *Collier's Weekly* will be used here to des-

ignate both *Collier's Once A Week, Fiction, Fact, Sensation, Wit, Humor, News* and *Collier's Weekly, An Illustrated Journal*.)

42. Theodore Roosevelt, "Cotton and the Chinese Boycott," *National Geographic Magazine* XVI (November, 1905), 516.

43. Editorial, San Francisco *Chronicle*, January 25, 1892.

44. "Chinese Sunday Schools," *Rocky Mountain News*, December 13, 1894.

45. Frederick J. Masters, "Can a Chinaman Become a Christian?", *Californian* II (October, 1892), 622.

46. Helen F. Clark, "The Chinese of New York," *Century* LIII (November, 1896), 104.

47. "The Chinaman in New York" (editorial), *Leslie's Weekly* LXXXIX (November 11, 1899), 378.

48. "A Plague of Men," *Illustrated American* XIV (October 7, 1893), 427.

49. Ibid., 428.

50. "The New Chinese Exclusion Act" (editorial), *Outlook* LXX (January 18, 1902), 153.

51. Truxton Beale, "Why the Chinese Should Be Excluded," *Forum* XXXIII (March, 1902), 53–58.

52. Addison Parker, "The Exclusion of the Chinese," *Baptist Quarterly Review* XII (October, 1890), 460–73.

53. "The Chinese Exclusion Bill" (editorial), *Harper's Weekly* XXXVI (April 16, 1892), 362.

54. Thomas Magee, "China's Menace to the World," *Forum* X (October, 1890), 202–3.

55. Archibald R. Colquhon, *China in Transformation* (New York, 1894), pp. 1–10.

56. J. Torrey Connor, "A Western View of the Chinese in the United States," *Chautauquan* XXXII (January, 1901), 374.

57. Phelan, "The Case against the Chinaman," p. 4.

58. Ibid.

59. Edward O. Shakespeare, "Necessity for a National Quarantine," *Forum* XIV (January, 1893), 582.

60. E. C. Spitzka, "Another Word on the Contagiousness of Leprosy," *Illustrated American* XXII (November 13, 1897), 628.

61. "How the Chinatown at Los Angeles Has Been Washed and Purified," Los Angeles Times, June 17, 1900.

62. "The Gospel in Oxford Place," Boston *Herald*, July 2, 1900.

2

The Chinese
in American Life
and Letters

"Was gal named Moll had lamb / fle all samee whitee snow, / Evly place Moll gal walkee, / Ba ba hoppee long too."—By an unknown caucasian translator

No important area of Chinese life eluded the scrutiny of free-lance writers, crusaders for moral justice, would-be authors, and others who fed the insatiable appetite of the Sunday supplements and cheap magazines. Few were the homes which escaped unscathed from the onslaught of feature articles, poems, and cartoons depicting the Chinese in barbarian posture. A clandestine visit to Chinatown at midnight arranged through a privileged contact with the local police and guided by a detective who "knew the secrets necessary to gain admission" won for the adventurer the right to speak with authority on all oriental problems. On Sunday and during the week the American version of Chinese sin and shame in all its glory and variety paraded through the front parlors of the nation's homes. Unsuspecting children learned of the brutality and mystery of Chinese life, unmitigated by close friendships with the objects of their young scorn. In their maturity they led their own children in the same paths, and the myths became reality to a new generation.

The part of Chinese life which received the most frequent attention during the years at the end of the century was the small oriental community which existed in a few large cities. As the Chinese population in the United States increased, these isolated gatherings of a people who appeared so utterly foreign to the Western eye drew upon themselves a character of their own. At one time there was a tendency to use several terms to describe these settlements, for example, "Chinese quarter" and "Chinese community." Soon, however, the more familiar designation of "Chinatown" became standard nomenclature, and the quotation marks disappeared. In order for a Chinese community to qualify as a recognized Chinatown, however, it had to consist of a fairly large Chinese population occupying its own quarters. At first only New York and San Francisco could meet these requirements, and for the purist only in "Frisco" could one find a true Chinatown. But by 1890 other cities such as Boston, Philadelphia, and Chicago were considered to have a small Chinatown.

It was easy for American eyes and nostrils to receive offense in Chinatown, and readers thrilled to the horrible experiences of caucasian visitors. The sensitivities of Elodie Hogan, sometimes free-lance writer, traveler, and crusader, were violated frequently during a visit to San Francisco's Chinatown, where she observed an "agglomeration of Oriental paganism," with "reeking sidewalks, foul with unknown trash; the nauseous odors vomited from black cellars; the wilderness of alleys; . . . and sphinx-eyed, crafty yellow men who glide along the narrow pavements."[1] Two years later another visitor to the same place described similar impressions gained from a tour of a boardinghouse. "In this [central] yard, in spite of all sanitary laws, all the offal and refuse collected in and about the establishment was deposited, so that the very potent 'celestial odor,' offal and opium combined, caused us to cut our visit to this establishment as short as possible."² When the visitor left, his tour led him into other sections of the Chinese community. "We went by way of some narrow, dark, and evil-smelling entries—past numerous closed doors, in the center panels of which were narrow slits through which came cautious hisses to attract our attention."³ The "tour" was conducted by a detective from the San Francisco police department.

The Chinese section had a fascination for global travelers, many of whom began their trip to the Orient in San Francisco's Chinatown. One female tourist, a rarity in 1890, found the air "thick with oriental odors of unknown origin."⁴ She observed workers in small cellar workshops laboring steadily on well past midnight. She climbed "rickety, greasy stairs" past rooms where "human bundles lay on shelves, overcome by poppy fumes," past "greasy hot kitchens" and "cackling cooks" preparing "midnight meals."⁵ Two years later another group of visitors were appalled at the "foul stench" and the "hideous and unspeakable filth" which made the Chinese quarter a "plague spot" in the fair city of San Francisco.⁶ Nothing they had ever seen in the East was "half so rank and filthy" as what they had observed in Chinatown.

The Chinese theater was a steady attraction for visitors, one of whom described the physical appearance of the hall overlooking the "reeking filth" of the market, reached by steep stairs and consisting of a long dirty auditorium desti-

tute of ornamentation or stage props.[7] The trampling, push-
ing, jabbering crowd and the terrible noise made it impossible to concentrate on the performance. "The fiddles
screech, trumpets blare, battles rage, drums and tom-toms
crash, pandemonium breaks loose, and the visitor rushes out
into the night to cool his throbbing brain."[8] Other visitors
could not comprehend why the plays had to be of such
length, from several hours to several days, or could not
understand what was going on in the absence of any but the
barest scenery. Those who could understand Chinese fared
little better because even though they understood the dia-
logue they were unable to endure the noise of the accom-
panying musicians. Almost all who came to see went away
more convinced than before of the barbaric nature of Chinese drama.

The eccentricities of Chinatown caught the eye of many
a visitor. The clothing of the Chinese appeared very peculiar
to the eyes of Westerners, with bright colors that did not
harmonize, pants for the women and blouses for the men.[9]
The written language was odd enough in appearance, but
even when translated it made little sense. Signs outside shops
carried outlandish names in poetical phrases bearing no
relationship to the actual business of the owner. The local
apothecary with its "beetles, snake bones, lizards, toads-
blood, and other tonics" highly amused Americans, who
were used to more sophisticated medical treatments. A naval
officer on leave from duty in the Far East noted that the
medicine which the Chinese needed worst, fresh air and
sunlight, was unavailable.[10] Funerals were a source of curiosity and amusement, as were the local religious temples or
joss houses. The idols and incense of these latter places, plus
the corpulent resident priest and the joss sticks which re-

vealed a man's fortune, strengthened the impression of the Chinese as heathens.

San Francisco's Chinatown was the source of much of America's acquaintance with Chinese communities, but the examples from other cities were similar. Denver's Chinatown was described by a local minister as "shabby, squalid, vile old Chinatown! It was the foulest, filthiest, most cheerless spot in all Denver."[11] Several years later the same sentiment was conveyed in a fictional account of a young girl's perilous experience in the same place.[12] New York's Chinese quarter was found swarming with humanity, where all men and women looked alike and where ignorance, superstition, and wretchedness characterized "this unwholesome side of New York life."[13] Mott Street in New York could not compare to San Francisco's Chinese settlement, but it was a local center for all the Chinese in the area. Furthermore, its inhabitants were the same because "the wearer of a cue can never be other, to the popular eye, than a 'heathen.' "[14] It appeared to the author that the character of the New York Chinese was the same as the character of Chinese everywhere. Their "utter failure to appreciate the virtue of cleanliness," the squalor of their environment, and their personal immorality were no different in New York than elsewhere. The last word on Chinatown, insofar as most Americans were concerned, may have been uttered by the mayor of San Francisco who suggested that "there is no remedy for the evils of Chinatown apart from its utter demolition."[15]

In addition to the impressions gained from an appraisal of Chinese communities, many Americans formed their opinions from activities which were considered characteristic of the Chinese in the United States. One of these was fishing on the California coast. Those who had any reason to be aware of the fisheries industry in California were highly indignant at the illegal methods of the Chinese, who were destroying the industry because of their practice of taking small fish and shrimp at all seasons. "It is generally agreed," a local fish and game official commented, "that the Chinese fishermen have little regard for the law (if they can evade it) and absolutely no consideration for the preservation of young fish from destruction."[16] Testimony was offered by the head of the fish and game department in San Francisco concerning the illegal apparatus and methods employed by the Chinese. Chinese fish camps were noted for their pungent odors and their dirty, rickety shacks, which even the beauty of Monterey Bay could not redeem.

Illegal fishing practices paled, however, in comparison with the criminal practices of the "Highbinders." This term originated in 1806 when it was used to describe Irish *banditti* who were responsible for a series of riots.[17] It was later applied to a secret Chinese society in San Francisco which had evolved from the Triad Society in China, a private organization patterned along the lines of the Chinese clan system and similar to the Italian Mafia. Highbinders were considered to be the controlling force in the Chinese underworld, and at their door all the crimes attributable to the Chinese were laid. The headquarters of the society was Spofford Alley in San Francisco, where initiations were performed and matters of highest importance discussed. Distinction should have been made between the Chinese Six Companies, which were benevolent secret societies, and the Highbinders, although this was not generally done. The Chinese consulate and leaders in the Chinese community, including the heads of the Six Companies, agreed that the Highbinders Society was nothing more than a band of assassins, blackmailers, and terrorists who made their influence felt in every Chinese community they could reach. But most Americans extended this characterization to all Chinese societies whatever their origin, with the result that every neighborhood organization took on criminal appearances. The inability to distinguish between the recognized but small criminal element among the Chinese and the remainder of the law-abiding community precipitated extensive misunderstanding.

The undeniably criminal character of the Highbinders was often offered as evidence that the Chinese were of an excessively criminal nature. Statistics were developed which were designed to prove that the Chinese population contributed a disproportionate share to the criminal population in the United States. One table based on the 1890 census showed that although the Chinese and Japanese made up less than a quarter of one percent of the foreign population, they were responsible for more than one and one quarter percent of homicides in the United States.[18] An earlier survey based on the census for 1880 demonstrated that the Chinese made up only .2 of 1 percent of the foreign population but constituted almost 1 percent of the prison population.[19] Such statistics as these convinced many people that the Chinese were a criminal threat to the communities where they lived.

The admittedly brutal methods employed by the Highbinders to maintain their influence received wide notoriety. The men who were dispatched on the society's errands were called "salaried soldiers." One such "soldier" was captured in Victoria, B. C., and instructions were found on his person detailing the procedures to be followed in the event that his mission failed.[20] If he was slain in the discharge of his duty, his family was paid five hundred dollars. If he was wounded, he got free medical help and ten dollars a month; or if he was captured, his family was paid one hundred dollars a year until his sentence expired. American authorities were warned by our diplomats in China to be wary of the secret societies because of their powerful position in the hierarchy of Chinese family life. The same organizations which controlled various aspects of Chinese society on the mainland often operated branches overseas.[21] Consuls who were familiar with the brutality which seemed to be a part of their activities in China cautioned officials in the United States to expect the same sort of behavior.[22] The common inability of the consular staffs to distinguish between genuinely criminal and merely fraternal or social societies encouraged misunderstanding on this question.

Opium smoking was held up to public light as another example of Chinese criminality and debasement. Descriptions of opium dens were as frequent as they were gruesome. A typical account of a visit would include such details as a room nearly filled with a single matress upon which "lay a woman smoking opium with a fierce eagerness. The sallow, swollen face told the tale of drink and opium. Her lips were pressed tight against the mouthpiece of the pipe . . . ; the veins of her forehead thickened, her cheeks flushed . . . she floated away. . . ."[23] Detailed drawings of the equipment necessary for pursuing the habit as well as prices and places where the drug might be purchased were published.[24] Some people feared that the habit would spread in the United States, and others testified to having seen large numbers of white women frequenting opium dens.[25] The percentage of the Chinese population which did use opium was variously estimated from less than 10 percent to a majority of all

Chinese. There is no way to ascertain the exact percentage of Chinese who used the drug; certainly it was greater than the Chinese themselves wished it to be, though probably no more and possibly less extensive than the current use of alcohol. In any event, however, the "foul curse" of opium was a bountiful source for anti-Chinese material.

No less horrible, but a little difficult to describe in a more Victorian age, was the female slave traffic. It might be possible to literally penetrate the depths of an opium den in order to expose its evil, but a similar course in a Chinese brothel was a more delicate matter for both author and reader. Yet one could speak in generalities and still convey the impression of malevolent evil. The normal produre, consistent with the practice in China of purchasing women for marriage, was for an agent to persuade a Chinese girl to come to the United States as a bride for a prospective husband.[26] Once the girl had passed through the immigration barrier as a bartered bride, she was conducted to the "Queens Room" in Chinatown where she was displayed for purchase.[27] The price was usually around six hundred dollars but might range above two thousand dollars in some instances. Part of the process involved the rendering of a contract between the young woman and her purchaser along the lines indicated in the following example. "Because, coming from China to San Francisco, she became indebted to her mistress for passage, _____ herself asks Mr. _____ to advance for her $630, for which _____ distinctly agrees to give her body to Mr. _____ for service of prostitution for a term of four years."[28] After the time specified had elapsed, the woman was free, though in practice she had little chance to escape from her predicament.

Prostitution was certainly not a common feature of Chinese life, but in American minds the fact that some women were brought into the country for illicit purposes clouded the conception of Chinese women in general. The exception was magnified until many Americans used interchangeably the terms woman and prostitute when referring to the mature Chinese female. The president of the Woman's National Industrial League of America, Mrs. Charlotte Smith, testified before the Senate committee on immigration that virtually all Chinese women in Boston were engaged in immoral enterprise. What is worse, she added, "educated American-born white slaves were bought and sold for as low as $2 per head, while Chinese women were prized at $1,500 to $3,000 each."[29] The committee members must have cringed under the wrath of Mrs. Smith as she described the state of Chinese female morality in Boston and the apparent discrepancy between the value of oriental and caucasian prostitutes.

The steady trickle of Chinese into the United States in spite of the exclusion laws was a running sore for those who wanted all Chinese excluded. "Chinese laborers cross our borderline between the United States and Canada disguised as clergymen, as nuns, as Quakers and as Indians; they come over the line by rail, boxed in barrels, covered top and bottom by potatoes; they come over sandwiched between bales of hay; they come in freight cars, buried under corn, wheat and oats. . . ."[30] The feeling against the Chinese was so intense that many years after the immigration legislation of the 1890s had laid the problem to rest once and for all, Alfred Thayer Mahan, one of the nation's most popular spokesmen for the idea of American destiny, expressed the feeling that he would rather go to war than permit any degree of "yellow immigration."[31] Mahan added, however, that unless he was very mistaken about his countrymen, the likelihood of any Chinese ever again entering the United States in any significant numbers was virtually nonexistent. Yet during the period when the debate over exclusion was at its height, there was considerable public frustration and anger over the means utilized by Chinese who entered the country illegally.

One of the prime geographical areas for illegal entry was in the northwest portion of the United States. The Chinese landed in Canada by paying the head tax and were brought from Victoria to landing points in northern Washington. Some slipped across the border between Washington and Canada at the many unguarded points in that wilderness area. The Honorable Watson C. Squire of Seattle described for his colleagues in the United States Senate the manner in which agents procured coolies in Hong Kong for entry into the country via Vancouver and Seattle.[32] The charge for transporting Chinese over the border on foot or by water across Puget Sound ranged from $25 to $50 a head. A full explanation of the manner in which Chinese obtained fraudulent entry permits by deceiving consular officials in China, as well as a plan for eliminating the practice, was offered by the consul at Canton.[33] Actually, the incidence of illegal entries was not nearly as large as commonly believed; but even so, most Americans generally accepted the notion that the devious means employed by Chinese coming into the country afforded ample proof of the general defects in Chinese character.

In addition, proof of Chinese criminal tendencies was thought to exist in the way in which some evaded the exclusion laws. Admittedly there were many instances of Chinese laborers employing a variety of subterfuges in order to establish their right to enter the country. The exclusion law did state, however, that Chinese who had been born in the United States could reenter if they offered proof of their status as a native American. In the view of many customs and immigration officials, especially those in California, it was in this area that the greatest degree of fraud existed. Even American consuls in China came under attack on this point as they were accused of issuing false certificates supporting claims of American birth. They defended themselves in part by pointing out that the Chinese were such wanton and skillful liars that it was often impossible to get the truth out of them.[34] So many Chinese claimed the United States as their place of birth that one federal Judge estimated that "if the story told in the courts were true, every Chinese woman who was in the United States twenty-five years ago must have had at least five hundred children."[35] The judge's estimate does not seem so exaggerated when the number of women who arrived regularly on the steamers is taken into account.[36]

Gradually, inexorably, although without any sort of plan, isolated irritations and points of view from widely separated areas of national concern created a separate place for the Chinese in American life. Words used in new ways and in different combinations formed a separate vocabulary of terms descriptive both of the Chinese and of the nation's point of view regarding them. The Chinese emerged in several well-identified roles in fiction, poetry, and drama by the end of the century. They were the subjects of numerous lectures offered at local Lyceums, where oral word pictures gave provincial minds their first glimpse of the Oriental. On the West Coast and in New York City and Chicago, Christian missions were maintained to save the heathen. In many households the laundry was taken around the corner to the

"Chinaman," and in a few the cooking and housework was managed by a Chinese domestic. Small boys and some grown men took their entertainment in the street at the expense of the Chinese. It was cheaper and often more exciting than the local theater. When talk got around to annexing Hawaii or the Philippines, tempers flared at the thought of bringing more "pig-tails" under the American umbrella. By 1890 the Chinese occupied a solid if minor place in the nation's life.

Perhaps the clearest indication of the low esteem in which most Americans held the Chinese was the growth and wide circulation of words associated with supposed Chinese characteristics, words which were meant to convey meanings of moral degradation. These words were usually derived from half-truths relating to Chinese behavior or were descriptions of actual physical characteristics singled out for the purpose of ridicule. Some words had no direct relationship to the Chinese but were designed primarily to evoke feelings of disgust when used in reference to them. In many instances the words were conscious slurs with no relationship to actual circumstances. Gradually the inaccuracies were accepted as legitimate descriptions of Chinese behavior and as factual in themselves. These prejudices, masquerading as facts, and the attitudes which accompanied them were incorporated into the American image of the Chinese.

The ethnic slur usually describes the point of view of its author better than it does its object, and the slang pertaining to the Chinese was no exception. The most characteristic word in use at the turn of the century to describe the Chinese was "Chinaman."[37] It carried the meaning of "one of them," or someone from "that place," and indicated inferiority, foreign origin, and a kind of subservient anonymity. A somewhat comparable example is the use of the word "boy" in referring to Negroes, the implication being that the individual possesses insufficient worth to be identified beyond the level of his particular racial class. "John Chinaman" or simply "John" is an example of this attitude whereby the individual concerned is not given the dignity of his own name with the implication that one designation can well serve for all such creatures.[38] Unfortunately, the term "Chinaman" is still in use today, although it continues to provoke resentment among the Chinese.[39]

Many expressions were related to distinctive oriental anatomical features and to what were presumed to be characteristics of Chinese life. For example, the terms "moon-eyed leper" and "yellow leper" were commonly used at the time that it was believed that the Chinese were particularly susceptible to leprosy. The designation of "yellow" was widely used in combination with other words such as "yellow-belly" and "yellow-boy" to connote cowardice, inferiority, and even barbarity, as in "yellow peril." The Sino-Japanese war in 1894–95 was styled the "yellow war," and Theodore Roosevelt referred to the Chinese as the "yellow race."[40] "Almond eyed" and "slant-eyed" had obvious origins, as did "pigtail," all of which were used to ridicule and disparage characteristics of Chinese appearance and custom. The term "Chinese" was rarely used as a natural description; instead it implied something foreign, harsh, and immoral, as in an editorial reference to tactics employed in the Senate during a tariff debate in 1890.[41]

Many words were used in a particularly harsh fashion. One of these was "Chink," which seems to have derived partly from Chinese mispronunciations and partly from a fertile caucasian imagination.[42] Whenever Americans searched their hearts for a description worthy of their most violent feelings of antipathy toward the Chinese, this word occupied a prominent place in the resulting phrase. Secretary of State John Hay regularly referred to the Chinese as "chinks" and to the treaty between Russia and China as the "Russo-Chink Treaty."[43] In a letter to Henry White he spoke of his concern for the "poor devils of chinks" and on another occasion he referred to the United States treaty with China as "our chink treaty."[44] In high places and low, in the U.S. Senate and in the streets of American slums, the Chinese were assaulted with this word and others like it.

Terms which created the image of darkness, whether in the Chinese soul or in Chinatown, and words which described the supposed pestilential herding instinct of the Chinese like "swarm," "mass," and "horde" conveyed impressions of animal-like inferiority and viciousness.[45] The range and variety of words was so extensive that almost any word applying to filth, social disease, deterioration, rot, and degradation can be found in descriptions of the Chinese.

American attitudes toward the Chinese were also shaped by a variety of folk-myths about Chinese life. There was the notion, for example, that all Chinese look alike, thus making it impossible to tell them apart.[46] During the congressional debates over the exclusion legislation in 1891–92, critics of the provision in the Geary bill for photographing all Chinese pointed out that since there was no way to tell them apart anyway, photographs would be useless. The expression "Chinaman's copy" referred to the supposed tendency of the Chinese to copy exactly any English-language document including mistakes and erasures and complimented his precision at the same time it disparaged his ignorance. Bret Harte fashioned one of his short stories about the Chinese in the West around this theme.

Many popular slang expressions used during these years were indicative of the American point of view toward the Chinese. One who craved narcotics was said to "have a Chinaman on his back." A "Chinese compliment" meant the make-believe acceptance of another's suggestion or exaggerated deference designed to cover up an unsavory scheme. "To give a Chinaman a music lesson" meant to offer a false reason for excusing oneself from an unpleasant situation. Someone with a "Chinaman's chance" was faced with an impossible situation, and a "Chinese watermelon" referred to a wax gourd because it was smooth and shiny on the outside but with an impenetrable shell which made the interior inscrutable. A "Chinese puzzle" was insoluble, and "Chinafication" referred to the situation in international affairs when a nation was unable to defend itself.[47]

In popular songs and on Broadway the Chinese were burlesqued and ridiculed for the amusement of American audiences.[48] *A Trip to Chinatown* played for 650 consecutive performances on Broadway between November, 1891, and August, 1893. "Chin-Chin Chinaman" and "Toy Monkey" were two songs from these dramatic efforts which lampooned the Chinese and achieved popularity beyond Broadway. Other moderately successful theatrical productions at the end of the century bore titles like *A Night in Chinatown, The King of the Opium Ring, Chop Suey One Lung, Chinatown Charlie,* and *Queen of Chinatown.* In 1899 *The Singing Girl* appeared with a score by Victor Herbert containing the song "Chink! Chink!" A musical comedy entitled *A Chinese Honeymoon* and several more comic operas contributed many popular songs about the Chinese during the next few years, such as "China Bogeyman," "China Dragon Blues," "Chinee Soje Man," and "Chinky China Charleston." All

in all, these are probably no worse than a random sampling
of songs relating to any minority group in the nation, yet
they were indicative of an attitude toward the Chinese which
had some serious implications for Far Eastern policy.

The Chinese also occupied a place in the fiction written
during the latter third of the century, though their impact
upon American letters in total was surprisingly slight. The
number of serious authors who gave more than passing attention to Chinese themes was small, and even among this
handful the Chinese were a minor emphasis. In view of the
excitement their presence caused on the West Coast and in
two or three other cities, it is somewhat puzzling as to why
this should be so. A possible explanation might be that readers who read the stories in the Sunday supplements and
cheap magazines and thus provided the bulk of the market
for the consumption of Chinese lore did not read book-
length fiction. It also seems to be true that the Chinese were
rarely considered worthwhile subjects for dramatic exploitation. When Chinese characters did appear, they almost always occupied inferior or ludicrous positions; seldom were
they treated as serious participants in the drama of life.
Thus, unlike other minority groups, the Chinese never
achieved a solid place in American folklore.

The author most frequently associated with the Chinese
was Bret Harte. The association was a strange one in some
ways because Harte did not write very much about the Chinese nor did he ever consider them very seriously. Harte's best
writing on the Chinese was done prior to his departure from
California in 1870. Later authors writing during the 1890s
merely echoed Bret Harte, and their writings lacked the vitality, clarity, and honesty of his fresh experience in the
west. The Chinese gave the same color to his episodes that

they did to the real experiences upon which the stories were based.

Even though the bulk of his writing pertaining to the Chinese was produced by 1870, it was Harte who provided a key note for the anti-Chinese sentiment of later years. In 1870 when he was the editor of *Overland Monthly*, under the pressure of a press deadline, Harte composed the poem which became the hallmark of the Chinese exclusion movement. As he sat at his desk looking out on the streets of San Francisco, he thought about two institutions without which life in the west would have been unrecognizable: four-handed draw poker and the Chinese.

First published in the magazine he edited under the title "Plain Language from Truthful James," the name was shortly changed to "The Heathen Chinee." The poem was an instant success in the east, though barely recognized on the West Coast. It was given recognition in England, where it was praised highly in the *Spectator,* and another version appeared in *Piccadilly Annual* in 1871. The poem was quoted by both critics and defenders of the Chinese, and there was some doubt about Harte's own motives, although Ambrose Bierce reported Harte as "greatly amused by the meanings that so many read into it," when in fact he meant nothing whatever by it.[49] The poem attracted such little notice in the west that Harte was surprised at its success among eastern magazines. It is doubtful that he had anything more in mind than a playful commentary on a familiar California scene.

The poem captured the point of view of many Americans, and for the following decades Ah Sin was a common pseudonym for Chinese characters. The term "heathen Chinee" was incorporated into American letters in a variety of ways, including a "Heathen Chinee Songster" and as the title of several short stories. The description of Ah Sin's dark and peculiar ways became a part of the national image, and Bret Harte was quoted many times on the floor of Congress during the debates on the Chinese question. Following are the lines which seem to sum up the thoughts of most Americans at the turn of the century, particularly the last three lines in the first stanza, which could be chiseled into the headstone marking the burial place of the last chance for a sympathetic understanding of the Chinese in this country.

> Which I wish to remark
> And my language is plain
> That for ways that are dark,
> And for tricks that are vain,
> The Heathen Chinee is peculiar.
> .   .   .   .
> Ah Sin was his name;
> And I shall not deny
> In regard to the same
> What that name might imply.[50]

Bret Harte was at his best in the short story, and it was here also that the Chinese were described for American readers in a most unforgettable fashion. His most effective scenes portrayed the vitality of western life in mining camps, small transient towns, and the back alleys of San Francisco. One such story was entitled *See Yup,* a parody on the notion that because of their slanted eyes Chinese could look up more readily than Caucasians. It described the adventures in the life of the Chinese who lived on the fringe of a small community of miners drawn together by their common desire to extract a fortune in precious metal from the hard

California earth. The presence of the Chinese was tolerated only because they provided the miners with two necessary services, that of attending to their soiled clothes and as a humorous diversion from their otherwise hard existence. The "pesky lot of yellow-skinned heathens," as the miners referred to them, were a never-ending source of amusement.[51] There was no more pleasant pastime than playing tricks on "John" like tying the end of his pigtail to the tail of a cat while both were dozing in the sun and then galvanizing the cat into action by a little lamp oil applied to a sensitive place. "John" would always rise to the occasion and roundly curse the "Melicans" who had played such a dirty trick on him.

The miners were far from the amenities of civilization, including medical aid, and often had to resort to home remedies when sickness or accident visited the camp. It was irritating that the Chinese were never affected when a siege of "dyspepsy" sent many hardy Caucasians to their beds. One miner who let his curiosity overcome his disdain visited one of the Chinese secretly to learn the source of oriental health. The miner came away with a powerful medicine (Bret Harte suggests that it may have been ginger) and was soon restored to robustness. The other miners laughed at their fellow who had sought the ministrations of a pagan and warned that one who associated with "Chinks" would soon be worshiping oriental gods. But it was silently noted that many late-night visits were paid to the Chinese in his shack, and the general health of the men improved markedly, though a noticeably pungent odor was added to the usual aroma of tobacco and whisky which permeated the camp. Later when a doctor from San Francisco visited the area, some of the miners casually inquired about his impression of oriental medicine. He chilled their enthusiasm for Far Eastern technology with a detailed description of the way in which the Chinese utilized dead rats, spiders, and other such material as ingredients for many of their medicinal compounds. Needless to say, the sale of ginger root declined drastically in the camp.

In the concluding episode of See Yup's adventures among the Caucasians, Bret Harte appealed to the traditional American sympathy for the underdog and placed the Chinese in a position where they could at least retaliate for the kind of abuse absorbed at the hand of their host. As a result of every mining operation in those days, a huge mound of rock and earth accumulated from the process of screening and washing the earth for gold. The tailings pile (or simply tailings, as it was called) often contained small amounts of gold but seldom in sufficient quantity to warrant working it. Tradition dictated that only Chinese could work the tailings and make any money from the effort because only they were capable of the kind of labor required. After their regular housekeeping chores around camp were done, See Yup and his friends would pick over the fresh tailings left from the day's work. Great was the surprise of the miners when they noticed that the Chinese were sending weekly bags of "dust" to San Francisco. Could it be possible, they wondered, that the tailings were so rich in gold as to supply the Chinese with a greater quantity of the precious metal than most men could obtain in a week's work at regular mining?

One morning early the miners quietly visited the tailings pile with their pans and to their amazement washed out gold on the first few tries. In great excitement they went to the Chinese and offered to buy the entire pile of tailings, which the Chinese had been careful to identify as their claim, and after some threats obtained their desire for twenty thousand dollars. See Yup was secretly delighted because, far from being reluctant to sell, the Chinese had salted the tailings with gold they had obtained over many months of hard work; and though it was true that a bag of gold went to San Francisco every week, the same bag came back a few days later hidden in the supplies brought into the camp by Chinese peddlers. When the miners realized in the succeeding days that they had paid a high price for worthless rock, they turned in anger on See Yup and his friends; but their shacks were empty, for they had left in the night for new territory.

Bret Harte viewed the Chinese in this and many other stories written about the west as simply a colorful characteristic of western life. He did not look upon the Chinese with any more personal animosity than most westerners, who had little contact with Chinese and saw them only as a part of the normal routine of living on the frontier. His western stories aroused little interest at first among those who lived there, but in other parts of the country, especially in the later years of the nineteenth century, his descriptions of the west and of the Chinese were a formative influence upon writers and others whose ideas about the Chinese were conveyed to America through the Sunday supplements and popular magazines. The "Heathen Chinee," with his dark ways and vain tricks, was a caricature which grew from the pen of Bret Harte.

Another literary source descriptive of the Chinese in American life was the writing of Ambrose Bierce, who was far more sympathetic toward the Chinese than Bret Harte, even though he never equaled the latter in the volume of his output. Ambrose Bierce was in many ways a critical commentator on his social environment, whereas Bret Harte was more of a teller of short stories which captured the authentic flavor of western life. But even though Bierce wrote about the tribulations of the Chinese in an effort to win more sympathetic treatment for them, his concern was largely lost amidst his descriptions of the peculiarities of Chinese life. In one story about mining Bierce described the abuse of the Chinese by the miners in the camps and had a mine foreman announce that "the Superintendent of the Mag Davis mine requests us to state that the custom of pitching Chinamen and Injins down the shaft will have to be stopped, as he has resumed work in the mine. The old well back of Jo Bowman's is just as good and more centrally located."[52] The humor of the story and its caricature of western life lead one to believe that such actions involved little sense of wrong-doing.

Several incidents were recorded of the Chinese settlement on the edge of a town being destroyed by fire either accidentally or purposefully during the years when the Chinese were spreading themselves throughout the west. It was not uncommon for the local people to show a noticeable lack of enthusiasm for putting out the fire unless it threatened other houses and buildings in the town. Bierce's indignation at this example of caucasian injustice was expressed in several stories and particularly in a poem written in reaction to the fire at Bakersfield, California, which almost completely destroyed the Chinese settlement while townspeople watched. The poem is entitled *A Dampened Ardor* and describes the day when "the Chinatown at Bakersfield / was blazing bright and high."[53] Streams of water directed at the sky failed to stop the flames eating into the dry shacks when "rose an aged preacher man / whom all did much admire; / who said: 'To force on you my plan / I truly don't aspire; / But streams, it

seems, might quench those beams / if turned upon the fire!"
The firemen turned instead upon the unwelcome defender
of the Chinese and "with jet of wet and small regret / they
laid that old man's dust."

Speculation about possible solutions to the Chinese problem occupied large amounts of space in the columns of the
San Francisco *Examiner* during the 1890s, and Ambrose
Bierce did not fail to offer his solution. "There is but one
remedy," he wrote in 1890. "I do not recommend it: to kill
the Chinese. That we shall not do! The minority will not
undertake nor the majority permit. . . . We could kill the
Chinese now, . . . but fifty years hence . . . the nation that
kills Chinamen will have to answer to China."[54] Bierce was
pointing out the extremes to which the hatred against the
Chinese had led some people and warning of the possible
consequences. He felt that if we pursued our present course
in abusing the Chinese who came to America, we might well
find ourselves at war with the Orient in the future.[55] His
prophecy evoked little concern in 1890, but readers now can
ignore his words less easily; it is apparent that present day
Chinese hostility toward the United States is in some part at
least a reaction to the events of earlier decades.

Several other American authors gave some attention to
the Chinese in addition to Bierce and Harte. Frank Norris
is probably the best remembered of these, with the possible
exception of Rudyard Kipling, whose accounts of his overseas journeys among the Chinese will be examined in a later
chapter. In *The Octopus* (New York, 1901) Norris mirrored
the general attitude toward the Chinese and helped to encourage the dislike and even revulsion which many people in
this country felt toward them. In one episode a young
woman who had entered "into the purlieus of Chinatown

. . . emerged, panic-stricken and out of breath, after a half hour of never-to-be-forgotten terrors."[56] Norris did not name the terrors, but their anonymity only increased the reader's reaction to the unknown horrors of Chinese life. In an earlier and less serious work, *Moran of the Lady Letty* (New York, 1898), he described the Chinese and "the blankness of their flat, fat faces, the dulness of their slanting fishlike eyes," and several pages later warned a Chinese that "when you try to get the better of white people you are out of your class."[57] In *Blix* (New York, 1902) Norris described San Francisco's Chinatown as well as Harte ever succeeded in doing, though he added nothing new to the well-established conception of a world of strange sights, smells, sounds, and mysteries too strange for the Western mind to comprehend.[58] These descriptions probably added little that was new to the reader's conception of the Chinese, but they undoubtedly reinforced an attitude firmly established through previous contact with Sunday supplements and cheap magazines.

Mark Twain produced a few short stories about the Chinese, and with his inimitable humor added to the caricature. One of these, entitled "Disgraceful Persecution of a Boy," was a satirical commentary on the arrest of a young lad on his way to church because he had paused to heave a stone at a "Chinaman."[59] What kind of persecution was this, wondered Twain, since the boy's parents undoubtedly would have commended their offspring's action because, as every one well knew, heaving rocks at the Chinamen was a pastime of the street which no self-respecting American boy could be expected to overlook. It might even be called the national pastime in San Francisco. Another story about "John Chinaman in New York" described the adventures of an unfortunate Chinese whose treatment at the hands of his American hosts did little to commend the experience of a visit to this eastern city to his brethren in San Francisco.[60] With the exception of a chapter in *Roughing It,* Twain wrote little else about the Chinese, though there were many slight references to them as they formed part of the background for his western stories. He was sharply critical of the injustices of his countrymen, but this did not lead him to express sympathy for the Chinese; rather, he seemed to view them as a pathetic example of a people unable to defend themselves and thus probably not really worthy of defense.

The work of one other author presented the Chinese in a derogatory light and undoubtedly helped to form the attitudes of many Americans. Atwell Whitney wrote more than two decades before the turn of the century, but his book is an example of the kind of fiction concerned with the Chinese which was readily available to the reading public in inexpensive editions.[61] The novel was an attempt to portray the evils of Chinese labor and the impact upon Caucasians which competition with the Chinese created. The flow of Chinese into the labor market was likened to a stream of sewage emanating from Chinatown, "a dark greasy, nasty little stream of distilled odds and ends," which filled the places previously occupied by Caucasians, poisoned the moral atmosphere, undermined the free institutions of the country, and resisted all efforts to stem its advance.[62] The book was obviously an example of polemical writing of an inferior sort, yet it represented a point of view familiar to many, and it must have had eager readers all too anxious to believe the worst about the Chinese.

Perhaps the most lasting impression made upon the readers of Chinese lore was that every "Chinaman" spoke in a curious tongue known as "pigeon English." It would have been difficult indeed to convince very many people that the Chinese in America had not developed their own peculiar version of the English language, and the notion that the Chinese developed a complete language structure as a means of communicating without actually having to learn English has persisted to this day. Considerable resentment was expressed by those who felt that the Chinese simply refused to make the effort to learn a new language in order to force their hosts to communicate on oriental terms, thus indicating again their complete refusal to accommodate themselves to the customs of their adopted country. It is probably true that many Chinese did not learn English, but this was more likely because they saw little advantage in attempting to master such a difficult language when their stay in America was to be only a temporary one. The oriental tongue found many Western sounds nearly imposible to master; thus it was inevitable that most Chinese spoke with a heavy accent.

Actually, the Chinese did not speak pigeon English; they simply spoke poor English, with characteristic mispronunciations and improperly accented words. (The term "pigeon," incidentally, was derived from the Chinese corruption of the word "business," and "pigeon" and "pidgin" were used interchangeably.) Pigeon English existed foremost in the minds of those who wrote about the Chinese, particularly those who knew them only slightly or not at all. The desire to attribute to them a manner of speaking which represented a corruption of basic English was simply one more indication of the readiness to characterize them as a strange and barbarous people. Americans who had read about the Chinese but had never met them believed firmly that all Chinese talked this way because that was the way nearly every author after Bret Harte made them talk.

At one point, possibly in the late 1880s, pigeon English threatened to become established as a minor dialect. The probable reason that it did not is that readers began to tire of the sort of verbal nonsense passed off as pseudo-Chinese dialect. The first verse of "Ping-Wing" is indicative of the sort of language attributed to the Chinese and supposedly used in their everyday communication: "Ping-Wing he pie-man son / He velly worst chilo [child] àllo Cantón / He steal he mother picklum mice / an thlowee cat in bilin' rice / Hab chow-chow up, an' 'Now,' talk he / My wonda' where he meeow cat be?' "[63] It is doubtful that any Chinese ever spoke in this fashion in Canton or anywhere else for that matter, or ever did any of the things attributed to "the worst child in Canton." The author, however, was convinced that his readers expected a "Chinaman" to speak in this fashion.

No significant literature of any quality was written about the Chinese. They were not immortalized in song or verse, and no dramatic presentation ever did much more than make rather bad jokes about their supposed physical and social peculiarities. The Chinese never grew to occupy a place in the nation's folk history similar to that of the Negro, the mountaineer, or the Yankee, and one of the most important reasons lay in their own attitude toward their presence in the United States. The majority of Chinese came here intending to stay only a few years until they accumulated enough money to return to their homeland and live out the remainder of their lives in comfort. They did not try to assimilate into American life because they did not intend to make a permanent home here, and their efforts to earn as much money as possible left little extra energy or time to devote to learning new ways of life in a strange country.

There are other reasons that the Chinese did not develop

a place of their own in the nation's literature. Like the Negro they constituted a people who were not native to the land, but the Chinese, unlike the Negro, did not enjoy a long period of useful labor which imbedded them in the social and economic fabric of the nation. The Chinese were brought here for the limited purpose of preparing the road-beds and laying the track which would form the western part of the nation's railroad system. When the transcontinental link was completed, they had to seek other areas of employ-ment in agriculture and mining, where they came into im-mediate conflict with non-oriental workmen who deeply resented the competition. The Chinese were never accepted as an indigenous part of the economic life of the nation as were the Negroes. They did specialize in certain occupations in the cigar and garment-making industries in some cities and the laundry business, but they won their place in these areas by displacing other workers.

The image of the Chinese which developed in American literature contained elements which worked against their ever occupying a prominent place. The Chinese never ac-quired heroic status, thus their lives could not be depicted in tragic hues. It is almost impossible to recall an incident in which a Chinese occupied the central place as a figure of daring, courage, and physical superiority. Occasionally, Cau-casians might be outwitted by the superior cleverness or trickery of their oriental brethren but never with any impli-cation except that of deviousness and dishonesty. Defeating the Chinese in any conflict did not reflect honor upon an opponent because no credit for heroic accomplishment could accrue from overcoming an insignificant adversary. A strik-ing example of this is that the Chinese rarely appeared as characters during the dime-novel phase of American literature because they simply did not offer sufficient potential for heroism. In effect, the image of the Chinese worked against their ever attaining a significant place in the American literary record.

This is not to say, however, that the treatment of the Chinese in American writing was not important. On the contrary, the descriptions of the Chinese and their way of life presented with unforgettable impact to every reader the picture of a people with strange and devious ways whose presence was a constant reminder of the contrast between the civilized Christian West and the barbaric pagan East. Few readers probably ever saw a Chinese except possibly from a distance, but such lack of firsthand experience was not permitted to stand in the way of firmly established convictions about the relative merits of an Oriental. The main effect manifested by all the writing about the Chinese was to convey an impression of a second-class human being inferior in all ways except those prized by some animals for the purpose of survival. He was an unwelcome visitor from a heathen land whose only purpose was to exploit his borrowed environment and return with as much profit as possible. It was a rare person who was able to distinguish between the word-picture of the Chinese and their actual situation. The written descriptions of their life in America reinforced the widespread misconceptions about them and spread and strengthened the prejudice against their presence.

It is not surprising that the animosity against the Chinese generated by the descriptions of Chinatown and life in the west resulted in open acts of hostility. People were antagonistic because they did not understand the Chinese. They did not understand why they had left their own land unless it was to exploit to their private advantage the country to which they had come. Because many Chinese made no pretense of wanting to settle permanently in America, most Americans concluded that the Chinese would seek their advantage wherever they could without regard for the interests of those among whom they lived. It is true that the vast majority of Chinese who emigrated during the later part of the nineteenth century were from the lower levels of Chinese society, members of the coolie class generally. They did not bring their families because of the cost, and they did not attempt to enter into the social life of their adopted country. With but few exceptions, however, they were honorable men prepared to work very hard and long for nominal wages by our standards. Yet few Americans saw in the Chinese anything but a threat to their own security. They reacted to them out of fear and with tragic consequences.

Chinese settlements in many towns were attacked, and the results were loss of homes and personal property, brutalization of the residents, and death. Most of the incidents, though not all, occurred in California towns like Vallejo, where the Fourth of July celebration got out of hand in 1891 and a gang of young toughs bombarded Chinatown with firecrackers. When the Chinese fled behind locked doors, several houses were set afire. In the confusion Chinese shops were broken into and looted, and when the flames had reduced one house to ashes, a distraught father was seen squatting with his head down beside the charred body of his young daughter. When a hoodlum ran up and kicked the body into the air, the grieving Chinese picked up a charred stick and beat the offender to death.[64] At Madeira, California, the Chinese settlement was burned at midnight, and sixty houses were destroyed. At Bakersfield the same sequence was repeated. First the houses were fired, then the fleeing Chinese were beaten and robbed. Up and down the West Coast, at Selma, Delano, Seattle, Tagus, Pixley, Borden, and many places too small and too isolated to have ever been remembered, the Chinese were hounded and harried out of their homes and jobs. In one year, 1886, in Washington, Idaho, Montana, Wyoming, and Oregon, twenty-eight Chinese were killed, and at Juneau eighty-seven were set adrift on a boat without food or water.[65] Fear and resentment fed by distorted, prejudiced tales about the malevolent Chinese flamed into acts of violence, and oriental lives were called into forfeit.

In Denver, Colorado, one Chinese was killed and some wounded when a mob got out of hand and dragged several laundrymen through the streets with ropes around their necks while onlookers showered them with jeers and stones.[66] In Pittsburgh a Chinese funeral procession honoring the death of a respected member of the community was attacked by a large number of hoodlums. They snatched the burning joss sticks, destroyed the printed prayers affixed to the grave, and pushed their way jeering and shouting into the midst of the ceremonies.[67] In Chicago, New York, and Boston incidents occurred when Chinese sought to establish laundries or work at jobs from which they previously had been excluded. At Rock Springs, Montana, on September 5, 1885, a Chinese village was stormed and burned by one hundred and fifty armed miners. As the houses blazed, the fleeing occupants, Chinese men and women, were shot and their bodies thrown into the fire. Forty-two were counted dead before the dogs and wild hogs ate the corpses.[68] Many of the incidents took place in the near-wilderness areas of the west, where small camps were established to pursue mining operations. One such camp was set up by

Chinese who were operating a placer mine on the upper regions of the Snake River in 1887. Rumor spread that they had found a rich location, and a plot was hatched to raid the camp, surprise them at their work, and make off with their gold. The plotters made their way to a point upstream where they constructed a river boat in which they floated down to the camp, surprising twelve Chinese who were shot in cold blood before they could flee or defend themselves. The raiders took $6,000 from the camp and before they left beat to death one of the twelve who had only been wounded and was caught trying to crawl into the woods. Eight more Chinese who arrived by boat at this moment to join their colleagues were also shot to death, and thirteen remaining miners were killed later as they worked their claim a few miles from camp. Altogether, thirty-three Chinese perished.[69] Claim-jumping was a familiar part of western life during the mining years, but the ferocity of the attack and the fact that no attempt was ever made to investigate the incident were characteristic of the general low regard in which Chinese life was held.

Western justice typically was applied with a rough hand, but when administered to the Chinese it was often characterized by unusual viciousness. In the town of Bridgeport, California, Ah Tia was a longtime resident (according to the standards of those transient days) who satisfied the town's need for a laundry and performed other odd jobs. He was not well liked, but neither was he disliked. He had a place in the life of the town, and as long as he performed his duties satisfactorily, he knew that he could stay. One evening during a poker game an Indian named Poker Tom, angered because of his losses, threatened Ah Tia and later in the evening waylaid him. Ah Tia killed the Indian in self-defense and threw his body in the river. When the body was discovered, Ah Tia sought refuge in jail; and the prominent members of the community, including the president of the board of supervisors, met to consider what ought to be done. Their decision was to release the accused to the local Indians to undergo their brand of retributive justice. The townspeople, deaf to his pleas for help, watched as Ah Tia was dragged off to a spot just outside the town where he was forced to stand in the middle of a circle of Indians wielding sharp knives. Without benefit of preliminaries he was promptly cut to pieces. Later, a shovel was required to scoop the remains into the earth.[70]

Incidents involving the abuse of the Chinese in the west and other places in the nation are part of the record of these years. Of course, these incidents do not tell the whole story, and it is possible to exaggerate their importance; but even in isolation the violence and cruelty involved can only reflect what must have been a general and deep-seated hostility on the part of white citizens. As noted by Mark Twain, throwing rocks at Chinese was a part of every boy's playtime activity in San Francisco, especially on "Oriental Steamer Day." When a ship bearing Chinese coolies arrived at the foot of Market Street, both children and adults would gather to jeer while the wagons bearing the Chinese were forced to run a gauntlet of missiles.[71] It was not suprising that children taught to revile the Chinese grew into men willing to commit violent acts against them. Nor was it surprising later that a nation which harbored deep-seated feelings of animosity toward the Chinese was slow to dignify a relationship between their country and ours with the degree of respect necessary for a sympathetic understanding of China's problems.

The American image of China was formed in a crucible of hostility and resentment fired by the heat of unreasoning fear and inflamed prejudice. The antagonism which marked the first prolonged contact between Americans and Chinese had a lasting effect on the nation's attitude toward the Orient. It is impossible to establish the precise relationship between popular attitudes and the actions of a single individual. It is equally impossible to deny the impact of broad-gauge experiences in the life of a nation upon the specific political acts of that nation. The men who helped shape our policy in the Far East—men like John Hay, William Rockhill, Henry Cabot Lodge, and Alfred Thayer Mahan—were men who harbored feelings of prejudice toward the Chinese that were both publicly and privately expressed. The atmosphere in which the nation's China policy was formed was not vacuous but filled with the winds of opinion blowing from San Francisco and Boston, from the upper reaches of the Snake River, and from Denver and New York. These currents, though not always strong, persisted, and over the years they strongly influenced the development of the country's relationship with China.

1. Elodie Hogan, "Hills and Corners of San Francisco," *Californian* V (December, 1893), 63–71.

2. W. H. Gleadell, "Night Scenes in Chinatown, San Francisco," *Eclectic Magazine* LXII (September, 1895), 381.

3. Ibid.

4. Elizabeth Bisland, "A Flying Trip Around the World," *Cosmopolitan* IX (May, 1890), 54.

5. Ibid., p. 55.

6. "In Chinatown a Slumming Party Sees Some Queer Sights," San Francisco *Chronicle,* January 16, 1892.

7. Frederic J. Masters, "The Chinese Drama," *Chautauquan* XXI (July, 1895), 436.

8. Ibid., p. 442.

9. "Chicago's Chinatown," Chicago *Tribune*, August 6, 1900.

10. W. A. Rogers, "A Chinese Prescription," *Harper's Weekly* XLIII (December 9, 1899), 1239.

11. J. L. Harbour, "A Funeral in Chinatown," *Christian Union* XLV (June 18, 1892), 1195.

12. "Slave to Opiates Lives off Garbage," *Rocky Mountain News*, July 8, 1900.

13. Arthur Hoeber, "New York's Foreign Quarters," *Illustrated American* XXI (January 16, 1897), 111.

14. Warren Taylor, "The Chinese Quarter of New York," *Munsey's Magazine* VI (March, 1892), 681.

15. James D. Phelan, "The Case Against the Chinaman," *Saturday Evening Post* CLXXIV (December 21, 1901), 4.

16. R. F. Walsh, "Chinese and the Fisheries," *Californian Illustrated* IV (November, 1893), 834.

17. F. J. Masters, "Among the Highbinders," *Californian* I (January, 1892), 62.

18. Sydney G. Fisher, "Immigration and Crime," *Popular Science Monthly* XLIX (September, 1896), 625–30.

19. W. M. F. Rand, "Immigration and Crime," *Journal of Social Science* XXVI (February, 1890), 66–78.

20. Frederick J. Masters, "Highbinders," *Chautauquan* XIV (February, 1892), 554–58.

21. Edward Bedloe to Secretary of State John Hay, July 7, 1898, *Despatches from United States Consuls in Canton*, National Archives (Washington: Government Printing Office, 1947).

22. William Martin to Assistant Secretary of State Robert Brown, March 7, 1906, *Despatches from United States Consuls in Hankow*, National Archives (Washington: Government Printing Office, 1947).

23. "The Opium Curse," *Illustrated American* IV (November 29, 1890), 551–52.

24. "Chinese Opium Fiends," Chicago *Tribune*, July 22, 1900.

25. "A White Girl Held Captive by Chinese," San Francisco *Chronicle*, January 15, 1892.

26. Eliza Scidmore, *China the Long-lived Empire* (New York, 1900), pp. 320–24.

27. Charles F. Holder, "Chinese Slavery in America," *North American Review* CLXV (September, 1897), 288–94.

28. Samuel Gompers, "Some Reasons for Chinese Exclusion," Senate

Document 137, 57th Congress, 1st sess., 1902 (*Senate Documents*, V.13 [Washington, 1902], 19).

29. *Congressional Record*, 57th Congress, 1st sess., 1902, 35, pt. 4:3667.

30. Terence V. Powderly, "Exclude Anarchist and Chinaman," *Collier's Weekly* XXVIII (December 14, 1901), 7.

31. Alfred Thayer Mahan to Sir Bouverie F. Clark, September 6, 1907, Mahan Papers, Library of Congress.

32. *Congressional Record*, 52d Cong., 1st sess., 1892, 23, pt. 4:3609.

33. Edward Bedloe to Secretary of State John Hay, September 10, 1898, *Despatches from United States Consuls in Canton*.

34. John Fowler to Assistant Secretary of State Francis B. Loomis, December 27, 1905, *Despatches from United States Consuls in Chefoo*, National Archives (Washington: Government Printing Office, 1947).

35. Allen McLaughlin, "Chinese and Japanese Immigration," *Popular Science Monthly* LXVI (December, 1904), 118.

36. "Steamers from Yokohama," San Francisco *Chronicle*, February 3, 1892.

37. Edward Harper Parker, *John Chinaman and a Few Others* (New York, 1901), p. vii.

38. Goldsworthy L. Dickinson, *Letters from John Chinaman and Other Essays* (London, 1901).

39. See for further examples A. A. Roback, *A Dictionary of International Slurs* (Cambridge, Mass., 1944).

40. Theodore Roosevelt to Cecil Spring Rice, December 27, 1904, Theodore Roosevelt Papers, Library of Congress.

41. "Chinese Warfare" (editorial), *Harper's Weekly* XXXIV (September 27, 1890), 751.

42. Adriana Spadoni, "Devils, White and Yellow," *Overland Monthly* XLIV (July, 1904), 80–84.

43. John Hay to Alvey A. Adee, September 4, 1901, and September 19, 1903, Hay Papers, Library of Congress.

44. John Hay to Henry White, May 22, 1903; to Alvey A. Adee, September 29, 1903, Hay Papers.

45. See also Lester V. Berrey and Melvin Van Den Bark, *The American Thesaurus of Slang* (New York, 1942).

46. Henry Codman Potter, *The East of To-Day and To-Morrow* (New York, 1902), p. 62.

47. For additional examples see Berrey and Den Bark, *Thesaurus*, and Roback, *Dictionary*.

48. Jack Burton, *The Index of American Popular Music* (Watkins Glen, N. Y., 1957).

49. William Purviance Fenn, *Ah Sin and His Brethren in American Literature* (Peking, 1933), pp. 45–46.

50. Bret Harte, "The Heathen Chinee," *Overland Monthly* XL (September, 1902), 234–37.

51. Bret Harte, "See Yup," *The Writings of Bret Harte*, 20 vols. (Boston, 1899–1914), XVI, 144–60.

52. Ambrose G. Bierce, *Collected Works*, 12 vols. (New York, 1909–12), XII, 320.

53. Ibid., V, 65.

54. Ambrose Bierce, "Chinese Immigration," San Francisco *Examiner*, 1890, reprinted in *Works*, II, 372.

55. Ibid.

56. Frank Norris, *The Octopus* (New York, 1901), p. 580.

57. Pp. 24, 232.

58. Pp. 62–63.

59. Samuel L. Clemens, "Disgraceful Persecution of a Boy," reprinted in *Sketches New and Old* in *The Writing of Mark Twain*, 22 vols. (New York, 1869–1909), IX, 143.

60. Ibid., p. 304.

61. *Almond-Eyed* (San Francisco, 1878).

62. Pp. 73–74, 168.

63. Charles Godfrey Leland, "Ping-Wing," in *Pidgin-English Sing-Song* (London, 1876), pp. 29–30.

64. W. F. Gray, "How We Treat the Chinese," *Independent* XLIII (December 31, 1891), 1940–41.

65. *Nation* LXI (August 22, 1895), 128.

66. Ibid.

67. Ibid., LII (April 2, 1891), 274.

68. Ibid., LXI (August 22, 1895), 128.

69. Gray, "How We Treat the Chinese," pp. 1909–10.

70. Ibid., pp. 1940–41.

71. Doremus Scudder, "Chinese Citizenship," *Outlook* LXXXI (December 23, 1905), 985–86.

3

Americans View the Chinese
in China

"By twos and threes / From out the mist / The weird Chinese / Glide forth to tryst"—Howard Sutherland

The issue before the Senate that spring was a familiar one to most of the members present; and if some of the senators had not actually taken part in previous debates, they nonetheless were thoroughly aware of the implications of the subject under discussion. It was not that very many of the men in attendance that afternoon seriously disagreed with the proposal before them or that they faced a particularly difficult choice; rather, it was simply a matter of keeping the public record straight as to their position. Thus when Senator Lodge rose to address his colleagues, it was not so much with the expectation that he would be able to influence votes but with the desire to state again the essence of his point of view. His support of exclusion, he said on April 12, 1902, was based not on any animosity toward the Chinese but on the deep conviction that the two races were so different that any mixing could only result in the degradation of the white race. "The Chinese are of the great Mongol family. We are of the Aryan race . . . with a different language, a different past, a different hope and a different future."[1]

Lodge's statement reflected the thinking of the majority of Americans searching for a means to justify their opposition to the presence of the Chinese in this country. As he explained it, the economic conflict between white workers and Chinese in this country was an inevitable result of the confrontation of two radically different peoples. "Theirs is the Mongol race; and when Chinese labor is brought into competition with our labor our labor can not meet it on the standard and in the environment that the Chinaman creates and lives. That is why, as I believe, the great mass of American people, with a strong race instinct, with an instinct which can not be overcome, believes they should be shut out."[2] The point, said Lodge, was not that all Americans who supported exclusion were followers of the labor-led sandlot agitators of the West Coast like Dennis Kearny; rather, it was much more basic, "a question of dealing with a people utterly alien to us, who never can become a part of our civilization."[3] In other words, argued Lodge, the deepest reason for the nation's opposition to the Chinese lay in its evaluation of them as an inferior race.

Privately Lodge did not express the violent hostility toward the Chinese which Theodore Roosevelt did in referring to them as an "immoral, degraded and worthless race."[4] But he made it very clear that American interests in the Far East and at home should be defended vigorously when necessary. He supported Secretary of State Hay's policy of keeping China open for trade to all the Western nations and said so more than once.[5] Lodge also shared in the common belief that the Chinese were an inferior race and virtually helpless in the absence of assistance from the West. Before the turn of the century he had written to his close friend in the British diplomatic service, Cecil Spring Rice, that he agreed completely with Rice's belief in the destiny of the English-speaking peoples in the East.[6] The only way that China could possibly become a modern nation, he said, was with the technical and spiritual assistance of the caucasian race. It was our duty, therefore, to supply the requisite leadership.[7] Lodge was sympathetic toward the ancient traditions of Chinese civilization, but his appreciation was at heart paternalistic. He did not despise the Chinese, but he supported their exclusion and believed that they were an inferior race.

Lodge's position was typical of the majority of people who reacted unfavorably to the presence of the Chinese in the United States. Their point of view was developed in part out of a reaction to descriptions of life in China in which the Chinese were characterized as a people deficient in most of the human qualities which were valued throughout the Western world. This attitude was not necessarily always expressed by the same people who had agitated for Chinese exclusion. For example, the labor unions tended not to be as concerned with the supposed cultural degeneration of the Chinese in China as they were with their presence in the United States. Yet it is true nevertheless that the same undercurrent of hostility which had stimulated anti-Chinese feeling in California also influenced the nation's attitude toward the Chinese in their homeland. Those who worked and traveled in China during these years did not reflect quite the same bitterness and intense antagonism which characterized the attitude of labor on the West Coast, but their attitude did reveal a deep hostility toward the Chinese and a belief in their inferiority.

Americans who traveled in the Orient and the far greater number who stayed home denegrated the Chinese largely because they were not American. Unfamiliar with Eastern ways, quick to criticize and deprecate customs which seemed strange, Americans were unable to appreciate the merits of a radically dissimilar way of life. Not a little of this feeling was based upon a fear of the unknown during a period when the nation's relationship to the rest of the world was being expanded in ways which required the restatement of national values. The United States was becoming aware again of the other nations and races inhabiting the world in a way quite similar to the experience of someone who, thinking he is alone in a dark room, suddenly discovers the presence of another. At first there is the shock of discovery and then the question of identity.

The Chinese in a sense were a newly discovered people, and the question of relationship between the two cultures was an implicit one, the answer to which contained ramifications of concern to everyone. If, for example, Western civilization was conceived of as resting at the peak of man's development and the United States as the emerging exponent of that civilization, then where was China's place on the mountain? Did she occupy an adjacent peak, heretofore hidden in the clouds and separate from the main body, a part of the same range, perhaps, but with its own distinct identity? If this was true, then serious questions must arise as to the relationship of these two people, both of whom claimed a position of leadership for the entire human race. It would be far easier to suppose that the Chinese were a distinct people but not a people of distinction. It would be more comfortable to maintain that the two peoples were separate entities, the one inferior to the other. In this way the need to explain a relationship which from the start proved to be awkward, embarrassing, and even threatening could be avoided.

Therefore, the proposition was vigorously put forward that the Chinese were an inferior race, a strange and barbaric people. Americans who traveled often got their first impression of the Chinese on a ship headed for the Orient, and for them their experience seemed to substantiate such an interpretation. There was no escaping the repugnance with which travelers described their contacts with the Chinese among whom they traveled. "Nothing can prevent their bringing on their own greasy and malodorous foods, which they strew over rich carpets, curtains, and couches as unconcernedly as on a yamin's stone floor."[8] The Chinese official who lounged about on the upper decks while his wife and family herded below in "the crowded promiscuity of the steerage" was held up as an example of typically unfeeling and barbaric behavior.[9] Travelers felt that it was more than a want for money which made the Chinese, sometimes of higher rank, huddle in the crowded quarters of the steerage.

The assumption of racial inferiority frequently led to unfavorable comparisons between the Chinese and the activities and appearance of certain animals. A traveler in China, for example, described her observations of Chinese tailors, stripped to the waist, at work in their shops. "When well fattened, their uncovered bodies suggest the animals which Americans enclose in a sty. The more like a well-fed porker a Chinaman becomes, the prouder is he of his looks, for a corpulent man is regarded by his almond-eyed brethren as a high type of humanity."[10] Chinese at work in the fields, on the river boats at Canton, or in the crowded city of Peking were described in terms which drew heavily upon images from the world of animals.[11]

Samuel Gompers, president of the American Federation of Labor, prepared a pamphlet in 1902 describing as he saw it the unanimous opposition of organized labor to the Chinese. The title page read, "Some Reasons for Chinese Exclusion, Meat vs. Rice, American Manhood against Asiatic Coolieism, Which Shall Survive?"[12] The pamphlet argued in part that the chief objection to the Chinese was that they represented an inferior race, as any neutral observer could readily ascertain from an inspection of their mode of living. The threat of the Chinese to American labor lay not simply in their willingness to work for lower wages but in their evident ability to exist at a level which Westerners would normally consign to animals. The pamphlet quoted from the report of a San Francisco commission charged with inspecting living conditions in Chinatown to indicate that only a subhuman specie could exist in this sort of environment, "with open cesspools, exhalations from waterclosets, sinks, urinals and sewers tainting the atmosphere with noxious vapors and stifling odors; with people herded and packed in damp cellars, living literally the life of vermin."[13]

The purpose of the pamphlet was not to provide an objective assessment of the Chinese but to present labor's case against them. Consequently, Gompers quoted an extensive passage from Rudyard Kipling's description of his travels in China—especially Kipling's assessment of Canton, which he found to be "a big blue sink of a city, full of tunnels, all dark, and inhabited by yellow devils."[14] Such charges today would lead one to question either the perceptiveness or the integrity of the writer; and in 1900 there were surely some who refused to interpret such descriptions of the living conditions of the Chinese (which *were* crowded and unsanitary in many cases) in the light of racial characteristics. But the emotional climate of the times allowed the charges to become widely accepted as truth.

American diplomats in China who had an opportunity to observe Chinese life firsthand, however, usually conveyed the same impression given by Gompers in his pamphlet. Charles Denby served for many years as our minister at Peking, and his son later followed him to the Orient. Denby's long acquaintance with the Chinese did not, however, make him sympathetic. His long experience with Chinese legal procedure as well as with their behavior before American judges convinced him that they were incapable of telling the truth. Furthermore, he said, "anyone acquainted with Chinese ethics knows that it is sometimes a duty for them to bear false witness."[15] He did not elaborate on his statement, but more than a decade earlier, in a letter to Secretary of State John Sherman, he had analyzed Chinese character. "In China there is no religious sentiment," he said, because "the people generally have no religion." Consequently the Chinese did not have strong commitments to their government or to any of the social institutions which form the bulwark of Western society.[16]

When Congress established a joint committee on immigration and naturalization and charged it with investigating conditions on the Pacific Coast with regard to feelings about the Chinese, Congressman Herman Lehlbach reported a similar interpretation by witnesses before the committee on the subject of Chinese morality.[17] Charles H. Dodd, for twenty-five years a resident of Portland, Oregon, and president of the immigration board appointed by the citizens of Portland, testified that "the Chinaman's idea of honesty and the American idea is different. The Chinaman's idea of morals in women and the American idea are as opposed as Heaven is to Hades. The idea of purity is something he does not know and can not appreciate."[18] Dodd went on to explain that the Chinese failure was a racial one, a defect in their character implicit in the very nature of their racial structure. To emphasize his belief, he shared with the committee his conviction that "you can not leave a girl in the house. If you had a daughter seven or eight or nine years old, you dare not leave her in the house if there is a Chinaman there. You must not do it. . . . They have no idea of pure morality— none whatever."[19] Testimony of a similar nature was recorded by the committee in other western cities, including Spokane Falls, Seattle, Los Angeles, and San Diego. In San Francisco, Alfred Fuhrman, president of the 16,000–member Federated Trades Union, testified that the morals of all Chinese were so low that in fact they had no morals.[20]

Shortly after the Geary bill had been passed by Congress in 1892, it was discovered that an extension of the date for implementation of the bill's provisions would be necessary. During the debate in the House over the McCreary bill, which provided for such an extension, the question of the nature of Chinese civilization arose. Congressman Samuel G. Hilborn from Oakland, California, devoted a substantial portion of his speech before the House on October 14, 1893, to explaining that the immorality of the Chinese was a result of the dissimilarity between the two races. "It is a contest between two civilizations," he said, "the Oriental civilization (if it can be called a civilization) and our own."[21] In comparing the two civilizations, Hilborn noted, one must be aware that even though we apply the term civilization to the Chinese and even though they can lay claim to a historical continuity extending back many centuries, theirs is a lesser civilization. They were a different kind of people whose very nature was threatening to Western civilization. In fact, when one examined their virtues and vices carefully, he must inevitably conclude that they were more nearly like barbarians than civilized men. Congressman Hilborn concluded his remarks with a statement which drew loud applause from the Congressmen present: "The Civilization of the Orient and the Civilization of the Occident can not exist side by side in America. One or the other must go down. Which shall it be?"[22]

Specifically, attention was drawn to the terrible cruelty of the Chinese. The reader of the 1890s and early twentieth century was spared few details in the effort to describe the qualities of Chinese punishment. Descriptions of Chinese trials, of the methods of torture, and of the peculiarities of the legal system were common. One feature which was particularly incomprehensible was the practice of substitution. If the criminal had enough money, he was able to buy a "pardon" which entitled him to the privilege of crucifixion instead of dismemberment, the advantage being that he would join his ancestors with his body intact. If he had a substantial amount of money available, he would hire a "substitute" who would take his place by confessing to the crime and submitting to the punishment.[23] Many Americans must have agreed with the editor of the Atlanta *Constitution* who concluded that "these people have no sense of the value of human life."[24]

Readers were informed that in most cases dismembering was not preferred by either the magistrates or the spectators because it was too easy to bribe the executioner to choose a knife designated for a vital spot such as the head or the heart.[25] The knives were stored in a basket, handles up, and the executioner was supposed to reach into the basket and select a knife without looking. Each knife was identified with a mark designating a particular part of the body, such as hands or feet, and had to be used for its designated purpose only.

So barbaric were the Chinese thought to be that any sympathy felt for them as a result of the war with Japan was totally misplaced because they were "cruel from the cradle."[26] Supposedly, their earliest environment bred this into them. "To torture animals, to attend and to gloat over executions, and to gaze on human suffering in any form, afford the keenest delight to the Chinese youth."[27] The Chinese system of meting out justice seemed to encourage excesses, for a man could not be punished until he had confessed to a crime. If a fine was levied and the accused could not pay, his only alternative was to submit to torture. Descriptions of such cases were provided, often in considerable detail and with illustrations.[28]

Lest the reader fail to experience the same horrors that supposedly had moved the observer, generalities were well supported with fact. Methods of torture came in different grades of intensity and ingenuity. The selection was influenced by the mood of the inquisitor as well as by the enormity of the confessed crime. The victim's ankle might be pulverized with a club, or he could be forced to kneel on a chain mat studded with sharp points. Beating with bamboo, judicious use of water, or a cord slowly tightened around the head might produce the desired result. "For certain offenders . . . the penalty is the 'Ling-chee,' or a 'thousand cuts.' This is too ghastly for detailed description, but suffice it to say that the victim is first crucified to a low cross, and then slowly sliced to pieces with a knife."[29] However, more detail was supplied, and readers were advised of the executioner's skill in prolonging the agony without inflicting a vital wound and of the crowd's delight at such exquisite entertainment.

According to eye-witnesses, the behavior of Chinese troops during the Sino-Japanese war supported the charge of barbarity. China was not a signatory of the Treaty of Geneva, which provided for the humane treatment of prisoners of war and for the employment of the Red Cross to ensure that such treatment was given. This fact was seized upon to buttress the claim that Chinese civilization had not reached the point where it could appreciate and recognize a level of humane behavior supposedly well established in the West. Consequently, humane consideration was shown only on one side during the war—the Japanese—whereas inhumanity ran riot on the other—or at least this was what the reader was asked to believe.[30]

A. B. de Guerville was a well-known correspondent whose accounts of the Sino-Japanese war were widely published in the United States. His account of the battle at Pen Yang when Japanese soldiers lay on the field under murderous cross fire was typical of the descriptions of Chinese cruelty in battle. "With the advent of night the Chinese scouted far and near and cut off the head and hands of every wounded foeman they could find."[31] And a few days later, on September 16, 1894, when Japanese troops entered the Chinese forts, "they found in several of them the frightfully mutilated bodies of their friends who had been made prisoners. Hands and heads were missing, others had been scalped, others lay with their eyes plucked out and ears slashed away."[32] The correspondent was convinced that the Chinese officials approved of the slaughter and mutilation of prisoners. In the papers which a Chinese general left behind him as he fled, circulars supposedly were found containing promises of rewards for "Japanese heads or parts of a head."[33] There can be no question as to the sort of impression left by these accounts.

It is perfectly evident, of course, that Chinese soldiers under the stress of war did commit acts of cruelty against their fallen foes and against civilians who were in the path of the conflict; but then, the soldiers of every nation have been guilty of similar acts. During the Sino-Japanese war the soldiers of Japan were guilty of the same sort of atrocities against the Chinese, but seldom was attention focused anywhere except on the latter.[34] Ten years later the Russo-Japanese war prompted another flurry of public revulsion, this time directed at the Japanese, who by 1904 were beginning to suffer from the same hostility previously directed at the Chinese. It was not difficult to discover acts of barbarity committed by the Chinese in wartime, nor was there any question of Chinese culpability. The conclusion that the Chinese were especially and uniquely cruel, however, does not bear up under examination. It is true that brutality was a part of life in the Orient; but it must have been difficult to single out the East as being very much different from the West when such features of Western civilization as the Crusades, slavery, and the Spanish Inquisition were recalled. The American image of China, however, was never meant to be a rational one. Therefore, the cruelty of the Chinese in both civilian and military life was inflated out of all proportion.

It was widely believed during these years that the ineffectiveness of the army in China was attributable to the basic lack of aggressiveness of the Chinese, an idea in ironic contrast to the belief in oriental brutality. Innumerable references were made to incidents in battle where the Chinese had fled from the conflict in abject terror, throwing guns, ammunition, and clothing heedlessly aside.[35] A United States naval officer described how Chinese seamen would wait until the battle was fully engaged and then take advantage of the excitement to try to escape from their ship. Chinese naval vessels, he reported, seldom carried lifeboats for fear they would be utilized by a mutinous crew.[36]

Chinese society paid honor to the scholar but not to the soldier, and everything about their way of life was thought to make the Chinese unfit for military duty. Minister Charles Denby observed that the Chinese were "without courage or spirit, and have a horror of war."[37] He did not foresee the possibility of ever being able to train them for duty in the army. The inability of the Chinese to drill was supposed to be due to their having to walk single-file in crowded city streets. Because the language relied heavily upon word accents, it supposedly was not suitable for uttering sharp, clear commands. The antiquated weapons, from infantry through artillery, were thought better suited for museum display, and in 1885 an illustration of soldiers actually armed with bows and arrows appeared in *Leslie's Weekly*.[38] It was true that the Chinese lagged far behind Western nations in the development of military weapons and were inferior to the Japanese in the development of military hardware. As late as the 1890s one of the tests for determining qualification for officer's rank in the Chinese army consisted of shooting a crossbow from a galloping horse. Yet it was ironic that one criterion for judging the quality of a civilization was its ability to acquire sophistication in the art of destroying human life. That the ineptness of the Chinese in warfare was considered a mark of barbarity was a fascinating commentary on the values by which a civilization was judged.

Contrasting somewhat strangely with the claim of Chinese cowardice and military ineffectiveness was the belief that they had a peculiar ability to endure pain and hardship. This attitude was substantiated in several ways, one of which was that the Chinese had a less highly developed nervous system than Caucasians. It might have been concluded that such a circumstance would make him a more effective fighting man, and perhaps there were those who argued along this line. But most people seem to have taken it as an example of the lower place occupied by the Chinese on the scale of civilization and proof that he had not developed as far from his animal origins as had the Anglo-Saxon.

Several accounts of the exploits of Chinese wounded men on the operating tables of front-line hospitals were recorded by American doctors. "Every one was amazed at the phlegm of the wounded Chinese. They made excellent patients; indeed each one was patience personified."[39] The author of these remarks did not impute any particularly heroic qualities to the Chinese; rather, he noted their desirability as model patients because their needs for the relief of pain were so modest. The ability of the Chinese to endure pain was frequently put to the test when chloroform was either unavailable or dangerous, and their performance under these circumstances was remarkable. One physician concluded that the many battlefield examples of a high tolerance for pain "support the conclusion that the Chinese nervous system is less highly developed than that of the Westerner."[40]

One medical research experiment compared the brain of a Chinese with that of a Caucasian and a chimpanzee. Experiments indicated that the Chinese brain weighed less than the "normal average brain" of the adult male and its convolutions were less complex.[41] The ratio of cerebral hemispheres to the cerebellum was eight and a half to one in the average man, five and three-quarters to one in the chimpanzee, and five to one in the Chinese. Unfortunately for scientific purposes little explanation was offered to supplement the bare details, but the implication for the layman was clearly one of Chinese inferiority.

The ability of the Chinese to adapt physically to difficult situations was cited as evidence of their limited evolutionary development. Because of their supposed lack of nerves, lower level of sensitivity to their surroundings, and lesser intelligence, they were thought to be able to endure in circumstances which would be impossible for a Westerner. One traveler observed that they felt no discomfort from being crowded together, were never distressed at monotonous, tiring work, and were indifferent to normal comforts.[42] The fact that Chinese babies were noticed lying impassively without wiggling was offered as proof that the Chinese had little need for physical exercise. The Chinese, driven by the pressure of overpopulation, had succeeded in adapting themselves to a variety of areas from the tropics to the Artic, and this was thought to be proof that they were able to adjust to any circumstances.[43] For example, a traveler waiting for his train watched a "Chinaman" pull himself up to a sitting position on the sharp edge of an open barrel, prop his feet on the opposite edge, and promptly fall asleep. These incidents and many more were commonly noted as proof of the ability of the Chinese to survive in circumstances where other men would succumb, with the implication that this was due largely to his arrested development.

To some Americans an incident of 1895 seemed to illustrate the deviousness and cruelty that were said to be part of the Chinese character. Henry Cabot Lodge evidently had such in mind when he criticized the actions of Secretary of State Walter Q. Gresham in authorizing the release of two Japanese students who had sought asylum in the American legation in Peking. Despite assurances of safe conduct the Chinese had executed the young men as spies. Lodge felt that Gresham "ought to have known what every intelligent schoolboy understands, that Asiatic standards of truth and honor, and Asiatic diplomacy, are utterly different from those of Europe and America, and that promises such as he accepted are of no binding force with an oriental."[44] The torture and murder of the two Japanese youths by the Chinese caused the editor of the Washington *Post* to "shudder with horror at its fiendish atrocity."[45] The Chinese were accused of practicing atrocious cruelties on the prisoners, and the resulting "ghastly picture of fiendish torture" was considered appalling.

This supposed deviousness in Chinese character was sometimes attributed to the powerful custom which decreed that one individual be held responsible for another's misfortune if in any way the first person could have alleviated or prevented the distress of the second. If, for example, a thief crossed through a backyard on his way to burglarize a store, then the owner of the property would be partly responsible to recompense the store owner for his loss. Such a system was thought by many Westerners to encourage suspicion of one's neighbors and a reluctance to admit to the truth in any situation lest the bystander be forced to accept responsibility for events beyond his control. In one instance a Western observer related how he had seen several Chinese men stand watching a woman drown a few yards from the bank of a slowly moving river without making any attempt to save her lest the effort fail and they be held responsible for her death.[46] The conclusion seems to have been that such a bizarre custom was typical of the deviousness of the Chinese.

One of the words most frequently used in describing the Chinese was the term "barbarian." For the people who used it, and there were a large number of them, it represented as forceful a word as could be applied to the Chinese in polite company. It had more overtones of savagery, depravity, backwardness, and inferiority than any other term, with the possible exceptions of "heathen" and "pagan." The editor of *Harper's Weekly,* commenting on the Sino-Japanese war, said that "the demoralization of defeat in war is now being felt and manifested by the Chinese, and although reserve and self-restraint are supposed to be Chinese virtues, it is very clear that they are superficial, and that the barbarism that is at the foundation of the Chinese character has again broken loose."[47] A few months earlier the same editor had characterized the Chinese as barbarians who had become gentle because they feared the power of Europe.[48] In these examples the word was used to imply mainly the concept of unprincipled and unrestrained aggressiveness. The use of the word was not limited to the English-speaking peoples, however, because the Chinese first described Westerners as the "red barbarians." Apparently they too were capable of cultural analysis.

When the Ku Cheng massacre occurred in the summer of 1895 and took the lives of eleven missionaries, the accounts emphasized the brutal and barbaric nature possessed by a people capable of such acts. The accusation was brought that the Chinese lacked the courage to fight effectively in the army but were capable of murdering people in their sleep. Such acts were a "barbarous blot on nineteenth century civilization."[49] Five years after the Ku Cheng massacre, during the Boxer rebellion, the same note was sounded. Chinese merchants who had just returned from Peking purportedly told of seeing "European women hauled into the street by shrieking Boxers who stripped them and hacked them to pieces. Their dissevered limbs were tossed to the crowd and carried off with howls of triumph. Chinese soldiers carried the bodies of white children aloft on their spears while their companions shot at the bodies."[50] Neither the accuracy of the report nor the conclusion that the Chinese were a people of uniquely barbarian character was ever questioned.

The term barbarian was often used to imply a sense of inferiority, backwardness, and coarseness. The Chinese were thought to belong to an earlier race which had not been in touch with the world's civilizations and was therefore "unfitted for the advancement which is now about to mark the world's history."[51] In 1895 some Americans were meeting the threat posed by a civilization about which they lacked even the most primitive information by deciding that it had long ago passed its prime. As the nation became more involved in the world near the turn of the century, it could not avoid succumbing to the always present tendency toward introspective analysis. The country had developed since infancy in an environment which constantly questioned the merits of every aspect of public life, and now as the nation became increasingly aware of rediscovered relationships with the rest of the world, especially China, it was natural and necessary to evaluate that ancient people. The result was a down-grading of everything oriental.

The attitude which developed had as its backbone an abiding sense of superiority, a fact which made itself apparent in the accounts of travelers. "My custom was to examine the window frames, and if I thought there was not enough air space I made as much more as I thought fit by poking holes in the paper with my walking stick."[52] The writer did not feel that the owner objected to this procedure because paper for windows was very cheap. The author may have been correct in his facts, but his attitude was unmistakable. A similar point of view was apparent in a description of cross-country horseback riding in China by a member of the American diplomatic corps who explained that among the relatively few diversions available for foreigners, riding in the country was one of the most popular. It was looked upon as an exhilarating sport because of the obstacles presented to horse and rider. In addition to traversing the rough ground it required agility to elude the anger of peasants who deeply resented foreigners galloping through young crops and leaping over the mounds where their ancestors sought peaceful repose.[53]

The sense of superiority implicit in the attitude of American diplomats was often quite apparent. Exasperation at the delay in trying to get satisfaction for missionary claims from Chinese officials caused the consul at Foochow to express himself with unusual candor. He had endured all the hostility and delay that he planned to, he said. He was tired of Chinese who refused to show proper respect toward Americans, and as far as he was concerned the only way to handle them anyway was with harshness. "They must be taught the lesson of force," he concluded.[54] The Reverend Doctor

Gracey was no newcomer to China, having seen considerable service as a missionary before entering the diplomatic corps. What he said openly was implicit in the attitudes of many consular officials. So dubious was he of the Chinese after many years among them that he no longer believed anything they said, even the Christian converts, unless he could establish its truth personally.[55]

The consul at Hankow revealed the same attitude. Shortly after the diplomats had been rescued from the besieged legations at Peking, he wrote to the assistant secretary of state. "The only way to deal with Chinese is with a club, and they will settle at once most graciously, and respect you above all men."[56] Most American officials were only mildly disturbed over the use of force against the Chinese. When an American missionary shot and killed a Chinese, the consul indicated concern over the appropriateness of his action but made no attempt to bring him under court jurisdiction.[57] Acts of violence against Chinese by Americans in China were common enough so as to attract little notice. When an American seaman on shore leave wrecked the British consulate, threw several Chinese in the river, and beat up two Chinese police who tried to control him, he was fined ten dollars.[58] Because Americans were not subject to trial in Chinese courts, the protests of the local police were to no avail. Consuls worked hard to protect the interests of American citizens but rarely gave much thought to the rights of the Chinese.

On another occasion a young American who was employed as a bank teller in one of the port cities described the manner in which he traveled the streets outside the compound. "If a Chinaman does not at once make room for me in the street I would strike him forcibly with my cane in the face."[59]

When questioned as to whether that sort of an act would go unpunished, the young man replied, "Should I break his nose or kill him, the worst that can happen would be that he or his people would make complaints to the Consul, who might impose the fine of a dollar for the misdemeanor, but I could always prove that I had just cause to beat him."[60] Americans in China resorted to force as a means of expressing their contempt for the Chinese with enough frequency to fix in the minds of many Chinese a strong resentment against their caucasian visitors. In many instances the root of this resentment traced back not to any particularly high-handed act but simply to the common practice employed by almost all Americans in China of referring to the Chinese as "boy" or "Chinaman." Their resentment was heightened because they felt that they were being treated as inferiors by people whom they in turn classified as barbarians. At the heart of the problem lay a familiar human weakness, the inability to judge other peoples by any standards other than one's own.

This attitude was quite clear from Albert J. Beveridge's description of an inspection tour of Manchuria which he conducted for the Senate in 1901. He was impressed with the vigor and ability of the Russians who were building the Trans-Siberian railroad. His descriptions of the towns built by the Russians to facilitate construction of the road emphasized the order, loveliness, and cleanliness of these places. Chinese towns, on the other hand, were "aggregations of corruption, disease and disorder."[61] He praised the Russian towns because there you could buy "bread made from American flour, American sugar-cured ham, American canned fruits from the Pacific Coast . . . American salmon from the Columbia, American canned meats from the central

West, and American condensed milk and cream from Illinois."[62] In Chinese towns, by contrast, all that you could find were strange, unappetizing, and inedible foods. The same standard by which the senator judged other peoples was utilized by many Americans in the Far East. The result was that the Chinese were viewed as far inferior to the people of the Western world when measured against the standard of Western civilization, particularly in its American expression.

The apparent inherent barbarity of the Chinese race was felt by observers to manifest itself most clearly in the social crudity of family life. Living accommodations which were coarse by American standards offended the eyes and nostrils of many, who returned with harsh descriptions of their experiences in Chinese lodgings. "This was my first experience of a Chinese inn and it made my flesh creep," noted one traveler in describing the central courtyard where animals, foul straw, and manure provided an unpleasant landscape for the weary traveler.[63] His room was on the ground floor partly occupied by coal stored for the winter and besieged by intrusive crowds at the door and window. "This went on all day, what with the stench of manure, distracting noises, windows unglazed, and inquisitive visitors, my lodging proved to be the worst I had ever had."[64] His description was typical of that recorded for American audiences by those who journeyed through the interior of China.

The huts of Chinese peasants were sometimes described as picturesque, but generally travelers found them to be thoroughly primitive in design, construction, and interior appointments.[65] The dwellings of poorer city people, who lived in severely crowded conditions and were never visited by foreigners because they did not dare to brave the hostility, were described only from a distance, but in many cases they were likened to cells or swarms. The houses of wealthy Chinese were also described in detail largely because these were places where Americans were more welcome. The placement of doors in other than a straight line so as to prevent the direct passage of evil spirits through the house and the uncomfortable, hard beds were a source of wonder. Visitors found the houses strange, sometimes attractive and even beautiful, but always indicative of an inferior understanding of architectural principles.

Travelers frequently emphasized the filth, poverty, and generally disgusting living conditions found in the cities. *American Architect* in commenting upon conditions in foreign cities editorialized that "China, however, stands first for the incredible foulness of its cities and their inhabitants. The Consul at Chefoo, Mr. Fowler, writes that in the center of the two cities reputed to be the cleanest in China he had himself seen cholera corpses decomposing, dogs eating the bodies of babies, and snakes crawling about among the masses of filth of every kind."[66] On another occasion a visitor to Canton who had allowed one day for his exploration of the city noted that "the rabble are a horrible nuisance to the sightseer in Canton, because, though they may not assault or insult the foreigner, they jostle against you disgustingly (from such a dirty people)."[67] A comparison between slum housing in New York and that in certain Chinese coastal cities was never offered.

A visitor to Shanghai was quite interested in the design and operation of the oriental sewage disposal system, and he described an early-morning encounter with men bearing uncovered buckets upon the ends of a carrying-stick through the narrow streets, where agility was required to avoid being splattered. These men transported their burdens to a waiting scow, which when filled was towed away to provide fertilizer for Chinese fields. As the buckets were dumped, some of the contents occasionally spilled into the river adjacent to the place where townspeople were filling water containers. "Small-pox, at the time of my visit, was epidemic in the town, and I brushed past men in the narrow alleys who were covered with eruptions; everywhere the ground was slimy with filth, and the state of the town was indescribable."[68]

The presence of large numbers of rats in the crowded areas in some cities helped to support the belief that rats were a major staple in the Chinese diet. The strength of this feeling may be better appreciated through the childhood experience of a Protestant minister in Pittsburgh. The author described his presence at a Sunday school program where lantern slides were being used to illustrate a talk on foreign missions. "It [the picture] represented a Chinaman reposing on a couch, when suddenly there emerged from the gloom a monster rat, whereupon the Chinaman opened his capacious jaws, and the rat aforesaid made a wild plunge down his throat. Soon another rat appeared and disappeared in like manner, and another, and still another. We youngsters screamed with delight and kept encoring the performance, so that the 'professor' was obliged to curtail the Biblical features of the programme in order that we might feast our eyes on the rat-eating Chinaman."[69] He could not exactly recall what relevance the "rat-eating Chinaman" had to the missionary program, but his first impression of the Chinese had never faded.

When a plague in China brought death to thousands in 1894, it was thought that the habit of eating rats was largely responsible. Americans were appalled at the supposed Chinese belief that the consumption of rats made the hair grow, produced "warmth" in the body, and was generally good for the constitution.[70] The subject was the occasion for a number of cartoons in a variety of periodicals. One of the cartoons consisted of two sequences: in the first one a "Chinaman" was shown standing before his tea cart on which the sign "Star Tea" was mounted; in the second frame the "Chinaman" was shown returning to his cart after a short absence during which the letters on the sign had been reversed by pranksters to read "Eat Rats."[71]

Eating habits and the attitudes and customs which characterized Chinese society were thought to support the picture of China as a strange and barbaric people. An interesting sidelight in this regard was the attitude toward Chinese art which prevailed in the United States. The conclusion of one art critic was that no true art could come out of China anymore.[72] It might be said that once, perhaps, China had produced art objects; but what was now passing for art in China was merely the duplication of ancient works and methods. So-called art objects from China should be more correctly called curios, and were really fit only for display in a museum. The viewpoint of this critic was not the exception. Travelers to the Orient and those who were especially interested in China spoke of collecting snuff boxes or jeweled swords just as one might collect stamps. There was almost no indication during the earlier years of the 1890s that Chinese art was judged on the basis of its own inherent creativity. The implication was that Chinese civilization had lost its power to create, and could only produce bizarre and picturesque objects which were prized for their novelty.

The status of women in China was a never-ending source of amusement, amazement, and indignation. American women were naturally disturbed at the position which Chinese women occupied. She was overburdened with social regulations and traditions to the point where she appeared to be little more than a bearer of children and the primary source of household labor.[73] The housewife was told that if she did not act according to custom her neighbors would laugh and speak ill of her. A gruesome picture was drawn of the cruel treatment meted out to the daughter in the family and continued on into marriage in the person of her husband's mother. Not until a woman had become a mother-in-law herself could she hope for any respite in her cheerless life.

The depreciation of women was thought to be largely responsible for the practice of infanticide, which was described in detail complete with an occasional illustration of places where the bodies of infant girls were left at the age of a few days. Many writers expressed shock and disgust at the attitude toward life which such a practice represented. Infanticide was one of the aspects of Chinese life that could always be counted upon to send chills through a reader. Images of day-old infants left on the rubbish heaps in filthy alleyways, deposited one upon another in small stone shelters, or thrown into the river always provoked charges of Chinese barbarity. An occasional brave observer attempted to deny the extent of infanticide, but readers did not want to be told about the good qualities of the Chinese.[74] They wanted to think of them as heathens and welcomed only those descriptions which supported this view.

The Chinese custom of foot-binding received a great deal of attention. Readers were amply informed as to the methods employed to reduce a foot of normal length to the maximum of five inches for ordinary girls and three inches for girls of high birth. Between the ages of four and twelve years the foot was tightly bandaged so as to bring all the smaller toes underneath, making the ball of the heel almost disappear by forcing it forward and creating a deep cleft in the sole of the foot.[75] The bandages were tightened regularly until the desired result had been accomplished. The pain was so intense that the legs were often allowed to hang downward over the edge of a board reducing the circulation and thus numbing the pain. Mothers slept beside their children, according to some accounts, and beat them with bamboo when they cried at night lest they awaken the household.[76] Two to five years were required to bring the distortion to "celestial perfection," and when it was completed, it was considered to be the mark of womanhood.[77]

Numerous observations were made about the custom, none of which reflected favorably upon the Chinese. The lack of vigor in China's defense against the Japanese was attributed by some to the enervating effects of foot-binding.[78] The extreme pain which accompanied the practice plus its crippling effect was thought to produce weakened, debilitated women incapable of fostering strong sons. Many women suffered pain through their entire lives, and it was believed that a large number died from complications resulting from the practice. The crippled feet often bled when stood upon for any length of time, and it was unusual to find a foot without at least one toe rotted away.[79] Americans seem to have been most dismayed by the pride which Chinese women took in their small feet. The only explanation for the custom, they felt, lay in the fact that the Chinese were an ignorant, superstitious, and benighted people.[80]

American readers of all ages absorbed descriptions of Chinese customs which strengthened their impression of China's strangeness. An article in *St. Nicholas* magazine, which was aimed at juvenile readers, characterized China as a place where city walls kept the people in, boys wore queer little shirts, and the women were kept busy at home making bird's-nest soup.[81] Marriage customs were thought of as not only strange but almost tragic in the extent to which they denied the possibility of a life of mutual understanding and respect. One traveler described the traditions which required so much of the wife and so little of the husband and concluded that "balancing the probabilities of jealousy, inward suffering, and outward quarreling one turns away sick with disgust from this picture."[82] Descriptions of funerals emphasized the curious pagan practices which were so carefully observed, from the practice of selecting a grave site to the small bits of paper scattered in the street after the funeral procession to help the spirit find its way.

The Chinese method of writing, with its curious little characters, seemed especially peculiar, and Chinese music was known for its harsh and unmelodic sounds. The dress and eating habits of the Chinese were different from any that Americans had ever known, and their habit of allowing their fingernails to grow to a great length made them seem grotesque. An illustration of the hand of a highly born Chinaman with fingernails from eight to ten inches in length must have repelled many Western readers.[83] At almost every angle from which the Chinese were observed they seemed totally foreign to the ways of Western civilization.

American medical men who went to China either as travelers or more usually as medical missionaries attached to the hospitals in the larger cities sent back accounts of their contacts with Chinese medical practice. A conversation with a successful Chinese doctor revealed that the Chinese were aware of veins and arteries but did not know their exact location.[84] They seemed to know nothing of hygiene and sanitation, but they were familiar with joints and knew how to treat dislocations. They were familiar with the theory of germs but thought of them as a cross between worms and snakes which hatched out in the body. In general, Chinese physicians were observed to be highly superstitious, revering the ancient practices of their fathers, who had taught them medicine, and having very limited perspective as to the real nature of medicine.

The superstition of the Chinese people easily matched that of their medical men. When a cold wave struck in a part of China where temperatures never dropped below freezing, the people gathered the ice from the trees and brought it into Hong Kong to sell for medicine.[85] The Chinese appeared to have fantastic ideas about the healing properties of some substances. Americans would use tigers' bones for fertilizers, but the Chinese used them instead for medicine.[86] Pills the size of pigeon eggs, oil rubbed on the temples as a cure for cholera, and dozens of other strange prescriptions seemed to indicate that Chinese medicine was hopelessly inferior to the West.

Superstition and greed were characteristics which seemed typical. Will Clemens described the latter when he wrote, *"Ch'ien, ch'ien, ch'ien*—money, money, money, is the real Chinese god."[87] Rarely did the Chinese rise above the greed for gold. It was not that they were a race of misers, he explained, but that they were buyers and sellers and gamblers. "You may pursue his soul but you cannot distract his mind from his one object in life—the pursuit of *ch'ien.*"[88] Because of their inherent dishonesty no Chinese could be trusted in places of responsibility, and this was why the development

of China could be carried out only under foreign direction.[89]
Henry Cabot Lodge wrote in 1895 that Orientals were so
radically different from Westerners, so thoroughly untruth-
ful by Western standards, that it was hopeless to expect to
establish communications with them on any reasonable
basis.[90]

Americans were startled and offended at how sharply the
Chinese attitude toward death contrasted with the attitude
in the West. "The common people of China are notoriously
indifferent to death," noted a geologist and science professor
at the University of Pennsylvania, "not because they hope
for another and blessed life, but because the national ancestor worship has set the eyes of the whole race backward."[91]
Examples of this attitude were plentiful. Women who took
their own lives so that their spirit might join the spirit of a
dead lover or husband were called "noble" in China. The
widespread practice of infanticide and the practice of hiring
a paid substitute to take the place of a condemned man
were incomprehensible to Western minds.[92] Committing sui-
cide in the house of an enemy in order to burden him with
the cost of a funeral and the exposure in the street of old
people near death were thought of as the acts of barbarians.

There was strong resentment over the treatment meted
out to foreigners by the Chinese. Numerous antiforeign
riots and massacres occurred during the 1890s, culminating
in the Boxer uprising in 1900. The missionaries were almost
unanimous in feeling that the majority of Chinese accepted
foreigners and that the attacks were due to a small group of
troublemakers. One minister attributed the attacks on mission personnel and property in part to a book by Chou Han
of Hunan, published in 1888.[93] It contained thirty-two pictures of a disgustingly blasphemous character describing the

Christians as hog-worshippers, killers of infants, and immoral and lewd persons. Diplomatic personnel placed the blame on the secret societies, who were stirring up antiforeign sentiment in order to establish support for their own political goals.[94]

For the most part Americans were unwilling to accept responsibility for the irritation caused by their own intolerant and often abusive acts toward the Chinese. By phrasing their explanations of the situation in a way which placed the Chinese in the wrong for resenting the presence of foreigners, Americans were able to continue to look upon themselves as representatives of a superior civilization. According to this view the Chinese were guilty of failing to appreciate the West and of failing to give way in the face of a more-advanced civilization. In order to preserve the interpretation of China as a decadent race and thereby maintain the notion of American superiority, it was necessary to avoid the suggestion that Chinese resentment of Westerners was as justifiable as Western resentment of the Chinese.

The term *barbarian* was the word which was probably the most descriptive of the attitude of many Americans toward China. In addition, however, the term *heathen* was employed in order to describe fully what many believed to be the moral depravity of the Chinese. The religious implications of the latter word were necessary in the minds of some to complement the impression of cultural and political inferiority conveyed by the former. Not only were the Chinese thought to be a backward people in the eyes of man when measured by his civilization, but they were also considered deficient in the sight of God. Unfortunately for a true understanding of Christianity and for the promotion of understanding between East and West, the people of the Western world had forgotten that in both Jesus the Lord and Paul the Apostle there existed men who were able to cross back and forth freely between East and West. By the end of the nineteenth century Christians had lost what little ability they originally had to conceive of God as equally Eastern and Western. In the eyes of those who ruled the North American continent, the people of the East were not viewed as fellow human beings under the same God. Nations in the West had been able to join together in happy wedlock Western culture and Western church. It was inevitable, therefore, that when the Chinese were judged inferior by the standard of the former, they were necessarily seen as inferior by the standard of the latter. To describe the Chinese as both barbarian and heathen was the natural consequence of religious nationalism.

The attitude of the missionaries toward the people among whom they labored reflects an inner paradox caused in part by the thorough mixing of Christ and culture in the Western world. The first principle of evangelization had to be the need of non-believers to hear the gospel of Jesus Christ; therefore, the greater the need of these so-called pagans, the more aggressive and widespread must be the effort to convert them. If the sacrifices of a particular mission field were great, as in China, then the evangelists invariably comforted themselves with the thought that the need for these sacrifices must have been even greater. The paradox occurred when it was necessary to face the unmovable theological tenet that since the Grace of God was irresistible no so-called heathen, no matter how depraved, could resist it. A human being who was saved in the religious sense became equal with all others who had undergone conversion. Thus the Chinese was viewed as a barbarian by the standards of Western civilization, but when he had undergone conversion, he was regarded as equal with all other Christians. The confusion which resulted from trying to apply two standards of judgment to a single human being was reflected in part in the antagonism with which missionary efforts were often met and in the long-term failure of the Christian church to establish deep and lasting roots in China.

Since the first requirement for a conversion experience was the presence of a sufficiently depraved subject, it was common for missionaries to describe the moral condition of the Chinese in the blackest possible terms. Samuel Wells Williams was a longtime resident and student of China. During his lifetime and for years afterward he was acknowledged to be one of the few experts on Chinese life and history in the Western world. He was often quoted by missionaries to substantiate their evaluation of the Chinese, whom he described as "vile and polluted in a shocking degree; their conversation is full of filthy expressions, and their lives of impure acts . . . the universal practice of lying and dishonest dealings; the unblushing lewdness of old and young; harsh cruelty towards prisoners by officers . . . all form a full unchecked torrent of human depravity [and] . . . moral degradation of which an excessive statement can scarcely be made. . . ."[95] Probably no missionary who was an honest bearer of the name could look into the depths of such depravity and not tingle at the thought of the possibilities for conversion.

Protestant missionaries almost exclusively looked upon the religious practices of the Chinese and the custom of ancestor worship as clear indications of their heathenish character. Many felt in particular that the latter practice of elevating members of the family was one of the prime causes of China's moral debasement. There was merit in honoring one's family, but carrying that honor to the excess of worship tended to deny the possibility of worshiping a god outside the family relationship. Missionaries discussed at length the terrible conflicts with their families which all converts in China faced. Unless the family was sympathetic toward the new belief, which it usually was not, the Christian Chinese had to struggle against the full weight of family tradition. Incidents were widely known where converts had defied family traditions to participate in the annual pilgrimage to a local temple or a traditional pagan celebration, at great threat to their own safety. Chinese religious practice was very imperfectly understood, and the presence of three distinct systems within one culture seemed to utterly confuse all observers including the missionaries. Rarely, Buddhism, Taoism, or Confucianism might be recognized as separate systems of belief; but their relationship with each other was unclear, and it was easier by far just to classify the Chinese as heathens.

This view of the Chinese was characteristic of virtually all missionary publications during the years at the turn of the century when the major missionary effort was launched in India and China, and it was this attitude which had such a powerful impact on American ideas about the Orient. Indeed, the only rationale which could justify the expenditure of life and funds in a missionary effort was the one which characterized the Chinese as being in desperate need of salvation. It was no wonder that they were looked upon as heathens in need of conversion. Because it was felt that they had strayed from the path, most missionaries were unable to appreciate the Chinese in their unconverted state. Missionary accounts emphasized continually their superstitious beliefs, strange customs, abnormal vices, and immorality. They could be, and were, converted, and the missionaries were intensely loyal to their converts; but that was the other side of the paradox. Meanwhile, the missionary did his best to describe the depths of China's heathenism and thus helped to solidify the attitude toward the Chinese as a strange and barbarous people.

The missionaries were highly selective in their descriptions of Chinese life. It was inevitable that their choice of topics led to distortion and to an unfavorable view of China. By emphasizing the cruelty, the strange customs surrounding the life of women, and the crowded cities, they reinforced the Western sense of superiority. Much of what they said was based upon actual conditions in China. Many female and also male children were allowed to die because their families could not feed them, and living conditions in the cities were often hopelessly crowded, with sanitary facilities reduced to a minimum. By selecting these and similar aspects of Chinese life, it was possible to cast China in the mold of a backward, barbaric people incapable of meeting the most elementary standards of the Western world.

But the problems which China faced in her efforts to provide for her citizens were seldom noticed. The political problem was little understood because the relationship between the ruling Manchus and the Chinese people was hopelessly vague in American minds. The transportation problem was largely ignored by observers, who could not comprehend the vastness of China's territory and the inaccesible nature of many regions. When Chinese died by the thousands in time of famine, the government was called heartless because it did not transport food to stricken areas. The basic social institutions of Chinese life such as the clan system were both misunderstood and unappreciated. The problem of keeping order in a country where in some regions the central government was only a name was not comprehended. The strong framework of ethical values in Chinese society remained unmentioned by those who saw only the unfavorable side of China. What was said about China was true to some extent, but because it was only a partial description, ignoring other basic factors, its effect was to distort.

The question as to why China was described in such an unfavorable manner does not admit of an easy answer. Part of the reason, however, lies in the expectations of the majority of the American reading public. The great gulf separating the two civilizations was too extensive to be bridged by the limited contacts which most Americans had with the Chinese. Many were familiar with coolie laborers and laundrymen, and had perhaps visited Chinatown; but rare was the American who had stayed in a Chinese home for even a few hours. The strangeness of Chinese culture was overwhelming. Readers could scarcely draw their eyes away from the descriptions of unusual adventures and the weird tales of Chinese life which appeared in all the popular magazines.

The standards which were used to measure the Chinese were impossibly unrealistic. Not only was it unrealistic to apply American values to a wholly different civilization, but those standards of judgment which were selected represented the brighter aspects of American society. Americans were thoroughly absorbed in the concept of national superiority and were unable to appreciate a civilization which lay almost totally outside of Western experience. Given their lack of understanding and their ethnocentrism, it was inevitable that Americans should judge China by the ideals of their own society.

When Americans were first introduced to China, they were startled. China looked threatening. Here was a civiliza-

tion with ancient lineage, with a claim to a longer and perhaps more profound acquaintance with the world. The beginnings of a solution to the dilemma posed by a disappear-
ing frontier were just being suggested in 1886 by Josiah
Strong, who wrote that America had a destiny not just on
the North American continent but on the entire globe. Then
suddenly, there loomed China with its claim to prior greatness. What destiny could there be for America in the Far
East with China there? The United States claimed to have a
peculiar mission to perform in the world. This claim could
not be justified unless China was found to be in need of the
American gospel.

The details of the solution were not fully developed until
1898. It was in that year and those following that the exciting
events in Cuba and the Pacific served to establish firmly the
broadened concept of an American destiny in the world. In
the early 1890s the country was still suffering from acute feelings of insecurity. There were glimmerings of a possible future for the United States as an evangelist of progress in
China, but for the most part China simply appeared as a
threat to American uniqueness. In order to meet the threat
the Chinese were described as a racially inferior, morally debased, and socially backward people. The threat was removed by claiming that there was no threat. If the Chinese
were inferior to the Anglo-Saxon race, then they could never
develop threatening proportions. In 1898 and after, the
threat of China was removed by the more sophisticated
method of emphasizing the responsibility of the superior race
for the inferior. But most Americans in the early 1890s contented themselves with a simple denunciation of the Chinese
as an uncivilized people.

Americans misunderstood the Chinese because they

needed to. Anything approximating an unbiased description of China was apparently too threatening to the image of America held by most Americans even to be considered. Those people in the United States who thought about the nation's enlarging environment seemed unable to face the possibility of China's being a great civilization and a possible power in the Far East, because it would require a reevaluation of basic values. As a result, the descriptions of Chinese life by American observers were designed to gratify their need to see the Chinese in an unfavorable light. Americans misunderstood the Chinese because they were unable to view oriental culture from any viewpoint other than their own. China was placed in an unfavorable light not primarily as a result of malice aforethought but as a result of a deep-seated sense of American superiority.

1. *Congressional Record,* 57th Congress, 1st Session, 1902, 35, pt. 4:4040.

2. Ibid.

3. Ibid.

4. Theodore Roosevelt to Henry Cabot Lodge, June 5, 1905, Lodge Papers.

5. Henry Cabot Lodge to Henry White, September 3, 1900, and to Brooks Adams, June 29, 1900, Lodge Papers.

6. Henry Cabot Lodge to Cecil Spring Rice, March 28, 1904, Lodge Papers.

7. Ibid., August 12, 1898.

8. E. R. Scidmore, "The River of Tea," *Century* LVIII (August, 1899), 548.

9. Ibid., p. 547.

10. Dora E. W. Spratt, "Earning a Living in China," *Lippincott's Magazine* LIX (May, 1897), 674.

11. Edward S. Morse, *Glimpses of China and Chinese Homes* (Boston, 1902), pp. 208–9.

12. Samuel Gompers, ed., *Some Reasons for Chinese Exclusion,* American Federation of Labor (Washington, D. C., 1902).

13. Ibid., p. 16.

14. Ibid., p. 9.

15. Charles Denby to William W. Rockhill, September 4, 1908, Rockhill Papers.

16. Charles Denby to Secretary of State John Sherman, December 11, 1897, *Despatches from United States Ministers in China,* National Archives (Washington: Government Printing Office, 1946) .

17. Lehlbach Report, House Document 4048, 51st Congress, 2d Session, *Public Documents* 2890, Vol. 6.

18. Ibid., p. 195.

19. Ibid., p. 204.

20. Ibid., p. 415.

21. *Congressional Record,* 53d Congress, 1st Session, 1893, 25, pt. 2:2529.

22. Ibid., p. 2531.

23. "Where Life Is Cheap," Atlanta *Constitution,* November 12, 1894.

24. Ibid.

25. "Chinese Execution," Washington *Post,* July 29, 1900.

26. A. H. Lee, "Chinese Cruelty," *Harper's Weekly* XXXIX (1895) , 182.

27. Ibid.

28. "Nameless Tortures," Seattle *Post-Intelligencer,* July 15, 1900.

29. Lee, "Chinese Cruelty," p. 183.

30. "A Ghastly Picture of Mongolian Savagery," San Francisco *Chronicle,* December 19, 1894.

31. A. B. de Guerville, "The Red Cross in the Far East," *Munsey's Magazine* XIV (1895) , 48.

32. Ibid.

33. Ibid., p. 49.

34. Editorial, Washington *Post,* November 17, 1894.

35. "A Few Shots Rout the Chinese," San Francisco *Chronicle,* December 19, 1894.

36. Eustace B. Rogers, "The War in Korea," *Harper's Weekly* XXXVIII (August 11, 1894) , 750.

37. Charles Denby to Secretary of State John Sherman, November 19, 1897, *Despatches from United States Ministers to China.*

38. "Chinese Army" (illustration) , *Leslie's Weekly* LXXX (February 7, 1895) , 91.

39. Julian Ralph, "Side Notes from the Asiatic War," *Harper's Weekly* XXXIX (May 11, 1895) , 448.

40. "Surgery in China" (editorial) , *Public Opinion* XVI (December 7, 1893) , 222.

41. "A Chinese Brain," *Nature* L (May 31, 1894) , 111.

42. James Ricalton *China through the Stereoscope* (New York, 1901) , p. 143.

43. John Fowler to Assistant Secretary of State Francis B. Loomis, August 10, 1905, *Despatches from the United States Consuls in Chefoo,* National Archives (Washington: Government Printing Office, 1947) .

44. Henry Cabot Lodge, "Our Blundering Foreign Policy," *Forum* XIX (March, 1895) , 11.

45. Editorial, Washington *Post,* December 1, 1894.

46. C. M. Cady, "Responsibility among the Chinese," *Century Magazine* LI (January, 1896) , 344.

47. "A Chance for Jingoes" (editorial) , *Harper's Weekly* XXXIX (August 31, 1895) , 817.

48. "The War in Asia" (editorial) , *Harper's Weekly* XXXVIII (October 13, 1894) , 963.

49. "The Massacre of Missionaries in China" (editorial) , *Chautauquan* XXI (September, 1895) , 765.

50. "Women Hacked to Pieces and Children Carried on Spears," New York *Times,* July 20, 1900.

51. "The War in the Far East" (editorial) , *Chautauquan* XX (January, 1895) , 491.

52. "Chinese Hostelries," *Current Literature* XXV (1899) , 35.

53. C. Smith, "Cross Country in China," *Harper's Weekly* XL (October 3, 1896) , 981.

54. Samuel L. Gracey to Assistant Secretary of State William R. Day, March 7, 1898, *Despatches from United States Consuls in Foochow,* National Archives (Washington: Government Printing Office, 1947) .

55. Samuel L. Gracey to Third Assistant Secretary of State Thomas W. Cridler, October 15, 1898, *Despatches from United States Consuls in Foochow.*

56. Levi S. Wilcox to Assistant Secretary of State David J. Hill, September 8, 1900, *Despatches from United States Consuls in Hankow,* National Archives (Washington: Government Printing Office, 1947) .

57. John Goodnow to Charles Leamen, April 28, 1902, *Despatches from United States Consuls in Shanghai,* National Archives (Washington: Government Printing Office, 1947) .

58. Edward Bedloe to Secretary of State John Hay, August 16, 1898, *Despatches from United States Consuls in Canton,* National Archives (Washington: Government Printing Office, 1947) .

59. Paul Carus, "The Chinese Problem," *Open Court* XV (October, 1901) , 608.

60. Ibid.

61. Albert J. Beveridge, "The White Invasion of China," *Saturday Evening Post* CLXXIV (November 23, 1901), 1–2.

62. Ibid.

63. Henry Lansdell, "Chinese Central Asia," *Nature* XLIX (January 25, 1894), 309.

64. Ibid., p. 310.

65. William E. Geil, *A Yankee on the Yangtze* (New York, 1904).

66. "China" (editorial), *American Architect* LXVI (December 30, 1899), 106.

67. Douglas Sladen, "The Oddest City in the World," *Frank Leslie's Popular Monthly* XXV (March, 1893), 343.

68. Edward S. Morse, "Latrines of the East," *American Architect* XXXIX (March 18, 1893), 171.

69. E. R. Donehoo, "John Chinaman," *Charities Review* VII (January, 1898), 914.

70. Claude A. Rees, *Chun Ti-Kung His Life and Adventures* (New York, 1897).

71. "The Chinaman" (cartoon), *Harper's Weekly* XXXVIII (November 10, 1894), 1076.

72. W. A. Cornaby, "Chinese Art an Index to the National Character," *Literary Digest* VII (October 28, 1893), 635.

73. Isabella L. Bird, *The Yangtze Valley and Beyond,* 2 vols. (New York, 1900), I, 21.

74. Herbert A. Giles, *China and the Chinese* (New York, 1902), p. 177.

75. "Domestic Life in China" Chicago *Tribune,* August 5, 1900.

76. "Lilly Feet," *Rocky Mountain News,* July 23, 1900.

77. "Foot Distortion in China" (editorial), *Public Opinion* XVII (June 14, 1894), 68.

78. Editorial, Atlanta *Constitution,* November 2, 1894.

79. "The Chinese Woman's Small Foot" (editorial), *Literary Digest* XXVII (November 27, 1897), 925.

80. A. Burlingame Johnson to Secretary of State John Sherman, September 1, 1897, *Despatches from United States Consuls in Amoy,* National Archives (Washington: Government Pringting Office, 1947).

81. Ruth Dana Draper, "The Chinese Giant," *St. Nicholas* XVII (April, 1890), 484–89.

82. Harriet L. Beebe, "Marriage in Nanking," *Chautauquan* XV (July, 1892), 473.

83. "A Chinaman's Hand" (illustration), *Literary Digest* XIII (September 26, 1896), 698.

84. William E. S. Faas, "A Chinese Physician," *Current Literature* XXX (June, 1901) , 739–40.

85. "News" (editorial) , *Nature* XLVII (March 30, 1893) , 516.

86. "Chinese White Wax," *Scientific American Supplement* XXXIII (February 20, 1892) , 13461.

87. Will Clemens, "Chinese Shops," *Lippincott's Magazine* LIV (August, 1894) , 282.

88. Ibid.

89. E. H. Conger to Secretary of State John Sherman, November 3, 1898, *Despatches from United States Ministers to China.*

90. Henry Cabot Lodge, "Our Blundering Foreign Policy," *Forum* XIX (March, 1895) , 8–17.

91. J. P. Lesley, "The Idea of Life After Death," *Forum* X (October, 1890) , 214.

92. A. Burlingame Johnson to Secretary of State John Sherman, September 1, 1897, *Despatches from United States Consuls in Amoy.*

93. S. F. Woodin, "Cause of the Riots in Yangtse Valley," *Independent* XLIV (June 16, 1892) , 18.

94. Samuel L. Gracey to E. H. Conger, August 4, 1899, *Despatches from United States Consuls in Foochow.*

95. John R. Hykes, "The Importance of Winning China for Christ," *Missionary Review* V (February, 1892) , 83.

4

Useful Aliens:

A More Favorable Evaluation

of the Chinese

"She was as pretty a little bit of Chinese bric-a-brac as ever evaded the Exclusion Act."—Frank Norris, 1894

By 1894 when Frank Norris wrote the lines above, American attitudes toward the Chinese were being swept into different channels by new currents of interest. The Geary bill had been enacted into law by that year, and to a considerable extent it marked a turning point in the development of the nation's image of China. From this point on a change in emphasis could be discerned in some of the public statements made concerning China. The criticism of the Chinese was less hysterical, and an appreciative note could be heard more often as commentators in the business and religious communities modified their points of view to accord with changing interests. The opportunity of the China market, the concern over the role of a strengthened China in world affairs, and the experiences of the missionaries, all had their impact on attitudes toward the Chinese.

The most important reason for the decrease in anti-Chinese feeling and the increase in expressions of sympathy was the effectiveness of the exclusion legislation. West Coast agitators had pictured the Chinese as a horde poised on the further shores of the Pacific waiting for a signal to advance across the ocean and sweep civilization from the North American continent. The rest of the nation adopted this viewpoint as its own. With the passage of the Geary bill, which added more restrictions to those imposed by the exclusion legislation of 1882, most Americans were satisfied that the nation had successfully defended itself from the Chinese threat.

Naturally there was a wide variety of emphasis in the more favorable viewpoint. At one extreme were a few who felt so strongly about principles of justice and equality that they argued for the application of these principles to the Chinese, even to the extent of opposing exclusion in any form. At the other were those who really had no admiration at all for the Chinese as persons but who would grudgingly admit to their occasional utility. The major reason for the existence of a more favorable point of view was undoubtedly that exclusion legislation had removed the bulk of the threat. In addition, however, there was an interest in obtaining more reasonable treatment for the Chinese for a variety of reasons.

For some the treatment of the Chinese, at least in its harsher extremes, was inconsistent with the American tradition of fair play. It "goes beyond the bounds of decency and humanity, and must seem intolerable to anyone not afflicted with the craze against the Chinese which began with the sand-lot orators of California and has got possession somehow of most of the politicians."[1] The editor of this liberal journal excoriated the exclusion legislation because it made it a crime for a Chinese to be found on the soil of the United States unless he registered. In 1892 the editor of the *Christian Union* wrote that the Geary bill, which had just been signed by the president, was a disgrace to the nation.[2] It was also an insult to China, and it would not be at all surprising if the Chinese retaliated, the editor added seemingly with hope. Religious feeling in some quarters was incensed when President Cleveland signed the bill. Thomas C. Edwards, educator, author, and Presbyterian clergyman, voiced a reaction common among missionary clergy when he said, "It is a political question, and that is why our noble senators and most unimpeachable President complete the iniquitous proceedings."[3]

A few people pointed out how the exclusion laws violated our treaty agreements with China. The editor of the *Nation* explained how Senator Sherman's fight against the bill had been in vain, "for the majority of both parties seem to believe that it is right to 'trample upon a treaty,' so long as it is a treaty with Chinamen."[4] The specific conflict referred to was that part of the Burlingame Treaty of 1868 in which the United States had promised never to exclude Chinese immigration, though it might limit or restrict it. Not very many people, however, agreed that the treaty had been violated by the exclusion laws, or were even concerned about the question.

By far the largest segment of American opinion approved of the exclusion laws in principle, even though some objected to the harshness of their provisions.[5] It was believed that although indiscriminate immigration was obviously undesirable, restriction ought to be consistent with our past treaties. It might even be preferable to let the Chinese come if the alternative was the weakening of the nation's good

name. "Undoubtedly this nation must throw some limitations on immigration to its shores," editorialized *American
Missionary*.[6] But this did not mean that the nation should
pass a bill which discriminated against races, violated a treaty
obligation, crippled trade, and might cause retaliation. The
retaliation referred to was that which might be brought
against missionaries in China, a possibility which caused
the clergy to advocate milder versions of the law.

In California a Protestant clergyman observed that interest in exclusion was abating and concluded that "the
Chinese problem, so called, has but little vitality, although
it is still a fruitful subject for newspaper editorials and sensational space-writing. The masses of Californians appear
to think that the present laws are reasonably well enforced."[7]
Orchard and vineyard owners were in favor of Chinese labor
because they could not get reliable workers from other
sources. The agricultural interests, therefore, formed a sort
of pro-Chinese party in resistance to the labor unions. "It
is an old story now that the politicians have far outrun the
desires of the people of the Pacific Coast in their anti-sinitic
fervors."[8]

Joaquin Miller, poet, amateur philosopher, naturalist,
and California booster, claimed to speak for California when
he said, "Californians, the real Californians, desire this act
modified, if not entirely abrogated."[9] Miller was enthusiastic
if somewhat unrealistic in his portrayal of the favorable side
of California opinion regarding the Chinese. "The real
Californian who bears the burthen of state hardly took note
of what was being done till too late; but now he wants the
whole thing undone."[10] He claimed to be speaking for the
real west when he said that property owners had never
wanted to discriminate against the Chinese. He laid the

blame for anti-Chinese activity at the feet of the labor agitator, who was nothing but a "beggar and a bully." The real laboring man simply wanted to work and never feared Chinese competition.

Miller's viewpoint was not widely supported, however, and an opinion which lies closer to the truth was that of a minister in Portland, Oregon. "The majority of quiet and order-loving citizens are glad the agitation ceased when it did, and that without the rupture of friendly relations with China the influx of an undesirable element into our population was brought to an end."[11]

The disappearance of the Chinese question as a domestic issue tended to soften hostility toward the Chinese, oftentimes to a greater degree than was warranted. Shortly before the onslaught of anti-Chinese recriminations in the debate over the Geary bill in 1892, it was observed that "outside of the labor unions and the hoodlums, nobody objects to the Chinese. They are preferred to Irish servant girls. . . . They work side by side with white workmen in factories, in orchards, and on farms, and fights are of rare occurrence."[12] This was a too optimistic conclusion, even though enthusiastic support for the Chinese did exist. The Chinese had been painted in vivid colors, but they had not lived up to their reputation, it was claimed. The Chinese were no more criminally inclined than other races, and Chinatown, instead of being the filthiest place in the city, had often proved to have a superior health rate. All the Chinese wanted was to be allowed to travel and work in the United States without being molested. They had no evil designs on the American way of life or on American prosperity. Such a picture of the Chinese, though not representative of American attitudes, was much less threatening.

The charge of cheap labor leveled against the Chinese was denounced as false. The *Yale Review* of February, 1896, carried an article by a professor of social science at the University of California in which the whole question of Chinese labor was examined.[13] The popular theory for the reduction of wages in California after 1870, explained the author, was the competition of Chinese labor. Because the Chinese would work for less, wages were driven down to a lower level. Although this might be true in a few areas, it was never more than a temporary development because as soon as the Chinese had mastered a skill they charged all they could get. An illustration of this was in Chinatown, San Francisco, where a Chinese clothing contractor was replacing his Chinese workers with white girls. In Sonoma County vineyards Chinese were being replaced with Portuguese because the Chinese demanded higher pay through their workers' associations. The Chinese in California may have aggravated the decline in wages, he opined, but they did not cause it.

A similar story was told about the Chinese in New York. The public had cried out against "Chinese cheap labor," noted a mission worker in New York's Chinatown, but such was not the case.[14] Chinese laundries charged higher prices than domestic laundries, and Chinese laundrymen got higher wages than laundry workers of other nationalities. The Chinese laundryman earned on the average from eight to fifteen dollars per week when other workers earned from four to ten dollars. Chinese cooks who worked in American homes were paid at least forty dollars a month and oftentimes much more. The truth about Chinese labor was that the Chinese worked for less when he had to, but as soon as he could command more, he would do so.

One reason for the lessening of anti-Chinese agitation was the feeling that the Chinese were no worse than the other immigrants who were coming to our shores from Europe. One writer even suggested that there was a worse class of immigrant than the Chinese. "Most men, if asked what class of immigrants they considered the least desirable, would answer, the Russian Jews."[15] Chester Holcombe, former member of the American legation in Peking, was one of a small number who were honestly sympathetic toward the Chinese. He thought that the exclusion of the Chinese on the grounds presently offered could only be interpreted as discriminatory. It should not be a question of Chinese immigration but of immigration from any country. Race, he said, is an inadequate basis on which to establish restriction or exclusion since all races have good as well as bad qualities in approximately equal proportions.[16]

The Chinese problem was also modified by the emergence of a new "question." The concern arose because of the increase of Japanese immigration at the turn of the century. In 1898 and 1899 slightly over two thousand Japanese arrived each year.[17] In 1900 the number jumped to 12,635 and by 1903 reached 19,968. The arrival of the Japanese immigrants constituted a new threat in the eyes of many. The Japanese population in 1904 based on immigration figures was estimated at 78,577.[18] Unofficial estimates ran much higher, however, and the Japanese were described as increasing at an alarming rate and "pouring in like a flood," so that they "must number well over one hundred thousand."[19]

It was not only the number of Japanese which was of concern but their supposedly inferior quality. A physician attached to a United States Public Health Service Hospital on the East Coast felt that "the Japanese coolie labor is [according to some observers who have made a special study of them] more undesirable than the Chinese."[20] The doctor based his statement in part upon his observation that the Japanese brought "more cases, absolutely and relatively, of contagious disease than any other nationality coming here."[21] He had noted that in 1903 one Japanese out of every thirty-seven who arrived was deported with a "loathesome or dangerous contagious disease."[22] Compared with such a threat as this, the Chinese seemed almost desirable.

The economic danger posed by Japanese labor was claimed by a few to be even more serious than that of the Chinese had been. The cry of Japanese cheap labor was quickly taken up by familiar voices. Senator Perkins of California emphasized the terrible danger to the wage-earners in his state posed by Japanese immigration.[23] In San Francisco the familiar cry of warning was heard about the oriental ability to work under conditions which would drive out caucasian labor.[24] Senator Perkins and John Young, editor of the *Chronicle,* had both been leading figures in the agitation for the exclusion of the Chinese. The chief point raised against the Japanese was their willingness to work for lower wages. The low wages paid in Japan where farm labor received less than a dollar and a half a month seemed terribly threatening. In the midst of such dangers the Chinese were forgotten.

The anti-Chinese viewpoint was also moderated to some extent through the acceptance of the Chinese into American life. "It is very gratifying to the tired farmer's wife to see her husband come driving up with a celestial, who presently having deposited his bed and valise in the place indicated, comes into the kitchen, places his little clock on the shelf,

ties on his apron, and proceeds to investigate the premises."[25]
The "celestial" was always courteous, very fond of the
children, and took to heart the interests of the family for
whom he worked. Two women who went to southern California for their health described their experiences with
Spanish house servants and concluded that the Chinese were
much to be preferred. The Chinese was still considered a
barbarian and a heathen, though not without some utili-
tarian value.

The Chinese were employed as domestic servants and as
general laborers. Strange though it may seem, there were
Americans who actually argued that the need for the Chinese was so great that seventy thousand ought to be admitted
at once into California.[26] It was argued that the Chinese were
needed to perform the menial labor which Americans
shunned and for reclamation of arid land and development
of mines and natural resources. Robert Ingersoll suggested
as early as 1893 that Chinese labor was of excellent quality
and ought to be admitted freely. True, they were not without fault, "some of them smoke opium, but the opium-
smoker does not beat his wife."[27] But whether they were
wife-beaters or not, he thought that the Chinese were needed
to help build the nation.

The usefulness of the Chinese was even more apparent to
those who contemplated the problems involved in the annexation of Hawaii and the Philippines. Frederick Williams,
son of Samuel Wells Williams and lecturer in oriental history at Yale, concluded that "we must dismiss old prejudices
and learn to consider the Chinaman in our Eastern de-
pendencies as an indispensable means to their economic
development. . . . His nearness to the Philippines Islands
and his ability and willingness to work in their tropical

climate render us at once unable to exclude him from those shores and almost helpless without his steady industry to exploit them."[28] The feeling that the Chinese were indispensable for the development of these areas was widely held. *Literary Digest* estimated that at least a hundred thousand Chinese would be needed for the industrial development of the Philippines alone.[29]

The outlook for Hawaii was similar. The suggestion was frequently made that the Chinese in Hawaii were of a different sort from those in San Francisco's Chinatown. In Hawaii they were an integral part of the population, and their loss would be a serious material disadvantage to the Islands. The Chinese were responsible for reclaiming swamp lands which could now be rented for twenty dollars an acre. They were the backbone of rice production and the sugar industry. No other laborer could endure the hard conditions which these jobs required. They were peaceful, orderly, obedient to law, industrious, and healthy; and they lived in comfortable houses. It seemed almost that the Chinese in Hawaii were everything that they were reputed not to be in the United States.

In California the Chinese were increasingly accepted as a normal part of daily life. The change was indicated more by a change in emphasis than by anything said explicitly. Visitors to Chinatown began bringing back stories of normal life there without mention of the dark and twisting stairways where one encountered "Chinamen" with similar traits of character. Articles appeared describing the criminal element among the Chinese without the usual conclusion that all Chinese were inherently criminal. A visitor from the east to southern California was reported as saying, "You have no distinctly foreign element, except the Chinese, and only a few of them.''[30] This remark was overheard in 1894, when many Californians thought that the number of Chinese in the state was alarming.

California magazines such as the *Land of Sunshine, Overland Monthly,* and *Sunset Magazine* published fewer articles on the Chinese during the 1890s than might have been expected if California feeling had been judged according to its newspapers. *Overland Monthly* began to use decorative material which was Chinese in design. The space at the end of an article was sometimes filled with a sketch of artistically arranged Chinese coins. Chinese proverbs were used in a way which reflected credit upon the Chinese. The absence of editorial comment was striking, particularly in such years as 1892 or 1902 when Congress was debating new exclusion legislation. Undoubtedly most people felt that the exclusion laws had solved the problem. They were working relatively well, despite some criticism, and people were generally satisfied with them. The Chinese who remained in California were absorbed to a large degree in the normal routine of everyday life and ceased to appear as a threat.

A similar conclusion can be drawn from the life of the rest of the nation. Boston was an example of a city where the Chinese rather quickly established themselves. The *Journal of American Folklore* published an article on the Chinese in that city in 1892.[31] They were described as good tenants, generous and helpful toward each other and with few bad habits. The lower class among them smoked opium, but not more than one-third was thought to have the habit. The upper class included several very wealthy Chinese who lived as well as many of the people in Boston. Their faults had been greatly exaggerated, they sent little money home, and though some did gamble, they never did so to any great extent. The description was undoubtedly a little optimistic, however, in view of the way in which the Boston *Herald* excoriated the Chinese during the siege of Peking in 1900.

There is evidence of increased acceptance of the Chinese from outside Boston also. In 1899 *Harper's Weekly* introduced a regular feature entitled "Chinese Proverbs" which treated its subject with seriousness and respect.[32] The number of Chinese students in American schools increased markedly after 1900. In 1901 the "Chinese Students Alliance" was organized at the University of California with eighteen members.[33] This was a self-help organization of Chinese students in the United States. By 1905 membership had increased to one hundred. In 1901 there were forty-six Chinese students in universities, the largest number at the University of California, with Columbia, Cornell, Yale and some others having a few. These examples do not necessarily imply that the Chinese were accepted on an equal basis, but at least they were permitted to occupy a more normal position in the nation's daily life.

Previously it was noted that the Chinese were portrayed in fiction as undesirable characters. Gradually, however, another image began to emerge. It was noted that Bret Harte's "Heathen Chinee" had started a flood of burlesque sketches which lasted for some time. But the Chinese were too solid to submit easily to caricature. "We have long recognized Chinese picturesqueness and we have regarded with curiosity Chinese character and customs, but we are only just beginning to understand them and their relation to the West. They have become a recognized factor in American life, consequently a fit subject for American artists."[34] The writer, an art student in San Francisco, was quite enthusiastic about the Chinese, even to the extent of being attracted by their "heathenism." She admired the role they had played in developing the unique character of California life. Her attitude, however, was not typical of most Californians.

The plots in fictional writing with a Chinese motif improved as human characteristics were emphasized. It became increasingly apparent that for some writers the bad qualities of the Chinese could be accepted along with his good ones because he was, after all, a member of the human as well as the oriental race. "At the core, all human nature is the same, and present incongruities and absurdities in our attitude toward the Chinese will fade away when we realize what true elements of picturesqueness, beauty, and variety, these beings from the farthest East have grafted upon . . . life in California. . . ."[35]

Evidence exists that Chinese customs began to be appreciated for their intrinsic value regardless of whether they appeared to have utility as judged by American standards. Chinese medical practices, usually caricatured as strange and grotesque, were given a sympathetic scrutiny by a writer for *Lippincott's Magazine* who was convinced that the herbal system of medicine practiced by Chinese medical men was in some ways more effective than that of American physicians.[36] Several instances were reported where patients of eastern doctors had been ordered to California in a last desperate search for health only to be cured in a short time by Chinese medicine. The fact that most white men could not patronize Chinese doctors because of heir high fees was taken to indicate a high demand for their services. More favorable descriptions of the Chinese method of preparing and eating foods suggested an attitude of greater interest and appreciation. In Oroville, California, a place where the

Chinese had often had their troubles, a Chinese banquet honoring local citizens was appreciatively described by one of the townspeople; and instead of emphasizing bird's-nest soup and shark's fins, the author noted the dignity and graciousness of the affair.[37]

Stewart Culin, director of the Museum of Archaeology and Palaeontology at the University of Pennsylvania, who wrote often on Chinese customs, criticized his readers for failing to appreciate the genius of the Chinese people.[38] American prejudice had had a field day with the Chinese, he said, and had supposed them to speak pigeon English whereas most spoke English very well. Americans in general had failed to appreciate the quality of the Chinese intellect. In particular, he described a Chinese friend who had attained substantial success in the difficult and complicated business of running a Chinese lottery. "In addition to his literary education, meager enough from a Chinese point of view, although in advance of any of his countrymen with whom I am acquainted, and ample and amazing to the western scholar, he possessed a vivid imagination and a refined and cultivated mind."[39] There is an obvious quality of sincere appreciation in these remarks which is in striking contrast to the condescension and hostility which marked so much of the American attitude of these years.

It seems improbable that Chinatown was ever looked upon as anything more than an evil curiosity during the years after 1890, but some writers did make the attempt. One visitor to the West Coast thought that the inhabitants of San Francisco failed to appreciate the treasure within their midst.[40] It ought to be called a beauty spot instead of a plague spot, she said, because here were collected the treasures and citizens of an ancient civilization. If the smell was bad and the living conditions crowded, this was due to the restrictions imposed by any city on its inhabitants. In some instances illustrations of Chinatown portrayed its more attractive side, and the Chinese were pictured as well-dressed men and women inhabiting clean and orderly houses adjacent to well-swept streets. Photographs of opium dens sometimes appeared with no more comment than that occasioned by an illustration of the corner saloon.

It was pointed out by some writers that the Chinese lived in crowded quarters because they were not allowed to expand into adjacent housing, but they did their best to make their living quarters as attractive as possible. They decorated their houses in bright colors, particularly red and green, and put them into as good repair as their means permitted. The balconies in particular were made attractive with lanterns and flowers, adding to the undeniable beauty of Chinatown. Comments on family life, complete with an illustration of a very attractive young girl entitled "A Chinese Flower," were sometimes highly favorable.[41] Perhaps it was still true that the Chinese had something to learn from us, concluded one writer, "but have we not something to learn from them."[42]

Americans on occasion even felt called upon to take up the defense of the Chinese. An effort was made by some writers to counterbalance the darker picture of Chinese character by a description of his high moral qualities. The tradition of social responsibility which made the Chinese responsible for each other in a way unfamiliar to Americans drew high praise. The Chinese placed no burden on the city for poor relief, and there were very few destitute Chinese because when a man was sick or in financial straits his relatives looked after him. The Chinese had their vices as did all men, but unfortunately for them, even their virtues were counted against them. The industriousness of the Chinese was known everywhere as were his patience and endurance, but these were not counted as attributes by those who feared his competition. "John" was abused because he was competent, complained one author, and "this is the real rub."[43]

The incidents of abuse which occurred from time to time seldom received much attention, but occasionally they were condemned. The Rock Springs massacre occurred earlier, in 1885, but it was such a gruesome affair that for several years afterward it was mentioned as a great stain on the American flag.[44] Probably the last major incident took place in Oregon in 1894 when the murder of ten Chinese in an ambush prompted the observation that if the Chinese were barbarous, Americans could hardly be considered as less.[45] *Literary Digest* explored the same thought and concluded that "we are as black as the Chinese."[46] These comments revealed as much concern for America's good name as they did for the Chinese, but there was an undeniable wish that justice be done and that the Chinese be accorded the same sort of treatment to which all men were entitled.

Among those who had the closest contacts with the Chinese were some who expressed feelings of deep sympathy for them. A minister in San Francisco who wrote frequently on Chinese topics, for example, described the curious procedures followed in a Chinese "joss house" and then concluded, "But amidst the smoke of sandalwood and wax candles, the kowtowing and tom-toming and jargon of Sanscrit litanies one can discover something good—a reverence for the brave, the wise and the good, and the expression of that universal truth, however grossly symbolized, that the grave is not the goal of human greatness; that wise words and noble deeds can never die."[47] Admittedly this quotation illustrates the religious faith of its author, and yet it also has strong overtones of those sentiments which are the basis for human brotherhood. Some men at least were able to look upon the Chinese as fellow travelers along the road of human experience, and yet admittedly these were the exceptions at the turn of the century, because for most Americans the great gulf between East and West had not been bridged.

Some Americans moderated their open expressions of hostility toward the Chinese because of feelings of embarrassment and even shame at the treatment accorded Chinese immigrants. Lyman Abbott, editor of *Outlook* and a liberal clergyman, was a staunch supporter of exclusion as necessary for the preservation of the American way of life. But he deplored the excessive brutality and abuse with which the Chinese were often greeted by immigration officials. The boycott of American cotton in China in 1905 was provoked largely by the personal indignities which the Chinese seeking admittance to the United States were forced to endure. President Roosevelt was reflecting the opinion of many Americans when he said that exclusion was necessary but should be conducted in a manner which supported the nation's reputation of just treatment for the people of all races. Religious leaders and diplomats pointed out that America had a right to exclude the Chinese but not a right to abuse them.

The more favorable comments on the Chinese in America, however, did not indicate a basic change in national attitudes. These opinions represented for the most part a small number of the better educated and more cosmopolitan members of society speaking out. Stewart Culin and Frederick W.

Williams, lecturer in oriental history at Yale, were men who spoke from the scholarly viewpoint. They had a professional interest in the Chinese rather than a personal one. The journals which published many of the more favorable articles were also professional magazines such as the *American Historical Review*, the *Yale Review*, and the *Journal of American Folklore*. Lyman Abbott, Joaquin Miller, and Chester Holcombe, minister, poet, and diplomat respectively, were careful observers of American affairs who sought to present a more sensitive analysis of the Chinese issue. Their efforts were supported by magazines with a similar interest such as *Arena, Outlook, Independent,* and *National Magazine.* In some cases these writers may have had a personal appreciation for the Chinese, but in most instances the favorable opinion resulted from a technical or a paternal interest in the subject.

In assessing the quality of American attitudes toward the Chinese, it is important to remember the difference between tolerance or acceptance and genuine understanding. Many people were able to accept the Chinese as a useful though alien part of the country's life. When overt hostility toward the Chinese diminished after the storm over exclusion abated, they took their place alongside men and women from many different places of national and racial origin and became a part of the fabric of daily life. This meant that for the most part they were ignored unless some incident occurred to draw attention to them. Undoubtedly, in many instances relationships based on genuine affection and understanding developed between the Chinese and their caucasian brothers; but publicly and nationally, even those who spoke favorably of the Chinese seemed to speak from a position of benevolent paternalism. If the Chinese were not to be viewed as an overt threat to America, it was nevertheless clear that they were an inferior people, the condition of whose society called for large doses of the healing and strengthening medicines of American wisdom. For the vast majority of people in this country at the turn of the century who had any awareness of the Chinese at all, whether he was loathed, tolerated, or appreciated, he remained still a "Chinaman."

1. "A Crime to Breathe the American Atmosphere" (editorial), *Independent* XLII (April 10, 1890), 10.

2. "The Outlook" (editorial), *Christian Union* XLV (May 14, 1892), 922.

3. "Chinese Question" (editorial), *Nation* LIV (May 12, 1892), 347.

4. Ibid.

5. Henry Cabot Lodge to Henry White, June 29, 1900, Lodge Papers.

6. "The Chinese Exclusion Bill" (editorial), *American Missionary* XLVI (May, 1892), 143.

7. C. H. Shinn, "Social Changes in California," *Popular Science Monthly* XXXVIII (April, 1891), 801.

8. "Chinese" (editorial), *Overland Monthly* XIX (May, 1892), 557.

9. Joaquin Miller, "The Chinese Exclusion Act," *Arena* XXXII (October, 1904), 352.

10. Ibid., p. 354.

11. A. J. Hanson, "The Chinese in America," *Methodist Review* LII (September, 1892), 714.

12. "The Chinese in California" (editorial), *Public Opinion* XI (July 25, 1891), 379.

13. Carl C. Plehn, "Labor in California," *Yale Review* IV (February, 1896), 409–25.

14. Helen F. Clark, "The Chinese in New York," *Century* LIII (November, 1896), 104–13.

15. Ida M. Van Etten, "Russian Jews as Desirable Immigrants," *Forum* XV (March, 1893), 172.

16. Chester Holcombe, *The Real Chinese Question* (New York, 1900).

17. Allen McLaughlin, "Chinese and Japanese Immigration," *Popular Science Monthly* LXVI (December, 1904), 117–21.

18. "Our Immigration during 1904," *National Geographic Magazine* XVI (January, 1905), 16.

19. "California's Chinese Missions" (editorial), *American Missionary* LIX (December, 1905), 311.

20. McLaughlin, "Chinese and Japanese Immigration," p. 119.

21. Ibid., p. 121.

22. Ibid.

23. George C. Perkins, "The Competition of Japan," *Overland Monthly* XXVIII (October, 1896), 393–403.

24. "The Question of Japanese Competition," San Francisco *Chronicle*, July 10, 1896.

25. Marie A. Kimball, "Chinese House Servants," *Chautauquan* XVII (May, 1893), 207.

26. Jee Gam, "Chinese Exclusion," *American Missionary* LVI (February, 1902), 99–108.

27. Robert G. Ingersoll, "Should the Chinese Be Excluded?", *North American Review* CLVII (July, 1893), 54.

28. Frederick W. Williams, "The Chinese Immigrant in Further Asia," *AHR* V (April, 1900), 503.

29. "Chinese Needed in the Philippines" (editorial), *Literary Digest* XXV (November 1, 1902), 548.

30. "The Right Kind of People" (editorial), *Land of Sunshine* II (December, 1894), 10.

31. Mary Chapman, "Notes on the Chinese in Boston," *Journal of American Folklore* V (October, 1892), 321–24.

32. "Chinese Proverbs," *Harper's Weekly* XLIII (July 15, 1899), 697.

33. "Chinese Students in America" (editorial), *American Missionary* LIX (March, 1905), 72–75.

34. Mary Bell, "The Chinese Motif in Current Art," *Overland Monthly* XXXI (March, 1898), 239.

35. Ibid., p. 242.

36. William M. Tisdale, "Chinese Physicians in California," *Lippincott's Magazine* LXIII (March, 1899), 411–16.

37. J. P. Bocock, "A Chinese Banquet," *Frank Leslie's Popular Monthly* XL (July, 1895), 91–94.

38. Stewart Culin, "Customs of the Chinese in America," *Journal of American Folklore* III (July, 1890), 191.

39. Stewart Culin, "Tsz' Fa or 'Word Blossoming,'" *Overland Monthly* XXIV (September, 1894), 250.

40. Mabel C. Craft, "Some Days and Nights in Little China," *National Magazine* VII (November, 1897), 99–109.

41. H. B. McDowell, "A New Light on the Chinese," *Harper's New Monthly* LXXXVI (December, 1892) , 3–17.

42. Ibid., p. 17.

43. "The Chinaman Abroad" (editorial) , *Public Opinion* XVII (November 1, 1894) , 747.

44. "The Point of View" (editorial) , *Nation* LXI (August 22, 1895) , 128.

45. Ibid.

46. "Outrages on Foreigners in China and in America," *Literary Digest* XI (August 31, 1895) , 516.

47. Frederick J. Masters, "Pagan Temples in San Francisco," *Californian* II (November, 1892) , 741.

5

China as an

Ancient Civilization

"If the testimony is to be taken on both sides, it simply amounts to this; the Chinese, as a nation, are not so bad as to be past help, and not so good that they cannot be made better."—W. C. Pond, Los Angeles, 1897

The Geary Act, the arrival of the Japanese, and an increasing acceptance of the Chinese in familiar occupations helped to modify antagonism toward Chinese immigrants. In the same way, heightened interest by the missionaries in the possibility of converting an entire people and the enthusiasm of some business leaders led to a reevaluation of attitudes toward Chinese civilization. The broader interests of mission work, the China market, and the role of China in international affairs had a formative influence on the American image of China as an emerging nation. As a result of these new concerns, the interpretation of the Chinese as a barbarian people gave way in part to the interpretation of the Chinese as an ancient civilization. Because of the nation's concern for its relationship with the Chinese beyond national boundaries, a more serious effort was made to understand China.

The fundamental problem faced by all who sought to reassess the Chinese was how to reconcile the accepted interpretations of Chinese life with expanded interests in the Far East. Statesmen and politicians who had argued vigorously for exclusion legislation on the basis of undesirable oriental characteristics now sought justification for expanding the nation's relationships with China. Businessmen who had opposed the activity of the Chinese in the United States now argued for an increase in trade ties. The missionaries too were eager to describe the opportunity existing in China for the conversion of millions. In each case an interpretation of China was offered which met the requirements of a particular point of view. The effort to establish a new interpretation of an emerging China anxious for American leadership was successful, and though the resulting image was slightly more favorable to the Chinese, it was still rooted in misunderstanding.

One of the best examples of the changed emphasis in America's image of China was the developing attitude of the missionaries toward the work there. It is a little hazardous to speak of a chronological development because all the elements of the missionary attitude toward China were usually present in some degree at all times. Neverethless, a definite change in emphasis is clearly visible. In the years before 1890 and in the early years of that decade, the Chinese were most often pictured as debased, immoral creatures in desperate need of Christian salvation. Gradually, however, the emphasis on their degraded state began to give way to an increased emphasis on the promise which they offered when changed by conversion to Christianity.[1] Descriptions of the heroic actions of Chinese Christians during the Boxer Rebellion came partially as a result of this change in emphasis.² Finally, the viewpoint of religious people toward China assumed an aspect of responsibility for the entire Chinese people. The emphasis on the conversion of individual Chinese gave way to a vision of converting the nation itself, with all its potential as an ancient civilization, into a giant Christian army. It was this viewpoint which was accepted with eagerness by the missionaries themselves and by the spokesmen for expansion. Not only did such an interpretation greatly enhance a missionary's concept of the importance of his "call," but it accorded well with the vision of America as a nation destined to lead the world.

The attitudes of members of the congregation in hometown churches were undoubtedly influenced by both the praise and the defamation of Chinese character offered by returning missionaries, as were the attitudes of members of the academic world by the favorable descriptions brought back by visiting scholars. Some of the most favorable accounts of China at the turn of the century were those found in professional journals or at least written by scholars whose intent it was to understand the Chinese and who thus brought home relatively favorable and sympathetic accounts of their researches and travels in the Orient.³ This is not to say that in every case such reactions were based on a deep understanding of the Chinese as human beings. In actuality many of the descriptions of the Chinese were devoid of any extensive appreciation of their way of life and appeared favorable only in relation to the vast number of aggressively hostile accounts. Yet it was still true that a small number of travelers, mostly professional men, brought back from the Orient favorable impressions which they in turn passed on to their readers. Although these accounts may not have had in themselves a significant impact on popular attitudes, they were indicative of an altered climate of opinion and of a serious effort to understand the Chinese better.

The appearance of the following story in a book published in the mid-1890s is indicative of the attempt to interpret Chinese life more sympathetically. According to the author who retold the episode, there was once a Chinese family in which the wife, tiring of her elderly mother-in-law, persuaded her husband to take his mother into the country-side, there to leave her to die of exposure and thus rid the family of a bothersome burden. The son took his mother on his back and began the journey under the pretense of taking her out for some air. On the way the aged woman remarked to her son that he had gladdened her heart ten times. The first was when he was born, and after much sorrow she knew she had a living boy; the second, when he smiled and she knew he was comfortable in her arms; the third, when he grasped an object with his hand and she knew he was strong; the fourth, when he began to walk and she knew he could take care of himself and be her helper; the fifth, when he went to gather fuel and thus help make a secure home; the sixth, when she gave him money and he went to the market; the seventh, when he went to school; the eighth, when he put on adult clothes and she knew she had a man to depend on; the ninth, when she got him a wife and he established his own home; and the tenth, when he now took her on his back to carry her out to get sight of the sky and fields that she might be refreshed and live the longer. As she talked, her son's heart softened, and he could not desert his mother who had loved him so well. The story itself is not unique, perhaps, but in his sensitive description of Chinese life the understanding and sympathy of the storyteller stand in sharp contrast to attitudes revealed in the congressional debates over the exclusion laws.[4]

The more favorable view of China was in some respects a transitional attitude leading from complete unwillingness to consider the Chinese as anything but inferior to the attitude that under Western leadership China's civilization might be redeemed. By redemption was meant the development of China along the lines of Western technology. According to this line of thought, America would share with China the secrets of progress and Western civilization. Businessmen could then see in China a great opportunity not only for trade but for an application of the principles of the gospel of wealth. By 1905 many Americans seem to have considered China as an example of the opportunity and responsibility which faced our nation in its new relationship to the world, though there was the concern of the minority with something called the "yellow peril." These ideas were not fully developed in the mid-1890s by any-means, nor did the antagonism toward China ever disappear; it only altered its form. The sympathetic view of China expressed all through the 1890s was influential in helping some Americans to express their anti-Chinese feelings in the broader terms of America's responsibility toward an inferior race.

An American engineer who spent two years in China as director of a survey for the Hankow to Canton railway, for example, introduced a more favorable note with regard to Chinese civilization. "We are wont to consider them as un-civilized; and so they are if measured scrupulously by our peculiar standards. But, on the other hand, they might say with some justice that we are not civilized according to the standards that they have set for themselves, founded on an experience of four thousand years."[5] The suggestion that it was only fair to judge China by her own ancient standards instead of by more recent Western standards was made by several writers. One writer who was in China with the United States Navy stated that "in our ethnological classifications we have these countries as half civilized, because we judge them by our own standards alone, but it may well be questioned if the fraction of culture we concede them may not be, after all, superior to the half which we retain in excess."[6] The willingness to judge China by her own standards indicated a definite modification in the judgment of her as uncivilized.

With varying purposes in mind some writers sought to make the point that, whatever we might say about China today, her civilization had ancient roots and had once been very highly developed. A minor controversy developed in some academic circles about whether or not Chinese civilization had its origin in Babylon. According to one scholar the similarity between Accadian and Chinese was so pronounced that it could only be concluded that the Chinese language had its roots in that of the former civilization.[7] Some scholars argued that the Chinese had discovered the North American continent before Columbus, and others pointed out how the Chinese had developed and used the mariner's compass centuries before Westerners had; consequently it was felt that perhaps because the Chinese had reached a high level of development many years ago, they no longer sought to improve themselves. Lyman Abbott noted that "the Chinaman's characteristic is not despair, which is hopeless aspiration; nor contentment, which is restrained aspiration; but self-satisfaction, which is absence of aspiration."[8] Although this is a qualified view of Chinese civilization, it is certainly a more sympathetic one than was generally current during the mid-1890s.

With the exception of a few isolated persons who for one reason or another had an interest in the Orient, there was virtually no instruction available in Chinese language, history, or philosophy in an American university prior to 1898. In that year John Fryer became Agassiz Professor of Oriental Languages and Literature at the University of California; but at Stanford, Yale, Harvard, and the University of Chicago there was no regular instruction in Chinese subjects prior to 1908, when Yale first included a course in Chinese literature into its curriculum.[9] At Columbia, however, the Dean Lung Professorship in Chinese was established in 1901 through an anonymous gift of $213,000 to found a department of "Chinese languages, literatures, religion and law."[10] Dean Lung had been a butler in the employ of Horace W. Carpenter, retired general in the French army, who later became an American citizen, when Carpenter in a fit of anger hit his servant over the head and later sought to make amends by asking Lung if he could reward him for his faithful service. Lung replied that the greatest problem facing the Chinese was a lack of understanding on the part of Americans and, therefore, urged that something be done to encourage greater awareness of the Chinese in America. Lung contributed his life's savings, some $12,000, and Carpenter made up the rest to establish a Chinese department and library at Columbia. Yet in spite of this happy event and the private interest of a few scholars, it is evident that little effort was expended at the higher levels of education to provide sound instruction in Chinese subjects.

Furthermore, an examination of some of the textbooks

available for use in the lower grades reinforces an impression that American schools insofar as they dealt at all with the Chinese were only repeating the oversimplifications about Chinese life which formed the substance of the body of knowledge about China available to most Americans at the turn of the century. Woodrow Wilson, for example, in his *History of the American People,* wrote that the "thrifty, skillful Orientals, who, with their yellow skin and strange, debasing habits of life, seemed to them hardly fellow men at all, but evil spirits, rather" presented a problem to white residents in California which could only be solved by "riot and slaughter."[11] Albert Bushnell Hart described the Chinese problem as similar to the Negro problem in his text on American history and concluded that Congress had done the right thing in excluding the Chinese.[12] Muzzey's *History* characterized the Chinese in the usual fashion as living on a few cents a day, being content with dirty quarters and poor food, and offering a general threat to all honest laboring men.[13] These and other texts devoted little space to the Chinese; and when they did refer to them, it was only to reiterate the accepted notions of the general point of view.[14]

Yet in spite of the unfavorable and insufficient attention given to the Chinese in textbooks and schools at all levels, it was from the academic and religious worlds that a more appreciative point of view issued forth. One example of the excellence of Chinese civilization was thought to exhibit itself in the attitude toward learning present among the people of China. Especially illustrative of the emphasis on letters was the manner in which literary examinations served as the selection process for governmental officials of all levels. The first step for a candidate who aspired to high office was to pass the local examination, where he might earn the equivalent of his B.A. degree. If he successfully overcame this obstacle, he then presented himself for the second degree or provincial examination. If he was among the 120 successful candidates out of thousands of competitors, then he would be highly honored by his home town and his future would be assured. A traveler in Peking at the time of the provincial examination was very favorably disposed toward the tradition of literary attainment. "It is difficult to decide which we should most admire: the genuine enthusiasm of all China for literary culture . . . or the marvelous ingenuity and precision with which this skill is tested, by a system of literary examinations hardly equalled and never surpassed by any nation in any age."[15]

That the Chinese were characterized as a literary people was sometimes thought to explain the seeming lack of courage in Chinese soldiers and the absence of warlike qualities among the general populace. But there were also those who thought that the strong literary tradition was a source of strength for China. Theodore Roosevelt suggested, for example, that the emphasis on literateness and other traditions helped to glue together the pieces of a sprawling, disconnected civilization.[16] Letter shops stood ready at all times of the day or night to serve the customer who wished to send a message to a distant part of the empire. Imperial messages traveled at the rate of sixty-six miles per day by runner or, if urgent, at the rate of 133 miles per day with horses. Ordinary business letters were sent at a slower rate. In many of the magazines specializing in missionary matters the possibility of spreading the gospel by means of appealing to the literati was discussed. The literary Chinese were so highly respected that, once converted, their influence over their countrymen would be very useful. The interest in Chinese

literature included articles on fiction, drama, and other matters of literary concern, and in all of these the attitude was
largely one of sincere interest and appreciation.

The religious and philosophical attitudes of the Chinese
were not considered as objectively as was their literary tradition, but there were some examples of a growing appreciation. The missionaries generally were not sympathetic
toward China's religions, although a writer in *Catholic
World* thought that missionaries should spend more time
understanding Buddhism instead of condemning it outright
as paganism.[17] The author found much to praise in a religion
which was a means toward the worship of God. Another
exception to the general religious comment on oriental religion was an article in the *American Journal of Theology*.
The author was W. A. P. Martin, one of the greatest ad-
mirers of Chinese culture and president of the University
of Peking. He argued that though the Chinese did not worship exactly the same god as Christians did, their belief
did leave room for such worship.[18] He thought that eventually the Chinese might recognize in their vague Power the
God of Christianity.

There was some praise of Chinese philosophy, particularly Confucianism. China could be forgiven much, thought
Thomas Magee, a highly respected real estate broker in San
Francisco, for preserving intact the memory of her great
philosopher.[19] W. A. P. Martin felt that the Chinese had
come closer to the heights in philosophy than the West
had realized.[20] The strong reverence, almost worship, for
the past in China, although criticized for its tendency to
produce backwardness, was also praised because it encouraged a well-balanced, mature attitude toward life. The
editor of *Monist,* himself a philosopher and interested in

China, concluded that "the whole Chinese civilization is saturated with the belief in the divinity, the perfection, and the unqualified excellence of its principles, doctrines, and institutions."[21] There were disadvantages to such a strong ingrown respect for one's own ideas, but there were also great strength and wisdom in such an attitude.

The Chinese language was thought by a few people to be one of the most attractive aspects of Chinese civilization. Instead of being "ear-splitting jargon," it was described as highly musical and quite like the notes of birds.[22] The language was thought to be rather easy to learn because there were no problems of syntax. Pure Chinese could be learned as easily as any foreign language, and, when learned, the student had access to a vast source of written material. Pure Chinese was seldom spoken, but all educated Chinese wrote it; and the language was described as full of energy of expression, directness of purpose, and natural logic. One writer even argued that Chinese might well become the universal language because a symbolic language eliminated all the problems of a phonetic language.[23] At the least, Chinese should be introduced and used in the professions in order to develop a means of consistent communication.

Some visitors to China belittled even the famous wall and insisted on its insignificance; but a few defended it as one of the great engineering feats in world history. A writer for *National Geographic,* which devoted the major part of several issues to China in 1900, thought that "the walls are so solid and inaccessible and the gates so well arranged and defended that it would puzzle a modern army with a first-class siege train to get through if any effort whatever were made for its defense."[24] The length of the wall was variously described as from 1,500 to 3,000 miles. Those who looked favorably upon the whole subject viewed it as a monumental engineering feat, though the majority of travelers thought it a highly overrated attraction. The canals in China were commented upon favorably, and it was argued that they provided efficient, cheap transportation as well as fertilizer from their muck bottoms for the farmers' fields, and with a little repair they would be the best in the world and a serious rival to any of the contemplated railroads in China.[25]

Chinese architecture in general was thought to be more distinguished for its engineering features than for its aesthetic excellence. Chinese civilization was so ancient that its architecture tended to be rather monotonous though undoubtedly thoroughly practical. The Chinese were excellent engineers and craftsmen, and their understanding of the quarrying, cutting, and placing of granite was superior to that of any people in the world. The legend of a mason who was put to death because he left a joint in the wall wide enough to drive a nail into was cited in support of their insistence upon excellence.[26] The Chinese arch and the principles of its design were the same today as in antiquity, and the pagoda, originally developed from the design of a tent, was described as China's most characteristic building.[27] Although China's architecture was neither as elaborate nor as highly developed as in Western countries, it was thought to be well suited to China's needs.

Some of the favorable comment was directed toward China's present achievements. Chinese justice was not all cruelty and bribery, as many writers had suggested. The ancient tradition of responsibility in China had produced a people who were a living example of the command that every man was his brother's keeper. The American consul in Foochow offered grudging acknowledgement of the ability of Chinese courts to keep order among their own people. An article in *Century* described the system whereby loads of gold and silver might be sent safely through the countryside without guards.[28] Travelers who stayed at the country inns in China were often suspicious at the insistence of the innkeeper that all valuables be deposited with him for safekeeping. What they did not realize was that the innkeeper would be held responsible for any loss to his lodgers, and in order to protect himself from a loss which might be disastrous to his business, he preferred to have custody of valuable items, which he promptly returned in the morning.

As an example of the system of responsibility in action, the story was told of an American who was carrying a quantity of silver home from a bank in Canton when a man suddenly rushed up, snatched the money from his hands, and disappeared down an alleyway. Unable to find the thief, the man made out a statement explaining the circumstances which he sent to the owner of the shop closest to the point where he had been robbed. The storekeepers along the street made good his loss. Such incidents as this suggested that the Chinese were more orderly and law-abiding than other races; it was certainly true that very few Chinese were held in jails, and there was no prison problem, as in the United States. There were probably more prisoners in one American county jail than were in jail in a whole province of ten million people in China. Descriptions of Chinese trials were common, and the orderly process of the law was highly praised.

An appreciation of Chinese customs was apparent in the attitude of a number of authors who agreed that filial piety was sometimes carried to extremes in China. "Still, it will be wise for us whose habits of life suffer from the opposite extreme . . . to recognize that all of them are pervaded with a noble spirit of respect for parents, which though exaggerated is none the less touching and ought to command our admiration."[29] An appreciation of Chinese folkways was difficult to acquire. The language was hard to understand because of its emphasis on word accent, and as a result much of the fine meaning inherent in all folktales could not be understood by foreigners. Yet with such a lengthy tradition some thought that Chinese folklore was a treasure house of human wisdom which had hardly been explored.

Chinese drama was praised for its lack of obscenity and sordidness, which were so prevalent in Western theater. Much of the strangeness of the Chinese theater was due to the foreigner's unfamiliarity with the customs and traditions of the Chinese people. Chinese music, for example, wrote the secretary of the Museum of Fine Arts in Boston, was not a hideous, unharmonic noise but a highly developed system which had evolved along different lines than in the West.[30] In fact, Europe was indebted to the earlier system developed in the Orient for some features of Western music. The music sounded discordant because the Western ear was not trained to appreciate the oriental system.

The Chinese were heavily criticized for the status accorded to women in their society and their attitude toward children, but the majority of Chinese homes were happy places where children were raised in an atmosphere of love and respect.[31] The clan system was not simply the source of secret societies but an outgrowth of the need for self-protection in a society where the government did not provide much in the way of police protection or social services.[32]

Defenders of China argued that Chinese civilization had contributed a great deal to the West. China at present was neglecting the sciences, but in practice she had contributed a great many scientific discoveries and developments to the world's store of knowledge. The discovery of the principle of magnetism and its application in the use of the compass was noted. European playing cards owed their origin to Chinese games which had utilized cards for centuries. Observations of birds and animals which resulted in the conclusion that animals utilized coloring as a protective device had predated similar Western studies. The discovery of ancient Chinese coins in an Alaskan grave encouraged a missionary among the Chinese in San Francisco to suggest that the Chinese had come to America long before the white man in order to civilize the Indian.[33] Numerous such items were cited in order to strengthen the case for an appreciation of China as a civilization in its own right and one entitled to a place in the world community.

The West had something to learn from the Chinese system of government, said the editor of the *Nation,* who commented in passing on "the guilds, habits, and superstitions of the wonderfully well organized people among us who have come from the freest country and greatest democracy in Asia."[34] The concept of China as a great democracy was suggested by several writers who thought that the system of examinations made it possible for anyone to rise to high rank and, therefore, made China the model of a democratic people. Not only was the Chinese government thought to be democratic, it was also praised for its high moral standard because "in theory of government the Chinese make large use of moral sentiments. For the preservation of order they rely on the better instincts of the masses, guided by the intelligence of the more educated."[35] This view was in sharp contrast to William Rockhill's observation that the Chinese government was the most corrupt of any nation in the world, but the attempt to describe China favorably persisted.[36]

The ability to distinguish between the different elements in China's governmental system was a sign that Americans were becoming more discerning in their perception of China. Li Hung Chang, for example, was recognized by a few political commentators as a highly influential person in Chinese politics but not the prime minister of China as many assumed, though again Rockhill felt that he was entirely untrustworthy.[37] Not all writers condemned China for her failure to prevent the missionary massacres in the 1890s, because it was felt that China was doing all in her power to handle a situation which at best was extremely volatile. It was recognized that China could not be thought of as a nation when she lacked a national consciousness and, therefore, should not be expected to act as a nation but as a civilization. The distinction between the Manchus and the Chinese was recognized by those who sought to explain the difference between dealing with the Manchu rulers and understanding the Chinese. A more sympathetic view of the Chinese was apparent as they began to be appreciated for their ability to govern themselves with intelligence and moderation in the face of so many difficulties not present in a more highly developed governmental system.

The sensational accounts of the experiences of travelers in China were countered by more appreciative and understanding reports. One author observed that it was "easier to call the Chinaman a heathen than to understand him."[38] In all his travels in China he had never carried a firearm, only a walking stick; and he had observed everywhere the natural, spontaneous kindness of natives toward foreigners with a reserved but sincere hospitality. The immorality of the Chinese was certainly no worse than elsewhere and possibly a little better. Crime was less noticeable, and most Chinese were thoroughly honest, with only an occasional example of sharp practice. In fact, the author concluded, the more time one spent there, the greater was the respect which one felt toward the Chinese. A traveler in Canton was impressed by the absence of policemen and the orderly procedure of the crowded traffic in the streets, where laborers with heavy loads were given the right-of-way over chair-borne officials.[39] The author thought that accounts of the horrible filth and odors were exaggerated, and was impressed by the absence of beggars and the intelligent use of available space for living quarters and recreation areas, a viewpoint which was in marked contrast to that of most American travelers to Canton and other Chinese cities.

A frequent contributor of articles on China and widely traveled in the Far East, Julian Ralph summed up a journey by houseboat with a description of the Chinese as people who "will live in my mind forever . . . as the jolliest, kindliest, most generous souls I ever found in such profusion anywhere in my roving."[40] During his travels on the Yang Tze River he had never bothered to lock up his valuables, and the servants who had been hired to assist on the trip proved intelligent, quick, trustworthy, and thoroughly capable in all respects. *Our Day* magazine reviewed Ralph's article and concluded that Ralph was a just traveler who, unlike most, found scenes of beauty instead of degradation, viciousness, and filth.[41]

The basic occupation of most Chinese was farming, and several observers marveled at their ability to extract the utmost from the soil. The careful utilization of every conceivable source of fertilizer from human to plant and animal was described in detail. The Chinese often sowed two crops together of varying maturity dates, such as cotton and wheat, so as not to waste any growing time. The soil was prepared carefully, and young rice shoots were planted by hand. If it were not for the marauding river pirates, the plagues of locusts, and the corrupt mandarins, the Chinese farmer's life would be thoroughly happy. If a man owned ten acres, he was considered quite wealthy; the average Chinese supported himself, his wife, two children, and his parents on as little as one-tenth to one-half acre of land. A people organized on such Jeffersonian principles as these could not fail to attract a little sympathy even from hostile Americans.

In addition to their achievements as an ancient civilization and as a respected modern people, the Chinese were viewed favorably by some because of their supposed inherent racial attributes. John R. Proctor, who because of his reputation for honesty in government was appointed head of the United States Civil Service Commission in 1893, thought that regardless of what was said about the corruption and deceit of the mandarin, the great mass of the Chinese people were "contented, sober, and industrious, with traditional habits of obedience to and respect for authority."[42] Even when measured against Western standards of civilization, the author thought it was doubtful that a population of four hundred million people who were as well-to-do and contented as the Chinese could be found elsewhere in the world. He viewed the Chinese as a race of naturally peaceful people who disliked aggressive ways, who were solid, industrious men willing to work at any task in order to provide for their families. When compared with the Japanese, the Chinese appeared to be the stronger race, with little tendency to indulge in frivolous activities on which the Japanese often dissipated their energy.

An American who spent fifteen years in China characterized the people as having the highest capabilities of any she had ever known.[43] Isolated instances of selfishness were more than balanced by their characteristics of self-respect, tenderness, heroic endurance, patience, and earnestness. Chester Holcombe, missionary in China, secretary and then chargé d'affaires of the Peking legation, and author of books on China, pointed out that the rule in Western lands was to misunderstand the Chinese. The author then described what he believed to be the true situation in China. What he had to say was not entirely complimentary, but his appeal for greater understanding on the part of Americans was indicative of a more favorable attitude.[44]

The attitude toward China of those connected with the missionary movement has been described as paradoxical. On the one hand the Chinese were viewed as racially inferior, as pagans in need of Christian salvation. But it was obvious that optimism, not pessimism, must eventually govern the missionary's attitude toward his work. Christian ministers at home and abroad believed that the Good News of Christianity had the power to change people's lives. Therefore, in the long run the missionary attitude toward the Chinese was a hopeful one. The Chinese might be depraved, but he was not beyond saving. The concept of a salvageable heathen existed alongside that of a degenerate people, and the former sometimes received more emphasis. It was only a short step from the concept of a redeemable human life to the concept of Christian responsibility, and if the Chinese were not hopelessly depraved but were, in fact, capable of conversion, then Christian nations as well as Christian churches had the duty of making the necessary efforts to accomplish the conversion.

The more favorable point of view was well illustrated in a small book entitled *God's Missionary Plan for the World* by James Whitford Bashford.[45] In spite of its somewhat pretentious title the book was a well reasoned and relatively honest assessment of the opportunities and difficulties facing Christian missionaries in several parts of the world. The author was a bishop in the Methodist Episcopal church who preached his first sermon at Foochow, China, in 1904 and in later years became a leader in the Christian church in China. On balance his point of view was about as reasonable as one could find during those years, since he made no attempt to exonerate the Chinese of all charges made against them but instead tried to recognize both their strengths and weaknesses. He found them to be an honest and conservative people, little different from human beings in Europe and America with the possible exception that they had a firmer devotion to their existing civilization and to their existing customs than did Americans.[46] His writing revealed an awareness of Chinese resentment at the imposition of Western tradition associated with the Christian religion and his own sensitivity for the problems created by the missionaries in asking the Chinese to alter their way of life in conformance with Christian teaching. He found the Chinese to be in need of Christianity but hardly the simple, backward, and depraved people described by so many visitors. He viewed the Chinese as pagans, but he was quick to underline their good qualities and to point out the opportunity offered to Christians to win these people over as friends and fellow workers in the vineyard.

Some Americans easily took the step from the responsibility felt by religious people toward individual Chinese to a feeling of responsibility for all the Chinese people. In this way religious responsibility was joined with the concept of America's duty to educate the world in the ways of progress. As a result of this happy combination, the nation could move steadily forward, secure in its knowledge of the truth, to distribute the fruits of religion, democracy, and commerce to a starved world. Before the step was taken, however, missionaries had to satisfy themselves that the Chinese as a people would accept Christian teaching. A missionary who invested many years in work among the Chinese both in the United States and China thought that the Chinese were as able to receive Christian teaching and as much in need of it as any other nation.[47] When the missionaries were attacked on all sides by critics who thought that a Chinese could never be converted and that the missionaries were wasting their efforts in the United States and in China, they often retaliated through articles in the various religious periodicals attesting to the faith of Chinese converts. Frederick J. Masters was a minister familiar with the work in China, and his article "Can a Chinaman Become a Christian?" concluded that he could indeed and that when once converted the Chinaman's faith was very strong, as witnessed by the loyalty of converts during the massacre of Christians in China.[48] The loyalty of Chinese Christians during the Boxer revolt was stressed heavily at the time, and many tales of the courage shown by Chinese in protecting the missionaries and their families were circulated in the United States through religious periodicals.

A more favorable attitude toward the Chinese precipitated a greater willingness to consider his religion as a preparation for Christian teaching. One writer, for example, presented a sympathetic description of Taoism in which he concluded that Lao-Tsze had introduced concepts familiar to Christian thought long before Christ was born. He felt that no one who had read the words of Lao-Tsze could doubt "that the mystery of the Most Holy Trinity was revealed to the Chinese five centuries before the coming of Christ."[49] Some missionaries had held that a Chinese was not really converted until he had given up his allegiance to the teachings of Confucius. Since Confucianism was virtually a way of life in China, this often proved so difficult that some people doubted whether a Chinese could ever be converted. But a happy way out was seen by W. A. P. Martin, who thought that there was no inherent conflict between the two systems. Confucius was not a prophet, not a god, but a perfect man; therefore, there was no conflict between Confucius and Christ.[50]

Another point on which some Americans modified their view of Chinese racial characteristics was that of the courage of Chinese soldiers. The accounts of Chinese cowardice in battle were balanced by others which presented a more favorable picture. Chinese troops were thought to possess great competence when trained and led by European officers under rigid discipline.[51] This view was supported by several correspondents and other observers in China who felt that his intrinsic qualities of bravery, obedience, steady nerves, endurance, and mechanical skill made it possible for the Chinese to develop into an excellent soldier. Stories of Chinese feats of skill and bravery in battle were circulated by those who were sympathetic toward the Chinese during the Sino-Japanese war.

The question of honesty among the Chinese had not been settled by those who argued that his ways were inherently those of deviousness and deception; many businessmen who were experienced in Chinese trade, as well as diplomats in China, made highly favorable comments about the integrity of the Chinese. It was believed by almost all of these men that the Chinese would usually make good on their contracts, including verbal ones, even if a drop in prices worked to their disadvantage. In fact, if a balance were struck between the wrongs committed by American and Chinese business-men, the Chinese would appear as the injured party in the majority of cases. Chinese banks were thought to be generally sound, and only a few small ones overextended themselves to the point of danger. The large banking houses enjoyed a reputation of scrupulous honesty.[52]

Part of the reason for the development of a more favor-able attitude toward China was the feeling that China might have a future after all. When a positive view of China was ad-vanced, the implication which followed necessarily was that China would move forward instead of backward.[53] America's role in this movement played an important part in such thinking after the Geary Act, and just as the religious view shifted from its emphasis on the individual Chinese to its emphasis on the entire race, so the more positive view of China involved Americans in new ideas about the nation's place in China's future.

The editor of *Harper's Weekly* spoke in just such a vein when he noted that hitherto China had been interesting al-most entirely as an illustration of a past civilization but that "today it is something more than this. At last the thought of the future intrudes itself."[54] The Sino-Japanese war stimulated many comments from observers who suggested the possibility of China awakening in order to take a new role in future world affairs. In reference to the war itself, one editor remarked, "It has evidently been God's plan for throwing China open to the fuller influences of the progressive spirit of the nineteenth century."[55] The role of the missionaries in opening up China to new ideas was recognized early in the 1890s, when it became clear that missionary schools, hospitals, and colleges were making an impact on conservative Chinese thought. Some writers even insisted that they could name the exact year or event which had worked a revolutionary awakening. As it turned out, however, arousing China from her lethargy would be a long process.

Signs of the awakening were evident for those who wanted to see them. In 1888 at the examinations in Peking, for example, it was thought noteworthy that a premium was placed on knowledge of mathematics and Western science. Of the candidates offering themselves for examination in those subjects, 5 percent would be allowed to pass instead of the usual 1 percent in the classics.[56] In 1893 the editor of *Public Opinion* noted the opening of new cotton mills, an increase in railroad mileage, and an increase in foreign trade as signs of a new awakening.[57] Li Hung Chang's visit to the United States in 1896 prompted recognition of his role in introducing progress into China. Two years later a national university was opened at Peking, and in the following year the ill-fated reforms of the emperor were hailed as the dawn of a new age for China. Every year during the last decade of the nineteenth century, articles were published announcing the beginning of a great period of railroad development for China. When plans did not materialize as rapidly as anticipated, no one was discouraged; instead, new prophecies of progress were advanced.

An author just returning from a long stay in China as missionary and diplomat noted that coastal defense guns manufactured in England were often defective and blew up, killing scores of Chinese. It was no wonder that the Chinese sometimes felt very hostile toward the West.[58] Foreigners hired to assist the Chinese government were often so imperious in their demands as to make it impossible for the Chinese to work with them. Li Hung Chang was never treated with the cordiality which he should have received on his journey to the capitals of the West, and the treatment of the Chinese in some countries was a blot on the name of Western civilization. Thoughts such as these worked a new emphasis in America's image of China. Instead of a second-class race, worthy only of condemnation and mistreatment, China began to emerge as a civilization with ancient resources and a hope for the future.

The favorable attitude toward China was expressed for the most part by a small group of men who were leaders in their professions. W. A. P. Martin spent a great deal of his lifetime in China, part of it as president of the University of Peking, and was very sympathetic toward Chinese culture.[59] Paul Carus was born in Germany, and his primary interest was philosophy. He published widely, including many articles in *Open Court,* an excellent liberal journal published in Chicago which came under his editorship early in the 1890s. He had a reputation for open-mindedness and honest scholarship. Thomas Magee was a real estate broker in San Francisco who forced his competitors to adopt higher ethical standards by setting an example for honesty with his clients.

He was an amateur Shakespearean scholar and also interested in the Orient. William B. Parsons led a survey party through the strongly antiforeign province of Hunan in 1898 and then pioneered the building of the first subway in New York City.

Chester Holcombe went to China in 1869 as a missionary, where he was in charge of a school for boys in Peking. He was a close friend of Samuel Wells Williams and served in a diplomatic capacity at the Peking legation during the 1870s and 1880s. Frederick J. Masters and W. C. Pond were men of great energy and honesty who carried on sympathetic ministries among the Chinese communities on the West Coast and in China. John R. Proctor was director of the Kentucky geological survey and was forced to resign under political pressure because he would not allow the governor's son to hold a job on the survey. His honesty won him a place as head of the United States Civil Service Commission in 1893. He was the author of several articles on China which appeared in *National Geographic*.

These men are representative of those who wrote sympathetically of China in the 1890s. Many of them were experts on Chinese culture with long experience in China; others had only a minor interest in the Orient. All of them, however, shared a common desire to rise above popular prejudice in their descriptions of Chinese civilization.

The sympathetic viewpoint expressed by these writers indicated a moderating in anti-Chinese sentiment. Their writings appeared all during the period from 1890 to 1905, and gradually the influence of their views increased. It was in the mid-1890s that a transition in emphasis occurred in the American attitude toward China. The threat of China was

no longer met by simple denunciations of the Chinese as uncivilized. Expansionist-minded men such as Henry Cabot
Lodge and Alfred Thayer Mahan were calling for a new
interpretation of America's destiny. These men agreed that
China was uncivilized, but they argued that even though the
Chinese were backward, this did not mean that there was no
hope for them in the future. On the contrary, ran their
argument, China's backwardness was merely another proof
of the need for American leadership, of the responsibility of
the superior race for the inferior.

The net effect of the more favorable view of the Chinese
was to make more plausible the notion that the white race,
and in particular the Anglo-Saxon race, had a mission to perform, that is, the rescue of the underdeveloped peoples of
the world from their backwardness through the means of
applying the techniques of enlightened technical and spiritual progress. The combination of the interests of wealth and
religion had already been developed into a sort of contemporary gospel which encompassed very nicely the needs of the
dominant groups in American society, business, and religion.
China provided a fertile opportunity for applying the new
gospel, an opportunity which was absolutely essential if
Americans were to be able to speak of their ministry to the
world, because how could there exist an American gospel of
salvation unless there were people to save.

Whatever the explanation for the nation's involvement in
China, however—whether because the Chinese were so debased as to be incapable of raising themselves up without
outside aid or because as a race they showed promise of
great achievement if given the proper direction—the under-
lying assumption upon which the entire attitude toward

China rested was that the Chinese as a race were inferior to the white man in every important respect. This assumption shaped the American attitude for decades to follow.

1. C. Campbell Brown, *China in Legend and Story* (New York, 1907).

2. A. H. Mateer, *Siege Days* (New York, 1903).

3. Arthur H. Smith, *China in Convulsion*, 2 vols. (New York, 1901).

4. A. M. Field, *A Corner of Cathay*, as quoted in *Dial* XVIII (April 1, 1895), 211.

5. W. B. Parsons, "Chinese Commerce," *Popular Science Monthly* LVIII (December, 1900), 201.

6. Eustace B. Rogers, "The War in Korea," *Harper's Weekly* XXXVIII (August 11, 1894), 750.

7. R. K. Douglas, "The Origin of Chinese Culture and Civilization," *Literary Digest* I (June 28, 1890), 260–61.

8. "The Awakening of China," (editorial), *Outlook* LXV (August 1, 1900), 855.

9. George Wilson Pierson, *Yale College: An Educational History, 1871–1921* (New Haven, Conn., 1952), pp. 706–13. See also standard histories of the other schools.

10. Brander Matthews et al., *A History of Columbia University 1754–1904* (New York, 1904), p. 298.

11. 5 vols. (New York, 1901), V, 185.

12. Albert Bushnell Hart, *Essentials in American History* (New York, 1905), p. 519.

13. David Saville Muzzey, *An American History* (Boston, 1911), p. 516.

14. See also Henry William Elson, *History of the United States of America* (New York, 1904), p. 846.

15. Charles Johnston, "Prince Hamlet of Peking," *Arena* III (September, 1900), 269.

16. Theodore Roosevelt to Cecil Spring Rice, March 19, 1904, Theodore Roosevelt Papers.

17. T. H. Houston, "A Chinese Holy Island," *Catholic World* LXIII (July, 1896), 445–55.

18. W. A. P. Martin, "The Speculative Philosophy of the Chinese," *American Journal of Theology* I (April, 1897), 289–97.

19. Thomas Magee, "China's Menace to the World," *Forum* X (October, 1890), 204.

20. W. A. P. Martin, *The Lore of Cathay* (New York, 1901).

21. Paul Carus, "Chinese Philosophy," *Monist* VI (January, 1896), 189.

22. "The Chinese Language" (editorial), *Frank Leslie's Popular Monthly* XL (July, 1895), 90–91.

23. "Is Chinese to Be the Universal Language" (editorial), *Literary Digest* XXII (January 12, 1901), 39.

24. "The Great Wall of China," *National Geographic* XI (September, 1900), 374.

25. George E. Anderson, "The Wonderful Canals of China," *National Geographic* XVI (January, 1905), 68–71.

26. C. T. Matthews, "Eastern Asia," *Architectural Record* V (January, 1896), 288–97.

27. Ibid.

28. Samuel L. Gracey to E. H. Conger, May 15, 1900, *Despatches from United States Consuls in Foochow*, National Archives (Washington: Government Printing Office, 1947).

29. Paul Carus, "Filial Piety in China," *Open Court* XVI (December, 1902), 764.

30. Benjamin Ives Gilman, "On Some Psychological Aspects of the Chinese Musical System," *Philosophical Review* I (January, 1892), 54–71.

31. William Barclay Parsons, *An American Engineer in China* (New York, 1900).

32. Ibid.

33. Frederick J. Masters, "Did a Chinaman Discover America?" *Overland Monthly* XXIII (June, 1894), 576–88.

34. "China" (editorial), *Nation* LII (April 23, 1891), 343.

35. W. A. P. Martin, "Book-Making and Bookselling in China" *Publishers Weekly* XLIX (May 23, 1896), 858.

36. William W. Rockhill, Lecture at United States Naval War College, August 5, 1904, Rockhill Papers.

37. William W. Rockhill to Secretary of State John Hay, September 2, 1900, *Despatches from United States Consuls in Shanghai*, National Archives (Washington: Government Printing Office, 1947).

38. Chester Holcombe, *The Real Chinese Question* (New York, 1900), p. 1.

39. Florence O'Driscoll, "In the City of Canton," *Century* XLIX (November, 1894), 62.

40. Julian Ralph, "House-Boating in China," *Harper's New Monthly Magazine* XCI (June, 1895), 3.

41. Review of Julian Ralph, "House-Boating in China," *Our Day* XV (July, 1895), 1.

42. John R. Proctor, "Saxon or Slav?", *Harper's Weekly* XLIII (November 25, 1899) , 1179.

43. Alice Morse Earle, "Travels in the Orient," *Dial* XVIII (April 1, 1895) , 211.

44. Chester Holcombe, *The Real Chinaman* (New York, 1895) .

45. New York, 1907.

46. Ibid., p. 7.

47. W. C. Pond, "The Los Angeles Chinese Mission," *American Missionary* V (May, 1897) , 162.

48. Frederick J. Masters, "Can a Chinaman become a Christian?", *Literary Digest* V (October 8, 1892) , 629–30.

49. George H. Trever, "Lao-Tsze and His System," *Methodist Review* LIX (March, 1899) , 233.

50. W. A. P. Martin, "On Chinese Ideas of Inspiration," *Andover Review* XV (May, 1891) , 472–81.

51. "Chinese as Soldiers" (editorial) , *Literary Digest* XIX (July 22, 1899) , 113.

52. Willard Fisher, "The Currency of China," *Yale Review* V (February, 1897) , 403–427.

53. Holcombe, *The Real Chinaman*, p. x.

54. "China Today" (editorial) , *Harper's Weekly* XL (May 30, 1896) , 538.

55. "Peace in the Orient" (editorial) , *Our Day* XIV (May, 1895) , 218.

56. Marcus L. Taft, "Chinese Education—Past and Present," *Missionary Review* III (September, 1890) , 697–701.

57. "China's Progress" (editorial) , *Public Opinion* XV (June 3, 1893) , 9.

58. Chester Holcombe, "Li Hung Chang," *McClure's Magazine* VII (October, 1896) , 427–36.

59. W. A. P. Martin, *The Awakening of China* (New York, 1907) .

6

China: The American
El Dorado

*"Our geographical position, our wealth, and our energy pre-
eminently fit us to enter upon the development of eastern Asia,
and to reduce it to a part of our economic system."—Brooks
Adams*

The nation formed its first impressions of the Chinese from
its reaction to immigration. Later, when the Geary Act had
laid their fears to rest, Americans readjusted their image of
the Chinese in the United States and in China in order to fit
more nearly with their concept of the nation's role in the
Orient and in the world. As the end of the decade approached, spokesmen for the enlarged view of American
world responsibility labored diligently in an effort to match
developments in China with their interpretation of the opportunities for national leadership. The key idea presented
by such men as Lodge, Roosevelt, Mahan, Beveridge, and
others was that China represented a unique opportunity for
the nation to establish itself as an example for other countries. In this sense China offered an opportunity for moral as
well as material advancement.

Brooks Adams carried the argument even further. As he

surveyed the American scene at the turn of the century, he, along with other thoughtful observers, was bothered by the new emphasis on material values and an apparent decline in the vigor which had marked American individuality. The passing of the frontier seemed symbolic of a basic reorientation in the nation's social structure. Adams was disturbed by the change, and in searching for an answer he turned to history. In *The Law of Civilization and Decay* he presented his theory that within human communities there was present a certain quality of energy—"cosmic energy," as he called it.[1] All human societies utilized this energy on the basis of attitudes of fear and greed. The attitude of fear produced an imaginative society in which religious and militaristic minds exercised control. The attitude of greed caused economic interest to predominate and money to become the source of power. In a society where money ruled, imagination was overcome, centralization took place, and the society ceased to move forward. The result was stagnation.

The present state of society, thought Adams, was a result of the action of historical forces. Human society tended to move from a position of decentralization, or barbarism, to one of centralization, or civilization. Motivation by fear gave way to motivation by greed. Gradually the source of energy was used up until man in his most civilized state lost his desire to improve himself and sought only to protect his position. The progress of civilization from vitality to stagnation was controlled by the forces of history which were akin to natural laws. He saw a grim future ahead for Western civilization and the United States. America had stopped moving, and what energy remained was concentrated on preserving the present level of attainment.

This point of view encouraged Adams to look upon China

with a hopeful eye. If, as his theory indicated, the United States was approaching the point of exhaustion, then some revitalizing act was necessary in order to permit survival. In the past, civilization had regained lost vigor through a barbaric infusion, and Adams felt that China might prove to be a source of such energy. If the United States could absorb the vitality still remaining in Chinese civilization, it would be possible to delay the process of disintegration in which the nation was involved. China occupied an important place in the future because the exploitation of her markets would mean the revitalization of American manufacturing and trade. Without such a stimulus Adams foresaw a bleak future for the nation.

Henry Adams shared many of his brother's concerns about the condition of American society at the turn of the century. His major concern was that the new economic age with its materialistic values had pretty well overcome the humanistic traditions of American society. Admitting that part of his pessimism was the result of literary posture, he believed nevertheless that society had approached and passed a fork in the road and that our present path led into a world of steel and steam where humanistic values would survive only as ornamentation or scrolls wrought in iron.

His concern with the demise of American society led him to view China as the last stronghold of those human values which had existed prior to the coming of the machine, even though he felt initially that the United States had no future in the Pacific.[2] Henry Adams did not accept his brother's elaborate interpretation of the reasons for the problems facing America and, consequently, did not view China as the nation's last hope. He used the imagery of the Virgin and the Dynamo to represent the conflict between humanity and the machine, and he felt that the last dwelling place of the Virgin was in China.

The significance of these two points of view lay not in the validity of their historical interpretation but in the curious process by which China was made to fit into the analysis of Western civilization which these theories offered. In Brooks Adams's eyes the nation should view China much as an expiring animal would view a piece of red meat. Henry Adams thought of China as a great reservoir of clear water, as yet unclouded by the excrement of man's material progress. For both, China represented an opportunity to gratify the peculiar needs of American society as they viewed them at the beginning of the twentieth century.

The ideas of Brooks and Henry Adams, of Lodge, Mahan, and Beveridge, brought into sharp focus the vision of China as a place of moral and commercial opportunity similar in its dimensions to the mythical golden country of El Dorado. China was portrayed as that distant and mysterious place which lay just beyond the grasp of the American nation. If that goal could only be obtained, it would resolve the nation's future uncertainty. It would satisfy the strong sense of mission for both missionaries and nationalists, and it would justify the economic interpretation of American life implicit in the Protestant ethic.[3]

It was for these reasons that the China market became not merely an object pursued by commercial enterprise but a symbol of the nation's potential for world leadership. Exponents of American opportunity in the Pacific were enthusiastic about the commercial possibilities offered by trade with China, and even though these spokesmen were seldom businessmen, it was clear to them that China was a treasure city which awaited the arrival of the United States.

It seemed natural that America should expand. It was part of the very character of Americans that they should constantly be reaching out for more trade, more territory, and more power. No satisfaction could come, according to this view, until Americans had captured the lion's share of the world's commerce.[4] The editor of *Leslie's Weekly* summarized the combined interests of politics and commerce when he said, "Our fingers itch for the world's commerce, and we are reaching out for it in the wake of Old Glory."[5] The star of empire had always moved westward for the United States, he thought, and it continued to move into the Pacific. A young man should now be advised to go not to the West but to the Pacific.

The prospects for trade in the Pacific seemed almost dizzying. If Americans could invade England's manufacturing centers and compete with the Englishman on his own ground, then think what might be done in China, where shipping distances favored the United States.[6] Charles Denby was United States minister to China for many years and a very outspoken supporter of America's opportunity in China. When Americans realized how well their manufactures competed with foreign goods in their own territories, he said, they could not help but be excited over the prospects for their manufactured goods in China. Americans did not need to fear the rivalry of any nation in the Far East because all the advantages which any nation could possess in world trade were held by the United States in China. China was the "greatest market of the world," he said.[7] William Rockhill was a recognized expert on Chinese affairs who possessed insight as well as experience. He thought that if the United States wished to extend its trade to China there was nothing standing in the way. The field was open to Americans, and it was their responsibility to avail themselves of the opportunity.[8]

The *Nation* editorialized in 1899 that "every time the dry bones of China have been shaken up, an increase of commerce has followed."[9] The editor had reference to the recent seizure of territory and the new concessions won by European powers. Repeatedly writers emphasized that the United States had everything to gain from the breaking-down of Chinese resistance to foreign penetration. If China could be opened up to Western influence, the potential of her market was so vast as to stagger the imagination. Writers envisioned hundreds of millions of customers waiting anxiously for American products. Statistics were eagerly advanced showing the amount of trade that would follow if every Chinese used one ounce of wheat a day or purchased one shirt and a pair of pants a year or did whatever he needed to do in order to utilize a certain product. China must be kept open, urged Denby, because one-fifth of the human race awaited the arrival of our goods.[10]

How could it be said that we had no interest in China, wondered the editor of *Overland Monthly*.[11] From Liverpool through the Suez Canal to the Orient it was a distance of thirteen to fourteen thousand miles, whereas from Hawaii to Hong Kong it was less than five thousand miles. The population of China was equal to that of all Europe combined, and in the past ten years trade had increased tenfold. In fact, in just three years, from 1895 to 1898, our export trade to China had increased from $3.5 million to over $11 million. China was a huge giant that was just coming awake, and her appetite for manufactured goods such as watches, bicycles, sewing machines, and electrical supplies would be insatiable when once aroused. In the face of these enthusiastic descriptions few Americans could stand unmoved.

One such person was Henry Cabot Lodge, who in speaking to the Senate on the matter of exclusion legislation in April, 1902, pointed out that even though he was in favor of such legislation, he did not wish the Senate to forget that "it is one of the visions and the dreams of my public life to see American commerce spread over the Pacific and become the leading commerce of the Orient."[12] He strongly supported Brooks Adam's contention that the economic future of the country would be determined in the Far East.[13] "For good or for ill we have come out of our hermitage," and with China in upheaval we were in the world to stay.[14] Virtually the same argument was made by Boies Penrose, senator from Pennsylvania, who suggested that trade with China was in its infancy and there was every possibility that future years would witness the rapid and profitable growth of commercial relationships with China.[15] Other speakers in the Senate during the round of debate over the proposal to extend exclusion legislation for another ten years offered arguments of a similar nature. Time after time the men who rose to speak about the problem of the Chinese hammered on the point that the nation was on the verge of an explosion in international trade which would propel American commercial interests in China into the forefront and leave behind the other trading nations of the West. Even though these same men went on to vote for exclusion, they insisted that the future of America in the Orient was bright beyond imagination.

The prospect of China opening up to railroad and industrial development stimulated several articles in technical journals. *Engineering Magazine,* for example, examined the potential for industrial advance in China and concluded that "the prospects for the next decade point to a demand in Asia for the greatest engineering contrivances and equipment ever known in the history of the world."[16] A whole new continent was being educated to the wants of the civilized world, and Asia would develop into an engineer's paradise where everything needed to be done. Industrial plants, roads, railroads, and buildings all begged for construction. The demand was unlimited, and all the United States had to do was to provide the men and machinery in order to reap the harvest.

The possibilities for American railroad development in China were described encouragingly by travelers also. American performance in this regard, however, was disappointing. An American syndicate finally took part in obtaining a concession for a railroad to be constructed from Hong Kong to Han Kau. The possibilities for profit seemed good because the line would run through areas rich in coal and iron deposits which had never been developed.[17] The American syndicate never capitalized on its opportunity, and far more hopeful signs existed in the sale of railroad supplies. Engines, rails, and couplings were sold in increasing amounts during the last years of the nineteenth century. Most of the material went into the building of the Chinese eastern portion of the Trans-Siberian railway. The topography of China, with its flat land, was ideal for construction purposes, and its large population seemed to offer great potential for a profitable operation. The opinion was voiced that American industrialists were overlooking an important field for development.

Cotton was another commodity whose sale in China encouraged Americans to speak of the vast potential of the Chinese trade. The *North American Review* noted in 1897 that "it is believed that the figures which show that the importation of cotton goods from the United States is annually increasing in value also attest that every advance in civilization by China will open new markets for such goods."[18] The value of cotton exports to China increased 40 percent between 1891 and 1897.[19] Exports of raw cotton increased from slightly over eighty-five thousand dollars in 1890 to almost thirteen million dollars in 1900.[20] These figures need to be qualified, but for those who read them in the 1890s and the early years of the twentieth century, they seemed to provide conclusive evidence of a growing opportunity in China.

Not only was the potential in China of vast proportions but the need of American trade for that market was also great. Several writers warned that the major problem facing the civilized world lay in the fact that its powers of production had outstripped its powers of consumption. The only way to avert serious congestion was to open up new markets and new fields of enterprise in undeveloped areas of the world. Arthur R. Colquhoun, correspondent for *Harper's New Monthly Magazine,* thought that China was a "world necessity."[21] The United States was emerging from her isolation and safety from attack. The best defense now lay in the acquisition of a strong position in world trade. A commentator in *Atlantic Monthly* felt that "a large and increasing foreign market seems to this country . . . an absolute necessity. . . ."[22] He saw such a market opening up in China and elsewhere and thought that unless the United States took advantage of its opportunity, it ran the risk of becoming a slave to the commercial monopoly of other powers.

Because of America's vital need to find new markets, it seemed clear to these same writers that the supreme concern of the United States in China must be a commercial one.

Minister Conger suggested from Peking that regardless of how the policy toward China was developed, whether in cooperation with England and other powers or not, the primary aim must be to protect America's right to share in the exploitation of China's resources.[23] The same point was made in a petition drawn up by several prominent New York firms and presented to the New York City chamber of commerce. The petition urged that the chamber of commerce acquaint the State Department with the desires of business interests in the United States in regard to the protection of trade opportunities in China.[24] George F. Seward, who had served as United States minister to China, urged that the importance of our market in Asia was at least equal to that of South America.[25] Trade was the key to the Far East, said the editor of *Independent*.[26] The desire for trade explained the interests of all the powers in China, including the United States, and we must protect our trade interests from the threat of foreign competition, he concluded.

When the Senate was listening to arguments presented by its Committee on Commerce in March, 1900, for sending a commission to China to gather information which would be helpful in encouraging trade between the countries, it was Jacob Gallinger of New Hampshire who offered the explanation as to why the Senate should support such a project. Not only was our trade much less than it should be, he said, but the nation as a whole was not as familiar as it could be with the tremendous opportunity which existed in China. The promise of Chinese trade was so great that it might well prove to be the single most important factor in determining which nation would come out on top in the coming struggle for world markets. "We need the Chinese trade," he said. "We shall need it even more in the coming years when our factories and workshops shall produce in still larger excess of our home demands. Within the very near future it will be decided what nations are to have their share of the commerce of one-quarter of the world's population."[27] If we did not make an effort to take advantage of the unlimited possibilities of the China market, he concluded, our nation might have to take a back seat to other world powers.

Gallinger was not alone in extolling the potential of trade with the Chinese. Many of his colleagues in the Senate and the House enlivened debates over exclusion legislation with purple descriptions of the fertile fields which lay undisturbed across the Pacific awaiting the touch of the American plow. Approximately eight years before Gallinger addressed his remarks to the Senate, John Morgan of Selma, Alabama, had spoken to the same body in a similar vein. "I look to the opening up of a trade with China on a very immense scale as being something that we are about to arrive at, and we shall find, as I think, that that is one of the most compensatory lines of commerce that we can possibly engage in."[28] China would become a great market for the wheat produced on the Pacific Coast and for the cotton of the South. If we were careful in our relationships with China and did not provoke her unnecessarily, we could look forward to a long period of increasingly profitable trade. Consul Bedloe wrote from Canton of the opportunity for American goods developing in China.[29] The details of this trade would have to be worked out in the future because the port facilities on the Pacific Coast, the necessary risk capital to open new and untried avenues of commercial contact, and the stimulation of a need for American manufactures and produce all lay ahead. But even though problems existed, many congressmen reflected a widespread point of view when they spoke with enthusiasm of the opportunities in the Orient.

The opinion in California emphasized the special interest which that state had in the development of commercial interests in China. The editor of *Overland Monthly* thought that it was the "height of folly to look complacently on the spoilation of the Chinese empire. . . ."[30] Every year our commercial relations with China had been strengthened until now she was practically a close neighbor. It was impossible that the United States should not be vitally interested in commerce with China, and as for California, that state stood to profit greatly from such trade. A few months later the same editor again urged the importance of the Far East for California. "For the moment the interest of the United States in the Chinese question is obscured by the Cuban war cloud; but to California it is of infinitely greater importance that American trade in China shall suffer no injury at the hands of Germany than that the Cuban Junta should receive recognition as a civilized government."[31] American industries, particularly in California, had outrun domestic markets, and the need for overseas outlets was acute.

The vitality of trade interests for some Americans was demonstrated by the boycott against cotton in China in 1905. The National Association of Manufacturers expressed alarm at the threat to a growing trade.[32] Exports of cotton cloth to China for a ten-month period ending in April had risen from sixteen million dollars in 1903 to forty million dollars in 1905.[33] In the same year *Outlook* editorialized that the Chinese had made a shrewd appeal to the American pocketbook which seemed to have much more effect than similar appeals to the American conscience.[34] A circular published by a literary society in Shanghai had urged a social and commercial boycott of all who sold, handled, or received American goods in China, and the editor feared that it was having some effect.

Concern over the impact of the boycott was reflected in the pressure brought to bear on consular officials in China by American business interests. Consul Martin wrote from Hankow that he had sought out the local *Taotai* and had explained to His Excellency Jee the need to end the boycott. He admitted that his efforts had little effect, and in all probability an application of force would prove to be the only effective remedy.[35] Consul Fowler wrote in a similar fashion from Chefoo. He suggested that sixteen years in China had taught him that the only way to end the boycott was through the use of strong pressure. In his view the boycott was being utilized as an issue by a variety of revolutionary groups to stir up antiforeign feeling.[36] He even admitted to Minister Rockhill in another letter that he had actually threatened several Chinese merchants with arrest if they participated in or encouraged the boycott.[37] Apparently some Americans could be moved to action against the Chinese rather easily when their economic interests were threatened.

The increased interest in the potential of trade with China and the increasingly widespread articulation of the apparent opportunity to expand American markets was reflected in a modification of the attitude toward China expressed by national and local legislators, some businessmen, editors, and other commentators on the nation's life. The debates over exclusion legislation at the turn of the century became more restrained, largely due to the oft-expressed idea that if the United States was to expand commercially in the Orient, then it was prudent not to offer unnecessary offense to the Chinese. This did not mean, however, that the provisions of the Chinese exclusion acts would be modified, but it did mean that Americans would be more discreet in describing the need for keeping the Chinese out of the country. There was more support for the argument that the Chinese ought to be classified with immigrants from other countries and not separated out for special treatment because of their supposed racial inferiority. As a matter of fact, it was just this aspect of the exclusion laws which gave the greatest offense to the Chinese, who felt that because they were not included in the general classification of immigrants they were being discriminated against because of their race; and of course, they were right.

Because China was touted by some Americans almost as though it were the new frontier, the freedom to malign the Chinese which had existed heretofore was considerably reduced. Even those who had been most outspoken against the Chinese—legislators and some labor leaders in California—were aware of the contradiction between the concept of the mission and commercial and cultural destiny of the United States in the Far East and the racial denegration of the Chinese at home. This was not to say that West Coast leaders were willing to alter their position on exclusion, but there were indications that even in California, at the heart of the antagonism against the Chinese, a new note was apparent in the old anti-Chinese refrain. People who had characterized all Chinese as barbarians and who had viewed their presence in this country as a threat to the American way of life were now faced with the possibility of establishing increasingly profitable commercial relationships with China as the nation extended its influence into the Pacific. In the South a distinct decrease in the openly expressed hostility toward the Chinese was apparent at the end of the nineteenth century, and several of the senators from cotton states, like Morgan from Alabama, became spokesmen for the cotton manufacturers' interest in an increased market for cotton goods.

The changed emphasis in the American attitude toward China was the result not only of an increased awareness of the concept of commerical opportunity but of a heightened conviction that the salvation of the Chinese people could be accomplished only through the application of large doses of the kind of industrial medicine which seemed, to some Americans at least, to be increasingly available in the nation at the turn of the century. The idea was that Chinese civilization lacked two ingredients which prevented a people with an ancient lineage from crossing the bridge into the modern era. If the technological knowledge and spiritual values of the Western world, particularly as expressed through the United States, were transfused into Chinese life, the result would be a sure and rapid growth from one of the most backward peoples on earth into a new creature of the twentieth century. In this way China was viewed as a kind of El Dorado, a place beyond the setting sun, which once reached would vitalize not only commercial profits but the sense of mission which made American hearts swell as they thought of the impact which their cultural and spiritual gospel would have on a people in need of uplift. The sense of accomplishment and the returning flow of gratitude which would accompany such missionary outreach was gratifying to contemplate.

It was not surprising, therefore, that the change in attitude toward China meant that Chinese commercial opportunities were regarded as more than a means to financial profit. They came to mean also the salvation of China as a new nation. A missionary with years of experience in China reasoned in

1905 that the way to preserve national integrity in Asia was to develop China's material resources, a method "which will not only enrich China and the world, but will help to arouse the people from their age-long sleep; and . . . will serve to maintain the empire's independence."[38] Americans were told that they should join with England whenever possible in exploiting concessions in China. There should never be any fear that the development of concessions was a form of national aggrandizement because they were inherently beneficial and in line with the best material interests of the Chinese empire. Gilbert Reid, a missionary well known for his educational work in China, wrote in *Forum* that America should cooperate with England in China because in this way the welfare of the Chinese people could be speedily protected through commercial development.[39]

The viewpoints of these writers should not be judged from the vantage point of a more cynical age. When the editor of *Harper's Weekly* reasoned that "we want out share of her resources, but we do not want it at the expense of our self-respect," he was voicing the common conviction that humanitarian and commercial interests were compatible in regard to China.[40] Humanitarian and commercial motives were so thoroughly mixed that it was folly to try to separate them. The missionary might be uneasy about capitalizing on the presence of the gunboat, but he seldom saw anything inconsistent in utilizing treaty concessions to further his work. The seasoned diplomat in China spoke of the responsibility of both merchants and missionaries for bringing Western civilization to China.[41]

Secular opinion was sometimes very hard on the missionaries in China, and historians writing about this period have often adopted a similar attitude, discrediting or at least seriously criticizing the work of the missionaries. There was a segment of public opinion during these years, however, which praised the missionaries for assistance in opening up China to Western ideas and particularly to trade. A writer in *North American Review* believed that the missionaries were breaking the hold of the past on China and that no other force of similar effectiveness was present in that country.[42] Businesmen who were interested in the development of a demand for American products in China often voiced the opinion that the introduction of Western ideas into China by the missionaries would help to create a need for American manufactures. It was felt by diplomats and others familiar with the situation in China that whatever the moral justification for missionary work, there was no doubt that the presence of foriegn communities helped to stimulate interest in Western merchandise.

The missionary in China had been sharply criticized for aligning himself with the commercial and national interests of his native land and thereby participating in the advantages won by the force of arms and profits. It was true that missionaries in China profited tremendously from the treaty concessions wrung from the Chinese during the nineteenth century, concessions which allowed them much greater freedom of travel and the protection of gunboats in their campaign to Christianize China. This alliance between the apostles of Christ and the apostles of American nationalism sometimes forced the missionary into tortuous paths of rationalization. In a great many instances, however, the men who worked in China recognized the dilemma in which they were placed when they accepted the protection of their own government in a land where they had come to speak about God's universal concern for all men without regard to national origin.

The alliance between the soldiers of the cross and the soldiers of the gun in a foreign land was in some ways, however, merely a reflection of a similar kind of alliance entered into by the men who sought profits in the missionary's homeland. There is no need to relate here the well-known relationship between Protestantism and business which was first articulated publicly by Max Weber, Ernst Troeltsch, Richard Tawney, and others. Many of the leading exponents of the cult of success through business were leading Protestant clergymen like Henry Ward Beecher, Lyman Abbott, William Lawrence, Horatio Alger, and others whose names were as familiar to the congregations who worshiped God as they were to the congregations who worshiped Mammon. It is fruitless to debate the issue of who allied with whom, but there is no argument about the existence of an alliance between business and Protestantism in American society. It may have been the religious who wished to glorify the success of business leaders who were predominantly Protestant, or it may have been business which sought moral justification for its practices as epitomized by the preaching of Andrew Carnegie. Whatever the sequence, it seems reasonable to conclude that the relationship between missionaries and merchants in China was not surprising in light of a similar alliance between religion and business in the United States.

Since China lacked the power to regenerate herself, it was up to the West to accomplish it for her. The responsibility of the West in the face of China's need was clearly stated by Minister Conger. He wrote to the secretary of state that it was his firm conviction that the only way that China would ever be reformed was through the agency of the foreigner.[43] When the dissolution of China appeared imminent to some observers in 1899, it was again emphasized that China was at the mercy of the European powers. The responsibility of America to throw herself into the struggle in order to preserve the commercial and political interests of both China and the United States seemed clear. A writer in the same year observed that "although civilization may not always seem to help him, it does far better by him when dispensed through forceful foreign hands. . . ."[44] The Chinese could not help himself, and therefore, the only alternative was outside assistance.

If China could not act to save herself, it was necessary to act for her. This line of reasoning had a strong influence on America's commercial policy toward China prior to 1905 and justified the responsibility which Americans felt to act in her behalf. Charles Denby, Jr., who had served as legation secretary in China under his father, admired the Chinese for their strength, intelligence, and endurance. But if it was necessary to humiliate China in order to bring her into the circle of nations, then it must be done because China could never do it herself.[45] China could not adapt to foreign ways through her own efforts because she selected mostly what was bad and ignored the good. Only foreigners themselves could discriminate between these qualities and select what was necessary for China.[46] The Chinese were capable of progress and possessed the necessary resources; all that was needed was for the West to show them the way.

The concept of China as America's opportunity and responsibility dominated the viewpoint of the nation's role in the Pacific. The annexation of the Philippines was urged because it would serve as a strategic point from which to establish the nation's influence in China. *Overland Monthly* spoke for California as well as the entire country when it reasoned that if the United States was interested in trade with China, the only sensible course of action was to utilize the Philippines in that trade.[47] In San Francisco the mayor and the president of the chamber of commerce agreed that the future of California dictated the retention of the Islands.[48] The editor of *Collier's Weekly* reasoned that the magnitude of the nation's present and prospective interest in China's foreign trade required that possession of the Philippines should be in American hands.[49]

So closely was the Philippine question tied in with China's foreign trade that the future prosperity of the Islands was thought to rest on that trade. The former chief of the Bureau of Statistics in the Treasury Department made the point that because of the dependence of the prosperity of the Philippines on the trade with China the question of annexation really involved the whole range of American policy toward China.[50] He argued that even though the United States had not planned to become involved in the Philippines, the possibility of using them as stepping-stones in order to strengthen our trade with China required that they be retained. Shipping interests, farmers and agriculturists, and manufacturing interests paid increasing attention to them, and Congress would do well to take that into consideration. The presence of the United States in the Philippines had enhanced the nation's reputation in the Far East and was sure to have favorable effects on trade. Alfred Thayer Mahan was one in particular who believed that possession of the Islands would increase our military effectiveness in the Far East and was entirely consistent with America's destiny there.[51]

Similar reasons were advanced for the importance of Hawaii. When China awoke, wrote one commentator, the United States would need to have at hand every facility that it possessed in order to profit from the new trade.[52] The nation's real stake in Hawaii was based on the value of the islands as a coaling station and harbor for ships in the Orient trade. The Navy would be similarly strengthened; therefore, the possession of Hawaii could not help but be a favorable factor in trade with China.

The problem of developing a diplomatic course of action in China was not discussed publicly in any but the vaguest terms. On one point, however, Americans seemed fairly well agreed. Any gains made by England would also benefit the United States as her close friend and even ally, if need be, in time of trouble. Charles W. Beresford was a British naval officer who went to China in 1898 on a special mission on behalf of the Associated Chambers of Commerce in England. On his return in 1899 he visited the United States and delivered several speeches emphasizing the unity of British and American interests. William Rockhill was so impressed that he wrote John Hay that "no one person has done more within the last few months to influence public opinion in the United States on the Chinese question than Lord Charles Beresford by his book, 'The Break-Up of China,' and by the speeches he has made."[53] The book was a good summation of the prevailing opinion that "the maintenance of the Chinese Empire is essential to the honor as well as the interests of the Anglo-Saxon race."[54] He pointed out that war could be avoided in China, and the trading and commerical interests of "the whole Anglo-Saxon race" could be secured.[55] When the British spoke of "spheres of influence," Americans interpreted this to mean "open door." Announce-

ments of new concessions won by England for the development of anthracite deposits or the construction of a railroad
were applauded in the United States. Because of the great
opportunities for trade existing in China, the United States
should not fail to support the policy of England whenever
possible. In this way China was looked upon as a source of
mutual profit to England and the United States.

The United States would profit from a relationship with
England in more than just a commercial sense. At the base
of expansionist thinking and concepts of responsibility toward another people were the implicit assumptions of race.
Americans were still feeding on Darwin and his interpreters.
China appeared to be an opportunity for exercising the
Anglo-Saxon genius for leadership. The open-door concept
had been developed into an international agreement by
Anglo-Saxons, and the statesmen who accomplished it desired to preserve the integrity of China as well as the availability of her trade. China was more than a commercial
opportunity; it provided a chance for the United States to
join her Anglo-Saxon brother in ministering to the needs of
an inferior race. As that favorite American naval officer
Alfred T. Mahan put it, "We have undoubtedly a difficult
road before us. I look at it with no light heart, but as a be-
liever in a Divine Providence, I do not lack confidence that
we shall be able to walk in the path in which, as it seems to
me, our feet are set for us."[56] Such an attitude was not
cynical but a serious expression of the burden of responsibility thought to be carried by a superior race.

The attitude toward the role of the nation in the Far East
was clearly illustrated by a cartoon appearing in *Harper's
Weekly* in 1899 captioned "Me and China."[57] The drawing

portrayed Uncle Sam and China standing in a doorway labeled "China." On each side of the door stood England, Russia, France, and Germany. Broken swords, guns, and other armaments littered the ground. Uncle Sam announced: "The door is open gentlemen." American opinion looked upon the role of leadership which the United States had acquired in negotiating the open-door agreement as an example of the sort of responsibility which the nation ought to assume in the world. The announcement of John Hay's diplomatic success was instantly recognized as an indication that the powers in China could look to the United States for leadership in solving the Far Eastern problem. China took on glamour as a place where America could demonstrate her right to be considered a world power.

The concept of China, and particularly of her trade, as the key to a successful future was a vision which attracted many who were caught up in the mystique of a kind of evangelistic nationalism in the 1890s and later. Yet, a more careful reading of contemporary sources and the studies of later scholars raise many questions about the accuracy of the predictions about China. Certainly, the image of China as a magnificent opportunity for the application of the gospel of American industrial know-how and spiritual power was real. But equally real were the circumstances which actually existed in China and which changed the quality of the dream to almost that of a nightmare when any attempt was made to make it the foundation of American policy in the Far East. What many Americans accepted and acted upon as real with regard to China, turned out to be the imagined product of an overpowering desire to see the world through the tinted glass of national egocentrism. The notion itself that

China represented a great business and religious opportunity was certainly real enough, but it was more a result of fond anticipation than frank analysis.

Even during the time when congressmen, editors, and religious leaders were extolling the virtues and promises of increased relationships with China, there were some voices of dissent and qualification. The editor of the influential *Nation* suggested in 1899 that even though those who argued for the need of expanding the nation's influence in the Pacific presented elaborate descriptions of the possibilities awaiting the American trader who journeyed to China, "with every explanation, the mystery of Asiatic trade increases."[58] Despite the predictions of a great future for Chinese trade, he believed that such trade remained very much of a gamble, a point of view also supported by John Barrett, traveler and commentator on Chinese affairs, whose enthusiastic descriptions of the opportunity in China were hedged by the admission that the practical value of the potential trade there depended to a large extent on the development of the necessary facilities for exploiting that trade.[59] There was additional support for Barrett's cautionary advice from others who felt that the potential of Chinese trade was essentially just that, a potential which was not likely to be developed except by the most energetic application of measures to encourage the creation of those instruments vital to an expanding trade.

An article in 1899 by the former chief of the Bureau of Statistics, who wondered how American cotton could compete with that of India, China, and Japan, foresaw a dim future for Western trade in the Orient.[60] In the same year Minister Conger expressed his doubts concerning the cotton market in China.[61] As China and Japan developed their ability to manufacture cotton goods, the cheap cost of labor would force American goods out of the market; and China's vast resources of oil would, when developed, compete disastrously with the American product. Industrial development in China would have a similar effect on the export of steel, machinery, and other industrial goods. Arguing from another angle, there was no certainty that China would develop along lines similar to Japan. Chinese conservatism was a potent drag on progress in China and might very well prevent the Chinese from ever advancing beyond their present state of backwardness. China would probably have to undergo a social revolution before it could become a significant market for Western goods.

Those who saw a great future in China were thought to have overlooked Chinese prejudice against Americans. The cotton boycott was held up as a warning that there were serious obstacles in the path of an increased trade with China. The editor of the *Commercial and Financial Chronicle* quoted an opinion from a letter he had received that "America seems to produce very little that the Chinese need."[62] The writer thought it improbable that China would ever change much since not even war had awakened her to a realization of her backwardness. Sir Robert Hart, who was inspector-general of Chinese customs for many years and became himself a part of Chinese tradition, thought that "China needs neither import nor export, and can do without foreign intercourse."[63] He felt that foreign traders would be able to dispose of their merchandise only "in proportion to the new tastes they introduce, the new wants they create, and the care they take to supply what the demand really means."[64] Those who sought to develop China, to build railroads, open mines, and start industries, should remember that "their eagerness to supply does not necessarily mean a corresponding demand. . . ."[65]

Support for these pessimistic reactions to the exorbitant claims advanced for the China trade comes from an analysis of the problems of industrialization in China at the turn of the century. In reality the Chinese market was a very feeble entity with little likelihood of improving in the foreseeable future. The myth of China's unlimited market of four hundred million people was responsible in part for greater foreign pressure and attention to China's domestic market than to that of Japan and seemed to fascinate Westerners, especially Americans, to the point of overlooking the difficulties of that market.[66] It is interesting to contrast the reaction in England and the United States at about the same time; in the latter popular enthusiasm was widespread but there was very little actual business participation, whereas in the former the decision was made by the Board of Trade that the actual and future market was not worth the effort and expense of developing it. The British Foreign Office also decided that the present trade from its Indian colony was worth far more than the undeveloped potential of the China trade. It was in the United States, where actual trade with China was minimal, that the strongest case was made for the China market.

The failure of the early efforts of the Chinese to industrialize can be attributed to several factors.[67] Chief among these is the inability of the Chinese merchant and government official to develop the kind of motivation which caused the Japanese to undertake successfully the cost of industrialization in the latter part of the nineteenth and early part of the twentieth century. The inability of the Chinese to create and harness for industry an agricultural surplus and the inability of Chinese home industry to win back the market taken over by foreign goods and to expand its feeble industry into a broad manufacturing base were important factors in the failure of China to emerge at this time when its island cousin was working so successfully toward the same goal. Also involved were the failure of China to adopt Western techniques and the unwillingness and ineptness of the government in providing leadership, although it was really asking the impossible to expect the imperial government of China in the 1890s to be able to offer direct and forceful leadership of the kind required to implement an economic revolution. Of all these factors, however, the greatest significance lay with the failure of leadership. "If China is ever to open the mines in the earth she must first open the mines that are in her eyes and mind."[68] Unfortunately the shafts were never sunk until later years, and the gulf between the promise and the reality remained unbridged.

Not only was the market for Western goods doubtful, but the means with which to exploit that market were woefully inadequate. American businessmen were deficient in the knowledge requisite for the effective conduct of commercial relations with the Chinese, partly because there were so few people who were knowledgeable in the ways of the Orient and partly because of the lack of interest in acquiring the information necessary to meet the special needs of the Chinese trade. Diplomatic officers in China often chided American businessmen for their inability to appreciate the most elementary fact that goods sent to China must be well crated in order to withstand shipment. The refusal to extend long-term credit, inexactness in filling orders, and a general attitude of superiority toward the Chinese hindered the development of trade relations. Furthermore, Americans were

not always noted for dealing fairly with Chinese businessmen, and claims for damaged goods were often refused and
the special requirements of Chinese import regulations ignored, resulting in increased expense for the Chinese.

Businessmen were hampered by their inability to understand either the language or the customs of the Chinese. Ad-
vertising circulars were distributed broadside among Chinese merchants, and ineffective as this method was under
the best of circumstances, it appeared ludicrous to the Chinese, most of whom were unable to understand the language
in which the circulars were printed. Because there was almost no understanding of Chinese attitudes toward color
and design, there was no recognition of the importance of
these factors in increasing sales. A red dragon on the pack-
age could boost the sale of an item considerably, whereas an
unlucky design or color—such as white, which was the color
of death—could inhibit sales no matter how good the product was; and the American businessman would be none the
wiser.[69]

The difficulty of finding men who were competent in
business and understood Chinese customs as well as the
language greatly hampered the sale of American goods. Usually the consuls had to be relied upon for contacts with Chinese merchants. But they were already overloaded with
duties, and although they did their best, American goods
were given a poor showing. Consuls continually described
the need for a manufacturers agent to represent American
products to the Chinese.[70] If an agent could not be engaged
to represent the firm, then a sample of the product should
be sent instead of descriptive literature; and exaggerated
claims should be avoided because the Chinese took the
manufacturer at his word until shown otherwise. It is hard to

believe that any American manufacturer who was serious about promoting sales in China would rely on the services of an underpaid and overworked consul, and yet it is evident that very few firms did send representatives. The Baldwin Locomotive Company and the Standard Oil Company were the major exceptions.

The need for information about the China market was recognized sufficiently to stimulate members of both the Senate and the House of Representatives to introduce bills calling for a commission to investigate the special problems of Chinese trade with the idea of encouraging increased exports by providing businessmen with information concerning the special requirements of trade in the Far East. The major debate over the commission occurred in March and April, 1900, in both houses, with support coming from a variety of sources but concentrating among New England cotton manufacturers, boards of trade, associations of manufacturers, and a few West Coast businessmen.[71] Representative W. P. Hepburn of Iowa, cosponsor of the bill with Senator Jacob H. Gallinger of New Hampshire, told the House that he had received petitions and telegrams from all over the country in support of the proposed measure from chambers of commerce and other business groups.[72] William L. Lovering of Massachusetts supported Hepburn in the House by pointing out that though the consuls undoubtedly did the best they could, they were overburdened with detail as it was; what was needed was a well-supported commission to investigate the situation and not only gather information but protect American goods from being copied and sold at a lower price in China. The British, French, and Germans had created such a commission, and it was imperative that the United States follow suit.

But in spite of a letter from the executive committee of the New York Board of Trade and Transportation, the New York Chamber of Commerce, and the National Association of Manufacturers, there was not sufficient interest in the proposed commission to enact the necessary legislation.[73] Champ Clark in the House thought that the consuls could provide all the information necessary and that the museum at Philadelphia had already been established to purchase and display foreign goods and thus accomplished the same objective for which the commission was being constituted.[74] Opposition also came from Democratic Senators James H. Berry of Arkansas and Francis M. Cockrell of Missouri, who protested that the commission was a Republican idea in a Republican administration to reward the worthy faithful with a trip to the Far East.[75] Though the bill was able barely to gather enough support in thhe Senate, it failed to pass the House, and on balance it appears that in spite of some obvious support from a few manufacturers there was no widespread enthusiasm at the time in taking even this halting step toward a practical exploration of the opportunity which some men claimed was the greatest opportunity ever presented to American business interests. Vigorous talk about the promise of the China market continued to echo in the halls of Congress and in the offices of businessmen, Protestant clergymen, and editors, but little concrete action was visible.

Despite the strong interest in America's commercial opportunity in China shown by some people, the general public seemed largely unaware of the Far East. Albert Beveridge complained in 1902 that Americans had "paid little attention to this immeasurable and near-by market and to this uncounted and interesting people."[76] A year earlier the *Chautauquan* was commenting on a petition presented by southern businessmen urging the government to protect the South's interest in China's cotton market, when it noted that the figures pertaining to the cotton trade would be news to most people because few people were even aware that the United States sold cotton to China.[77] In 1905 the effort to develop a profitable trade with China was looked upon as still very feeble. A writer in *Sunset Magazine* described how the people of the Pacific Coast looked toward China as the coming market for exports and how "the little army of commercial Americans who are laying siege to the fortress of Oriental prejudice and European competition have done their work with little support from home."[78]

A curious feature of the attitude toward Chinese markets was that a great many businessmen showed no interest at all in trade with the Orient. The *Commercial and Financial Chronicle,* which claimed to represent the industrial and commercial interests of the United States, published many issues between 1890 and 1905 without a single editorial comment or article on China. The isolated instances where China received attention were in most cases brief news items. American businessmen were criticized by foreign observers for caring only for the present and not the future, and if this were true in regard to trade with China, it might help to explain the lack of interest. If an immediate profit could not be gained, there was no interest in developing commercial relations further. Whatever the reason was, and it may have been partly that business was good elsewhere, it is a clearly observable fact that American commerce moved very slowly into the area of oriental trade.

The difference between the imaginative and vivid picture of commercial opportunity in the Orient painted by enthusiastic interpreters of the nation's new role in world affairs and the reality of American trade with China was brought into sharp focus by an examination of the quantity and dollar value attached to that trade during the 1890s and early 1900s. The use of statistics relating to the China trade is fraught with difficulty because in addition to the chance for error or misconstruction, shipments of American goods were often lumped together by the Chinese with goods from England, and therefore no figures exist which measure precisely the extent to which American goods were treated as British in origin. Furthermore, from the American side there is no way to distinguish with absolute accuracy between goods sold to England and other countries for resale in China and goods purchased by those countries for domestic use. Thus the exact extent, quality, and dollar value of American exports to China and the precise shape of the China market cannot be determined with absolute accuracy. Given these limitations, however, it is possible to analyze the relative fluctuation from year to year in terms of total goods as well as the relative importance of the trade when compared with the totals for trade with all countries.

Perhaps the most startling part of the picture revealed by the figures relating to exports during the period between 1890 and 1905 is the relative insignificance of the Chinese market when compared with total United States exports. In only two years during this period did exports to the Chinese Empire and Hong Kong together rise above 2 percent of the total of exports to all countries.[79] Furthermore, during each of the twelve years between these dates the total China market never exceeded more than approximately 1½ percent of the total of all goods shipped abroad, and in five separate years the total was 1 percent or less. It is possible that even these figures might be high because many of the goods shipped to Hong Kong found their way into the international market rather than into the domestic market in China. It is clear, therefore, that the actual amount of goods sold to China by American firms was inconsequential when compared with the amount of goods delivered to European and other ports. Even our Latin American market, which was small, exceeded the Chinese market in every year except one during this period, and in thirteen of the years was two or more times greater.[80] Our trade with Europe averaged about 75 percent of total exports, and it was on this trade, not the Chinese, that American businessmen focused their attention, in spite of the noisy demand to look to the East for profits.

Not only were our exports to China embarrassingly slight when compared with the total for the nation, but the wide fluctuations from year to year and the imbalance between exports and imports further diminished the quality of the China market. The fluctuations in the dollar value of the trade, indicated by the fact that during most of the period between 1890 and 1905 the difference between one year and the next was seldom less than a 50 percent increase or decrease and in three instances the variation exceeded 100 percent, made it extremely difficult for a manufacturer to gear his production to the market.[81] The businessman who decided to enter the competition for customers in China accepted the risk of wide fluctuation in the demand for his goods. Looking at the Chinese market as a whole, it is apparent that on only three occasions during the years under examination did United States exports to China exceed imports. There is no doubt that the Chinese trade was very important in the thinking of some Americans, but the figures relating to that trade do not indicate that it was of importance to any considerable number of businessmen.

The only exception which must be made concerns the two industries whose products accounted for a lion's share of the country's exports to China. Another look at the classification of goods involved in the China trade reveals that cotton and illuminating oil together accounted for more than 50 percent of exports to China in every year between 1891 and 1905 except one, with the average for those years slightly above 58 percent.[82] The sale of cotton alone in China during this period amounted on the average to more than 40 percent, and in 1902–3 it constituted more than one-half of the value of all goods sold to China.[83] Thus although it was true that trade with the Orient was of little significance to businessmen in general in terms of actual profits, it was highly significant to the manufacturers of fuel oil and cotton cloth. The latter particularly depended upon the Chinese market for a substantial portion of its sales. Between 1891 and 1905 the sale of cotton goods to China constituted never less than 22 percent of all cotton sold abroad and ranged as high as 53 and 56 percent in 1902 and 1905 respectively, with 34 percent representing the average per year for the period.[84] These figures clearly indicate that cotton manufacturers, with one-third of their sales in China, had an important stake in the development and protection of a Chinese market.

After cotton and illuminating oil the most important classifications of goods were railroad supplies, including steel rails and locomotives from the Baldwin works, wheat and flour, and various kinds of machinery. None of these goods however, approached the importance in the market attained by cotton and oil. Manufacturers of these other classes of goods had some interest in developing outlets in China, but the only one of them to act upon its interest in any significant way was the Baldwin Locomotive Company, which sent its agent and mechanics to China and even brought several Chinese back to the United States to be trained in its own shops as mechanics. Yet even this company did not sustain its efforts to develop trade contracts, and when railroading failed to develop strongly in China as it had been thought it would, the interest in a Chinese market for railroad supplies fluctuated widely.[85] Thus with the exceptions of cotton and oil and possibly railroad manufactures, there was very little interest by any segment of the American business community in taking the steps which would lead to a firm and expanding market. There was little enthusiasm for risking capital in an area where little was known about the nature of the market, where demand fluctuated widely, and where profits were uncertain.

Additional insight into the divergence between American hopes for the Far East and the existence of any practical or effective plans for developing the China market on a broad scale is gained from an examination of the viewpoint offered by a number of congressmen with regard to the exclusion legislation of the 1890s and early 1900s. In 1902, for example, when the renewal of the bill passed in 1892 was under consideration, William P. Dillingham read a number of telegrams to the Senate from such business leaders as Claus Spreckels, Levi Strauss, W. C. Ralston, and others protesting that the exclusion of legitimate Chinese merchants as proposed by the new legislation of 1902 would damage trade with China and the development of a port at San Francisco.[86] Dillingham also quoted from John Foord's testimony before the Commitee on Immigration when Foord was representing the American Asiatic Association, the American Association of China, and the American Asiatic Association of Japan, organizations having an interest in trade amounting to three-fourths of the nation's trade with the Far East. Foord testified that further restrictions on Chinese students and merchants seeking entry into the United States would constitute an insult to the Chinese and might well damage our trade.[87] Clarence Carey, a member of the American China Development Company, was quoted by Dillingham as having warned that further restrictions might well hamper the efforts of the company in building a proposed 950-mile railroad beween Hankow and Canton.[88]

Yet the interest expressed by businessmen who were essentially interested in developing the port of San Francisco and the hired representatives of a development company which failed to develop anything in China made little impact on most congressmen. The exclusion question had been solved many years before, and the only congressmen at this point, in 1902, who were feeling any new pressure to change their previous stance were a few from the cotton states who were being urged not to make any moves which might offend the Chinese and reduce the sale of cotton. Senator McLaurin from South Carolina, for example, agreed that everyone was still in favor of exclusion but urged that in the light of the impact of the Boxer Rebellion upon cotton sales perhaps it would be wise to avoid any new restrictions which might offend the Chinese.[89] The same thought was voiced by Jeter C. Pritchard of North Carolina, who put it more strongly when he suggested that new restrictions might well prove disastrous to cotton manufacturers in the South.[90] However, these were small voices of caution in a chorus of assent.

The sentiments of most senators were undoubtedly summed up by John H. Mitchell of Oregon, who introduced the new and even harsher exclusion bill of 1902 by saying,

"It [exclusion] has become one of the great policies of the country, as firmly supported and almost as thoroughly acquiesced in by all political parties, as the Monroe Doctrine."[91] Samuel Gompers testified before the Committee on Immigration that the proposed bill represented the widely held opinions of the members of the American Federation of Labor with regard to the Chinese problem and urged its passage.[92] His testimony, as well as the arguments of the committee, one of whose members was Henry Cabot Lodge, were presented to the Senate. The debate covered the same ground gone over in other years, with the same claims being advanced with regard to the supposed inferiority and undesirability of the Chinese. Opponents of the bill did not question the principle of exclusion but simply argued that no additional restrictions were needed.

The most interesting aspect of the debate was the frank recognition that even though it were conceded that exclusion legislation might have a detrimental effect upon trade with China, there was no question as to which concern had the greater priority. As Henry M. Teller of Colorado put it, "If I knew that the passage of a proper exclusion bill would destroy every dollar's worth of trade between us and China, I should vote for the exclusion bill. I know that the trade between here and China is not worth the admission of Chinese hordes into this country, and if I had to choose between the two I should take the exclusion."[93] Teller was only stating openly the principle upon which senators had been acting for years. The actual interest in trade with China in terms of voter motivation was not nearly sufficient to counterbalance the strong resentment against Chinese immigration. Henry Cabot Lodge spoke enthusiastically and often about the nation's destiny in the Pacific and the opportunity presented by the possibility of trade with China; yet he was firmly on the side of exclusion and justified his position by arguing that domestic regulations relating to immigration would not hurt our commerce in the East.[94]

Lodge may have been satisfied with his own argument, but there is considerable evidence to suggest that the Boxer Rebellion of 1900, which reduced the sale of cotton in China from 40 percent to 28 percent in 1901, and the cotton boycott of 1903, which reduced cotton exports to 17 percent in 1904, the lowest figure since 1891, had considerable influence on the market for American goods in China.[95] If Lodge was right in thinking that exclusion had little or no impact on trade, at least one cotton senator, Furnifold M. Simmons of North Carolina, was unconvinced, and said rather plaintively to the Senate that though he would vote for the bill, it was with considerable reluctance because of the pressure he was under from the cotton manufacturers in his state.[96] The bill in a modified form later passed the Senate with only one negative vote, and it thus became apparent that though the idea of a flourishing Chinese trade was tantalizing, Congress was not prepared to let it affect its legislative acts.

Secretary of State Hay summed up the matter very succinctly in a letter to Minister Conger in Peking. Conger had advised Hay by telegram of the deep resentment felt by the Chinese toward the immigration treaty of 1894. Chinese officials were urging that the treaty be extended for one year at the most and that a new and more favorable treaty be negotiated within the next few months. Hay advised Conger that the suggestion of the Chinese was "quite impossible." Furthermore, he said, "not only would it be impossible to secure the approval of the Senate to another treaty as favorable as the present one, but it would, as well, be doubtful whether any treaty looking toward the regulation of Chinese immigration into the United States could be secured."[97] In the absence of any treaty at all "the way would be open for more stringent legislation by Congress." In view of the hostility against Chinese immigration and the Chinese in general, Hay thought it would be far better to urge the Chinese to be content with the present treaty because a worse condition could easily prevail if it were allowed to lapse.

The ambivalence in the nation's attitude was strikingly apparent. On the one hand, Americans constructed an image of China out of the notion that beyond the waters of the Pacific there arose another continent whose people were so numerous and whose perimeter was so vast that it constituted an opportunity of sufficient magnitude to affect the entire course of the nation's growth. Without access to the Chinese market, it was reasoned, no nation would be able to continue the pace of its economic growth, which in a capitalistic world was keyed inexorably to the availability of markets. The idea of the China market was an integral part of the concept of America's historic place on the enlarging world stage which lay open before the nation at the turn of the century. The desire of Americans to conceive of an economic and spiritual mission to the world created the need for a people toward whom that mission could be directed. China quickly came to represent a market for American goods as well as the American gospel, and without the opportunity which China offered, some of our country's most enthusiastic evangelists of the American way would have had no place to preach.

Yet the dream of economic opportunity and mission, important and influential enough though it was in shaping national attitudes toward the Chinese, was not based upon a reality of circumstances which would allow the vision ever to become more than a hope. Hardheaded businessmen could not be persuaded to risk capital in a market where they felt themselves at a disadvantage because of the lack of information and the solid indicators of sufficient demand to insure profits. The outcome might have been different if American businessmen had aggressively developed a market and pushed hard to expand it. Yet considering the reluctance of the Chinese to embrace innovation, it was unlikely that such a development would occur.

The most imaginative and vocal descriptions of the commercial opportunity in China were advanced not by businessmen but by politicians, diplomats, missionaries, and others who looked favorably upon the idea of America expanding her authority into the world. In large part the cry which arose to encourage the exploitation of markets in the Far East was raised by these men in order to gather support for the concept of America's expanding destiny in Asia. Not so much out of a desire for trade did these men argue but out of an emotional involvement in the vision of America as the prophet of progress through industrial development. If indeed China could be restored through such progress, then America's claim to be the evangelist of a new order in the world was eminently justified.

1. New York, 1895.

2. Henry Adams to Henry Cabot Lodge, August 4, 1891, Lodge papers.

3. Henry Cabot Lodge to Cecil Spring Rice, August 12, 1898, Lodge papers.

4. Charles Austin Bates, "American Trade Expansion," *National Magazine* XV (December, 1901), 292.

5. "Enormous Possibilities of the Pacific Coast" (editorial), *Leslie's Weekly* LXXXVIII (August 4, 1898), 82.

6. Bates, "American Trade Expansion," p. 291.

7. Charles Denby to Secretary of State, John Sherman, February 14, 1898, *Despatches from United States Ministers to China*, National Archives (Washington: Government Printing Office, 1947).

8. William W. Rockhill, "The Outlook in China," *Collier's Weekly* XXVIII (January 4, 1902), 15.

9. "China" (editorial), *Nation* LXVIII (March 30, 1899), 236.

10. Charles Denby to Secretary of State John Sherman, February 14, 1898, *Despatches from United States Ministers to China*.

11. "Our Interest in the Orient" (editorial), *Overland Monthly* XXXII (October, 1898), 382–83.

12. *Congressional Record*, 57th Congress, 1st Session, 1902, 35, pt. 4:4036.

13. Henry Cabot Lodge to President William McKinley, October 22, 1900, Lodge Papers.

14. Henry Cabot Lodge to James Ford Rhodes, June 29, 1900, Lodge Papers.

15. *Congressional Record*, 57th Congress, 1st Session, 1902, 35, pt. 4:4157.

16. Alexander H. Ford, "Russia's Field for Anglo-Saxon Enterprise in Asia," *Engineers Magazine* XIX (June, 1900), 367.

17. "American Enterprise in China" (editorial), *Outlook* LX (October 22, 1898), 460–61.

18. Thomas R. Jernigan, "Commercial Trend of China," *North American Review* LXV (July, 1897), 69.

19. "Statistics of American Trade with China," *Literary Digest* XVI (February 5, 1898), 154.

20. O. P. Austin, "Foreign Markets for Our Manufacturers," *National Magazine* XV (December, 1901), 299.

21. Arthur R. Colquhoun, "Eastward Expansion of the United States," *Harper's New Monthly* XCVII (November, 1898), 933.

22. H. N. Fisher, "The Development of Our Foreign Policy," *Atlantic Monthly* LXXXII (October, 1898), 558.

23. E. H. Conger to Secretary of State John Hay, March 1, 1899, *Despatches from United States Ministers to China*.

24. "The Week" (editorial), *Outlook* LVIII (April 16, 1898), 310.

25. George F. Seward, "A Future for China," *Independent* L (January 13, 1898), 42.

26. "Notes" (editorial), *Independent* L (January 27, 1898), 118.

27. *Congressional Record*, 56th Congress, 1st Session, Vol. 23, pt. 4:3268.

28. *Congressional Record*, 52d Congress, 1st Session, 1892, 23, pt. 4:3565.

29. Edward Bedloe to Secretary of State John Hay, February 11, 1898, *Despatches from United States Consuls in Canton*, National Archives (Washington: Government Printing Office, 1947).

30. "America's Interest in China" (editorial), *Overland Monthly* XXXI (February, 1898), 178.

31. "Our Interest in the Orient," p. 480.

32. "Alarm over the Chinese Boycott" (editorial), *Literary Digest* XXXI (August 12, 1905), 203.

33. Ibid.

34. "The Chinese Boycott" (editorial), *Outlook* LXXX (July 29, 1905), 794-95.

35. W. A. P. Martin to Assistant Secretary of State Robert Bacon, February 8, 1906, *Despatches from United States Consuls in Hankow*, National Archives (Washington: Government Printing Office, 1947).

36. John Fowler to Assistant Secretary of State Robert Bacon, December 18, 1905, *Despatches from United States Consuls in Chefoo*, National Archives (Washington: Government Printing Office, 1947).

37. John Fowler to Minister Rockhill, August 3, 1905, ibid.

38. C. K. Edwards, "China's Renaissance," *Popular Science Monthly* LXVII (September, 1905), 393.

39. Gilbert Reid, "American Opportunities in China," *Forum* XXVIII (April, 1899), 242.

40. "The Partition of China" (editorial), *Harper's Weekly* XLIII (December 9, 1899), 1226.

41. John Goodnow to Senator C. K. Davis, March 17, 1899, *Despatches from United States Consuls in Shanghai*, National Archives (Washington: Government Printing Office, 1947).

42. Francis E. Clark, "The Empire of the Dead," *North American Review* CLXXI (September, 1900), 388.

43. E. H. Conger to Secretary of State John Hay, November 3, 1898, *Despatches from United States Ministers to China*.

44. J. Barnett, "America in the Pacific and the Far East," *Harper's New Monthly Magazine* XCIX (November, 1899), 919.

45. Charles Denby Jr., "The Crisis in China," *Independent* L (January 13, 1898), 42-43.

46. E. H. Conger to Secretary of State John Hay, November 3, 1898, *Despatches from United States Ministers to China*.

47. "Two Opinions of Oriental Expansion" (editorial), XXXII (October, 1898), 364-68.

48. Ibid.

49. "An Alliance with England or with Russia?" (editorial), *Collier's Weekly* XXI (July 2, 1898), 2–3.

50. Worthington C. Ford, "The Commercial Relations of the United States with the Far East," *Annals* XIII (May, 1899), 117.

51. Alfred Thayer Mahan to Colonel Sterling, December 23, 1898, Mahan Papers.

52. John R. Proctor, "Hawaii and the Changing Front of the World," *Forum* XXIV (September, 1897), 34–35.

53. William Rockhill to Secretary of State John Hay, August 28, 1899, Hay Papers.

54. Charles W. Beresford, *The Break-Up of China* (New York, 1899), p. iv.

55. Ibid.

56. Alfred Thayer Mahan to Colonel Sterling, December 23, 1898, Mahan Papers.

57. "Me and China" (cartoon), *Harper's Weekly* XLIII (December 23, 1899), 1312.

58. "Notes" (editorial), *Nation* LXVIII (March 16, 1899), 205.

59. John Barrett, "America in China," *North American Review* LXXV (November, 1902), 660.

60. E. H. Conger to Secretary of State John Hay, March 15, 1899, *Despatches from United States Ministers to China*.

62. "Effects on Trade of the Opening of an Additional Chinese Treaty Port," (editorial), *Commercial and Financial Chronicle* LXI (August 8, 1885), 182.

63. Robert Hart, "China and Her Foreign Trade," *North American Review* CLXXII (January, 1901), 58.

64. Ibid.

65. Ibid., p. 71.

66. Albert Feuerwerker, *China's Early Industrialization* (Cambridge, Mass., 1958), p. 56.

67. Ibid., p. 39.

68. Ibid., p. 36.

69. "Suggestions for Labels and Trade Marks in China" (editorial), *Scientific American* LXXVII (January 22, 1898), 51.

70. W. A. P. Martin to Francis B. Loomis, September 15, 1905, *Despatches from United States Consuls in Hankow*.

71. *Congressional Record*, 56th Congress, 1st Session, 1900, 33, pt. 6:4877.

72. Ibid., pp. 4876–77.

73. Ibid., pt. 4:3268–69.

74. Ibid., pt. 6:4876–77.

75. Ibid., 23, pt. 4:3265.

76. Albert J. Beveridge, "Winning the Markets of the Orient," *Saturday Evening Post* LXXIV (March 22, 1902), 1–2.

77. "Cotton" (editorial), *Chautauquan* XXXIII (September, 1901), 556.

78. Wallace Dana Evans, "American Railroad Building in China," *Sunset Magazine* XV (August, 1905), 368.

79. Statistical Abstract of the United States (Washington, 1906), pp. 154, 179–80, 214, 216, 220.

80. Ibid.

81. Ibid.

82. *Statistical Abstract* (Washington, 1896), pp. 274–76; (Washington, 1906), pp. 214, 216, 220, 269, 283, 286, 288, 304, 323, 333, 337, 341, 349, 426–28, 443.

83. Ibid.

84. Ibid.

85. E. H. Conger to Secretary of State John Hay, December 7, 1898, *Despatches from United States Ministers to China.*

86. *Congressional Record,* 57th Congress, 1st Session, 1902, 35, pt. 4:3938.

87. Ibid.

88. Ibid., p. 3939.

89. Ibid., pp. 4092–93.

90. Ibid., p. 4094.

91. Ibid., p. 3654.

92. Ibid., p. 3665.

93. Ibid., p. 3991.

94. Ibid., p. 4036.

95. *Statistical Abstract of the United States,* pp. 216, 220, 323, 327, 341.

96. *Congressional Record,* 57th Congress, 1st Session, 1902, 35, pt. 4:3771.

97. John Hay to E. H. Conger, February 19, 1904, *Despatches from United States Ministers to China.*

7

The Awakening Dragon

"The idea of endowing an inferior or backward race with the institutions of a more highly developed civilization has at present a great charm for the American people."—Paul S. Reinsch, 1901

"There are three races who can work but there is only one that can swarm."—Rudyard Kipling

The impact of the events of the year 1898 turned many eyes toward the East, and while a great deal of attention was focused on Japan, the Chinese were also scrutinized afresh. The fundamental hostility toward the people of China, particularly those who found their way to American shores, had moderated somewhat because of the effectiveness of the restrictive immigration laws, and a change in emphasis can be discerned in the public remarks of men whose interests caused them to focus on the Far East. The change seems to have been brought about by an increased awareness of the possibility of the nation's participation in Eastern affairs. It was no longer sufficient merely to express hostility toward the Chinese or to argue from a paternalistic point of view for the appreciation of an ancient civilization. The war of 1898 was not the cause of an about-face with regard to national interest in China so much as it was an occasion for the expression of a growing concern among many Americans for the implications of an expanded world position. The Spanish-American War did not alter basic attitudes toward the Chinese, but it did underline the growing need for a more careful articulation of the nation's relationship to China.

In the same year that the United States turned the corner into the twentieth century, the nation faced the task of explaining to itself the nature of its interests in China. Secretary of State John Hay became the focus of public acclaim in 1899 when he won international support for the American version of the old idea of the open door. When the policy was tested the following year during the Boxer Rebellion, Hay reaffirmed the nation's intention to preserve the integrity of China. Cotton-mill owners in New England and cotton producers in Alabama spoke to their representatives in Congress about their concern for the protection and development of a China market. Alfred Thayer Mahan warned that the future greatness of the country hinged upon its ability to control the sea and urged that every effort be made to acquire coaling stations and bases on the China coast. Brooks Adams was certain that any civilization which failed in the competition for markets would begin the turn downhill toward its eventual demise. These and other voices were heard as the effort to articulate the nation's relationship to China went forward.

Workmen who feared and despised the Chinese, politicians who exploited the emotional reaction, clergy and business people who pointed to an unlimited opportunity, all engaged in the debate. Woven into the fabric are the threads of a paradox which forms an inseparable part of the garment of American opinion. The most striking characteristic of the attitude toward the Chinese at the turn of the century was the contrast between the hostility and fear expressed by labor leaders like Samuel Gompers and the enthusiasm and expectation of missionaries to China like Bishop James W. Bashford. When the question of China and the Chinese was raised, whether in parlors, in clubs, or in Congress, enthusiasts for both points of view vied with each other to establish contradictory arguments. On one side was the conviction that if the Chinese ever succeeded in putting their own house in order, they would rapidly engulf the world with their superior ability to survive and even prosper under difficult circumstances that would defeat a less tenacious and talented race. The counter argument held that the Orient constituted the last frontier for the Western world from the standpoint of the economics of international life and from the religious point of view a never-to-be-repeated opportunity to win the world for Christianity. An understanding of the paradox represented by these two points of view is essential to an understanding of the American attitude toward China.

During the latter part of the nineteenth century, Americans in their public pronouncements, with few exceptions, rejected the thought of China as a great or even a potentially great nation. Indeed, China was viewed not as a nation at all but as a racially backward and inferior people. The fact that measuring China by the standards applied to Western nations was grossly unfair escaped the notice of most people, and it was the exceptional person indeed who understood the greatness of China's ancient civilization. But as events in the Far East and at home focused more attention on the Chinese in the world, speculation increased about the future of China as a potentially powerful nation in the Western meaning of that word. In the light of increasingly well articulated interpretations of America's destiny offered by the expansionist-minded, it became neither possible nor desirable to dismiss China with the simple explanation of racial inferiority. Indications of a growing Chinese nationalism plus the need to demonstrate the nation's capacity for leadership combined to change the emphasis of the attitude toward China. The Chinese were still described as an inferior people but were viewed less as an innocuous race in a strange land far across the Pacific and more as an opportunity for American spiritual, cultural, and material know-how to prove itself, and even as a dark barbarian threat if allowed to grow unchecked by the influence of the West.

When China took several tentative steps forward on the world stage at the turn of the century, Americans reacted to the advance essentially in two ways. If it was indeed true that the dragon was awakening, then the nation, and even the world, was faced with either harnessing it or preparing to meet it as an enemy. The challenge posed by the dragon was viewed as an opportunity of the greatest magnitude for Americans to demonstrate their skill at renovating and modernizing backward peoples, thus establishing more firmly than ever the nation's claim to world leadership among the supposedly secondary races of the world. If, on the other hand, the challenge was not met, then the presence of an aroused and populous race represented as serious a threat to the Western world, and to the United States in particular, as had ever been presented. To a few Americans at least the potential entrance of China into the world arena required a renewed effort to articulate the nation's relationship to the flowery kingdom.

China had been "awakening" for so many years that it seemed as though Americans would become discouraged by the repetition. But every fresh claim that purported to show

that China was at last ready to move down the road of progress was met with new interest. The prophetic instinct was
evident in the 1890s among those who thought they had the
special ability of being able to determine the exact moment
when China turned the corner and left her backwardness
behind. Nevertheless, taken together the events of the 1890s
and early 1900s indicated a pattern of China's continuing
awareness of Western ideas.

Americans had already begun to notice signs of change
when Li Hung Chang was recognized and supported as the
greatest proponent of progress in China. Sympathy with his
attempt to win respect for Western methods was widespread.
Schools, hospitals, roads, bridges, and improved agricultural
methods were attributed to his efforts.[1] Chang Chih Tung
was also recognized as an advocate of progress, as was Sheng
Ta-Jen, a leader known for his desire to develop a modern
railway system and whose popularity rivaled that of Li Hung
Chang.[2] Sheng Ta-Jen promised that China could build her
own railroad without foreign aid because she had the capacity
to produce the necessary rails and equipment. This attitude
appealed strongly to the Chinese. The traditional Chinese
antagonism toward railroad development seemed to be breaking down somewhat, and the emperor himself had come out
in support of a line from Peking to Hankow as early as 1890,
according to one report.[3] The new emphasis on railroad
development was thought to be not only a sign of China's
new interest in Western progress but would in itself encourage the growth of additional modern enterprises.

Hunan had long been recognized as the province most opposed to foreign influence. It was the source of anti-Christian
propaganda and of much of the agitation against missionaries and other foreigners. An engineer who had worked in

China observed in 1900, however, that even in Hunan there were signs that Western ideas were making headway.[4] Electric lights glowed in some cities, and explorations to determine the vast extent of the mineral resources were being conducted. The resources of the province, it was felt, would play an important part in the deveolpment of China.

At the urging of K'ang Yu-wie, the emperor embarked upon a series of reforms in the summer of 1898. He proposed the establishment of a new medical college in Peking, the improvement of naval training facilities, and the inauguration of a system of budgeting. These and other reforms prompted a reaction by Empress Dowager Tzu-hsi, but the signs of progress could not be erased. Even the sacred tradition of the literary examinations was bending before the force of Western ideas. At Kuikiang two men were said to have gotten their degrees after only one month of study.[5] They offered themselves for examination in a new subject, chemistry. Even though their mastery of the subject was slight, the examiners knew nothing at all and were afraid not to pass them. One candidate obtained his degree by writing the Ten Commandments and commenting on them in an essay entitled "An Examination of the Great Code of Laws of the Western Nations."[6]

It all added up to the growth of a nationalistic spirit, wrote the consul at Shanghai. Everywhere in China, he said, there were signs of a growing spirit of patriotism. The main cities of the empire were connected now by telegraph, and "newspapers have sprung up in great numbers and are being widely circulated and read, even by the coolies, and the freedom of speech in these newspapers is beyond even our habit."[7] The growth of a public opinion was evident and the nation was becoming unified, he thought. "This new national feeling does not seem to have reached the officials; it is only strong among the mercantile and the lower classes. But it is so strong and thoroughly diffused among these classes that one has the feeling all the time that a leader arising who will stand honestly for the development of China and firmly for the maintenance of the integrity of China will have the country unitedly and enthusiastically supporting him."[8]

In 1905 some perceptive observers noted that, even though the boycott of American goods was a matter for concern, the movement itself testified to the beginnings of Chinese nationalism. The editor of *Literary Digest* agreed that the boycott was disturbing but felt that it was natural for the Chinese to express resentment toward the United States. "We can not expect to maintain an open-door policy for trade in China with one hand, while holding a closed door against Chinese immigration with the other."[9] The Chinese were beginning to realize, concluded the editor, that pressure could be exerted on foreign nations by means of trade restrictions. The list of grievances published by the Chinese guilds in Canton in connection with the boycott clearly indicated the extent of Chinese resentment.[10] Prominent among the objections was the unfair treatment accorded Chinese who sought admittance to the United States. Unnecessary delays, regulations abusive to personal rights, and a general arbitrariness in the American attitude toward the Chinese were condemned.

The importance of China was steadily increasing in Western eyes. As early as 1897 the editor of the *Nation* argued that China had become one of the most important posts in the diplomatic service of the country.[11] Two years later *Harper's Weekly* noted that the post had grown tremendously in importance and that the best possible man should be given the responsibility.[12] The editor wondered why McKinley was removing Denby when he was obviously the best qualified man for the position. In 1903 a professor at the law school of the University of West Virginia pointed out that in the nineteenth century the biggest question was the balance of power in Europe, in which the United States had had only an academic interest. But now in the twentieth century it appeared that the major question would be the balance of power in China, and in this question the United States had very important economic and political interests.[13]

The awakening of China caused American interest in the Far East to increase, though never in a steady or uniform manner. The dramatic events—the massacres of missionaries, the two wars, and the civil strife—each created fresh interest. Although the sum of these incidents was to increase the attention paid to the Far East, there were many slack periods when events in Cuba and the Philippines occupied the center of the stage and the subject of China often did not rate even a passing notice. A careful study of American interest in the Far East would probably reveal that Japan was the real focus of the nation's concern rather than China. Those who paid the most attention to China were men whose interests naturally included the problems of the Far East, such as missionaries, diplomats, political leaders involved in expansionist thinking, and a few businessmen. Popular opinion was often ill-informed, or as a Presbyterian clergyman in Pittsburgh put it in 1903, "The civilized world has shown a disposition to maintain a deep-seated attitude of whimsical disinterestedness" toward China.[14]

However, even though interest in China was mercurial and at its height never very pronounced during these years, the importance of the nation's relationship with the Orient was not minimized thereby. The national image of China was dependent to an overwhelming degree on the kinds of attitude reflected in public statements near the turn of the century. It was not only that these years were the formative ones in the development of the nation's image of China, because certainly the opposition between Chinese immigrants and California workers between 1860 and 1890 was crucial in terms of developing hostility toward the Chinese in this country. Yet the fifteen-year period which saw the nation achieve an awareness of its role in the world was an extremely important one in terms of our attitude toward the Orient. It was a period in which the renewed emphasis upon the importance of American leadership had to be adjusted to events in the Far East as observed from the West. Even though Chinese affairs were not of major interest to the country as a whole, the impressions gained during this period figured importantly in the formation of the Chinese image.

As the attention of Americans was directed increasingly, if unevenly, toward China, questions concerning the nation's interests arose. What did Americans desire in China, and how should they achieve their goals? Two items came immediately to the front in response to this question: the United States sought to preserve the integrity of China and to protect American treaty rights. John Hay outlined these goals when he announced the policy of the open door as the nation's official attitude toward China. The United States, he said, sought a solution to the Chinese problem which would bring about permanent safety and peace, preserve the territorial and political integrity of China, protect all treaty rights, and assure free and open trade.

In a letter to Paul Dana, who was then editor of the *New*

York Sun, Hay explained that the government was opposed to the dismemberment of the Chinese Empire and felt certain that public opinion would not support any attempt to take part in the spoilation of China.[15] At the same time, however, he assured Dana that he was keenly alive to the opportunities offered by an opening-up of China. More than a year later, during the Boxer revolt, when the foreign legations in Peking were held under siege for several weeks and feeling against the Chinese was intense, he insisted to Henry Adams that everything would be done to ensure that in the negotiations following the revolt the integrity of China would be preserved.[16] American policy in China was basically a question of doing what was right, he told the New York Chamber of Commerce in November, 1901. Paraphrasing Proverbs 22:29 he said, "Let us be diligent in our business and we shall stand . . . asking nothing, putting up with nothing but what is right and just. . . ."[17] As Hay envisioned the nation's relationship with China, we would protect our own interests, of course; but it was certainly in the nation's interest to exercise moral leadership through the justness of our actions. We had little else to rely on in the Far East except our own righteousness, as he indicated when he wrote Theodore Roosevelt in 1903 that "the strength of our position is entirely moral."[18] The United States was sincerely interested in maintaining the integrity of China, according to Hay, as well as in the opportunity to establish the righteousness of our leadership.

William Rockhill, who played a crucial role in its formulation, emphasized in 1900 that the United States had proposed the Open Door policy not just to provide commercial opportunity but to defend the integrity of China.[19] Rockhill summarized the fears of many Americans when he said that unless China protected herself either by accepting foreign assistance or by instituting her own reforms she was doomed to partition. It was not likely that China would reform herself; therefore, it appeared that only steady pressure from the West could prevent dismemberment. If China was unable to rescue herself, then the United States had an obligation to do so. Since the European powers seemed determined to pursue their interests in China, America in a very real sense was China's only hope. Many Americans seemed to accept the conclusion that to refuse the responsibility offered by China was to deny the meaning of America's mission to the world.

Lyman Abbott, the editor of *Outlook,* defined the majority view on America's commercial interests in China when he said, "A few gentlemen . . . are announcing that if China is to be partitioned we must have our share, but these gentlemen are without following. The preservation of American treaty rights through any changes of sovereignty which may take place on Chinese territory is seen to mark definitely the limits of our interest in Chinese affairs."[20] Comment from a number of magazines supported this view. Two years later, in 1900, Abbott reiterated his belief that from the beginning the administration had only two distinct objects in view in China. The first was to preserve the integrity of China, and the second was to protect the rights of American citizens and American trade.[21]

There was less certainty about the methods required to implement American goals in China. One viewpoint called for a policy of friendship. The policy of force, of intimidation and criminal aggression, had been followed for many years and it had failed miserably, thought a lawyer who had been deputy consul general in Shanghai from 1889 to 1892.[22]

"All Europe is not strong enough to carry China on its back."[23] Force would not solve the problem; instead, an appeal should be made to China's reason and good will. Albert Beveridge wrote in the *Saturday Evening Post*, "Why should Americans not keep their hands off, cultivate China's goodwill, and increase their trade by force of friendship won by kindness?"[24] Instead of combining with England or Japan, the United States would do better to follow a unilateral policy. Edwin Maxey of the law school at the University of West Virginia offered statistics to show that trade with China had prospered because of America's policy of friendship.[25] The policy of friendliness did not cost anything, and yet it would profit the United States better than any other method.

However, the men who were closest to the China problem shared the common feeling that the only way to deal effectively with the Chinese was by the use of force. Rockhill, who noted the problems which would arise from an attempt to subdue China by superior foreign force, nevertheles said, "I do not think that a good thrashing will hurt China in the least—in fact it is the only tonic which seems to suit that queer country."[26] Ten years after his remarks to Alfred Hippisley, in a lecture delivered at the Naval War College he outlined in considerable detail his program for China. While expressing respect for their industriousness, he observed that in order to control China "direct pressure by armed force will at all times be necessary and the Chinese Government must be kept in as weak, inefficient and corrupt a state as possible. To secure the policy of the sea powers in China, the presence of force is essential, in view of the vacillation and weakness of the Chinese Government."[27] Because of the "racial peculiarities of the people" he did not advise the massive use of force in subverting Chinese ideals to those of

Western civilization. But he left no uncertainty as to the only sure method which could be employed in advancing American interests in China. Rockhill had spent many years in China, but despite his long acquaintance he had no affection for the Chinese.[28]

Alfred Thayer Mahan, though not directly involved in making policy in China, was nevertheless close to the center of the group of men who put together the so-called large policy, which envisioned an American destiny in the Far East and in the world. Mahan's personal attitude toward the Chinese was only expressed by implication in his public statements, but in a letter to his close friend Admiral Bouverie Clark in England he described how he thought the Chinese ought to be treated. "As regards the Chinese, I found out something in my experience with my children. When they have done wrong, if you insist on their doing something they just refuse to do it. Consequently after some disastrous failures, I adopted this plan which always worked. I required no amends at the moment, no promises for the future. I just gave them a good shaking and let them go."[29] Others shared his point of view—for example, Secretary of State John Hay, who told his friend and publisher Henry White that "the open hand will not be so convincing to the poor devils of chinks as the raised club."[30]

Those who were closest to the Chinese, our consuls and ministers in China, showed a nearly uniform dislike for them and a propensity to use force in their relationships with them. Charles Denby, who was American minister to China for many years, was consistently rude and arrogant in his dealings with Chinese officials.[31] It was necessary to be very careful about the rules of protocol when dealing with the Chinese because of the immense importance attached to custom in Chinese life. But Denby went to extremes in insisting on the prerogatives of his office. The consul in Chefoo, John Fowler, noted that he had on more than one occasion threatened Chinese officials with arrest if they acted contrary to American interests.[32] In Foochow the consul advised that he had developed the only sure way to get satisfaction from the Chinese on any matter. Deal harshly with them, he said, and teach them the lesson of force.[33] The consul in Hankow stated that "the Chinese officials gain their points more frequently, by making fair promises and putting off the final settlement of a case."[34] Deception was their normal method, and the only way to bring them to terms was with a club. There were a few exceptions, consuls who were sympathetic toward the Chinese, but the majority were both arrogant and hostile in their relations with them.

The belief in using force in China was widespread. A writer in *Harper's Bazaar* in 1900 thought that "the gatling gun must blaze the way, shrapnel and shell must knock civilization into the most bigoted and most stubborn race in the world."[35] Forceful intervention was suggested as the only means of educating such a backward race in the advantages of Western civilization. Finley Peter Dunne, the great humorist of the era, caricatured this attitude in his inimitable way. Mr. Dooley remarked to his friend Mr. Hennessy that there would probably be a celebration when the troops arrived to civilize China. "I'd like to hear th' sojers singing 'Gawd r-est ye, merry Chinymen,' as they punchered thim with a baynet." Mr. Hennessy thought that it would be a good thing and would civilize the "Chinymen." " 'Twill civilize thim stiff," said Mr. Dooley.[36] A professor of law writing in the *Sewanee Review* objected to the suggestion that a forceful policy meant "shooting Christianity into the heathen."[37] The government would merely be discharging its duty in protecting its interests and its citizens.

The United States had an obligation to protect its interests in China. The preservation of the integrity of the Chinese people and an insistence on the observance of treaty rights would assure the development of these interests. America also had a commitment in China, an obligation to serve as China's protector. The explanations of the Open Door policy offered by Rockhill and Hay, the descriptions of the missionary endeavor, and the claims of a developing market in China. The history of Chinese-American relations was referred to as the story of America's friendship for China. Unpleasant factors in these relations, such as Chinese exclusion, were played down because a new and vocal element in the United States was interested in China not as a barbarian people but as a protégé of the West. It was a part of America's interest to fulfill its duty in regard to China, to preserve intact in American eyes the image of America's responsibility to the world.

This feeling explains to a considerable degree the role of the United States in the peace negotiations concluding the Russo-Japanese War and the interference in Chinese affairs in general during the same period. Theodore Roosevelt was very explicit about the sense of responsibility which he felt toward the Chinese. "I intend to do the Chinese justice," he said, "and am taking a far stiffer tone with my own people than any president has ever yet taken. . . . We must make it evident both that we intend to do what is right and that we do not intend for a moment to suffer what is wrong."[38] His desire to do what was right for the Chinese combined with his strong sympathy for the Japanese help to explain his role as peacemaker at the conclusion of the Russo-Japanese war.[39]

As he wrote to John Hay in 1904, "We may be of genuine service, if Japan wins out, in preventing interference to rob her of the fruits of her victory."[40] His opinion of the Japanese, like Lodge's, had "risen enormously" as a consequence of the war, and he felt that they were a very "high minded" people indeed.[41] There is considerable doubt as to whether the American concept of justice in the Far East was consistent with the best interests of China and Japan as these nations interpreted them. But there can be no question of the sense of responsibility felt by political leaders in the United States.

American responsibility toward China was also closely tied to events in the Philippine Islands. The *Bibliotheca Sacra* discussed the problem at length in 1899.[42] The author, a Congregational clergyman, viewed the struggle in the Pacific as a conflict between races. Because of the growing solidarity of the world, he felt that the United States was "destined" to be in the Far East and the Pacific. Part of this destiny was the obligation of the superior race to the inferior —the obligation to protect and encourage the peoples of the Philippines and China. It made no difference whether the actions of the United States in the Philippines were right or wrong because the nation had a responsibility there. "We cannot unboil the egg."[43] The author believed that God still controlled the destiny of the nation and that the United States could not shirk its duty even if it wanted to.

A similar viewpoint was expressed in the same year by Robert T. Hill of the United States Geological Survey. He described the recent expansion of the nation as due not to governmental intent but to the "culmination of great forces acting through the individual atoms of society which moved irrelevant to any preconceived political plan."[44] The superior quality of American citizens gave them a special responsibility toward the Pacific. No longer could Americns regard the province of their destiny as the land alone; they now owned an interest in the ocean as well. These would be empty words unless the United States took an actual part in guiding the development of the people in the Philippines. The nation's presence in the Philippines could be explained as the working-out of America's destiny, but unless the United States actually exercised the required leadership, the vision of an American mission to the world would fade.

The responsibility of the nation toward China was phrased in similar terms. In 1903 a writer for *Political Science Quarterly* concluded that the United States had now become a world power of the first rank and must accept the responsibility of its new position. "Destiny has forced us into a position which we did not dream of assuming a few years ago."[45] The editor of *Outlook,* Lyman Abbott, wrote in 1900 that the duty of America as a Christian nation was plain.[46] She had a responsibility to fulfill toward China which dictated friendship, not force. The United States could not treat China with inhumanity or take any part in partition because the Chinese expected America to defend China's integrity. A Presbyterian missionary in China and president of Union College at Tungchou wrote, "The hope of China is not in itself. The realization of its best thought must come from without. Christian civilization will bring to China a truer conception of the nature of man, a better understanding of his relations and duties, of his dignity and destiny."[47] If China could not help herself, it was obviously America's duty to assist her.

A mission worker among the Chinese in New York in describing her experiences indicated that one of the basic assumptions which underlay her attitude toward her work was that the Chinese should be Americanized.[48] The reason for this, she felt, was that simply by forcing the Chinese into the mold of American life he could be civilized. The two terms "Americanization" and "civilization' were identical in meaning for her.[49] Civilizing China meant exporting the sentiments closest to American hearts. A professor of physics at Canton Christian College thought that Americans, by helping China to establish her independence, would also be helping her to enjoy the dearest principle of American life, freedom.[50] Paul Reinsch, political economist and later United States minister to China, wrote in *Forum* that the American people were delighted with the idea of exporting American civilization to the Chinese. His remark was made in 1901 when interest in China was at a high point, and it was certainly true that many people at that time were thoroughly enamored of the idea of instilling American principles in the Chinese.

The missionaries were held in high esteem by some who believed that they had an important role to play in fulfilling America's responsibility toward China. Alfred Thayer Mahan expressed the hope that Americans would not neglect to inculcate spiritual as well as material ideas in the Chinese and joined his voice with others who were convinced that the missionaries had the special responsibility of introducing the Chinese to Western values.[52] Shortly after the liberation of the Peking legation in 1900, Sir Robert Hart wrote a rather alarming appraisal of the situation in China.[53] He spoke of the possible threat of a Westernized China and concluded that only foreign intervention or the Christianization of China could prevent such a threat. He thought partition unlikely and Christianization difficult, but recognized the special responsibility of missionaries in China.

Diplomats often spoke favorably of the work of the missionaries and of its importance.[54] A diplomat who was familiar with China believed that "the most potent force for the uplift of this country was not trade or commerce or diplomacy, but Christian missions. The missionaries are doing more for this land than all other foreigners combined."[55] Lyman Abbott quoted the opinions of several well-known diplomats in *Outlook*.[56] John W. Foster, former secretary of state and counselor to the Chinese government in negotiations with Japan, thought that the only hope of China was in Christianity. John Barrett thought that antimissionary talk originated in "the superficial gossip of treaty parts."[57] Furthermore, he said, "we cannot think of withdrawing the messengers of Christianity from Asia until we are ready to withdraw the merchants of commerce and the ministers of diplomacy."[58] Missionaries had a special place in the thinking of those who looked upon China as America's responsibility.

The opinion of missionaries themselves covered a wide range of attitudes during the years from 1890 to 1905. The Chinese had been described as barbarian heathens in order to emphasize their need for Christian teaching. On the other hand, the ability of the gospel to convert any human being, including a "Chinaman," certified to the salvageability of the Chinese. Now the missionaries were caught up in the idea of converting a whole nation to Christianity. The restoration of a single soul to a state of grace was an exciting event in the life of a mission worker, but to be involved in the work of restoring an entire race was a calling worthy of the greatest of men. When missionaries considered their endeavor in this light, the massacre of thousands of Chinese Christians and dozens of missionaries by the Boxers seemed not too great a price to pay.[59]

A Presbyterian missionary in China, writing in *Century Magazine,* described the opportunity. "Let the spirit of Christianity regulate the intercourse of the nations with China in some moderate measure and she will be preserved in her integrity, her institutions will be reformed, and the best capabilities of the people will find their realization in a just and beneficent government and in an enlightened and purified society."[60] No Christian could shirk his duty in the face of such a clear mandate. The deaths of converts at Peking did not seem fruitless, and the slogan calling for the evangelization of the world in one generation did not seem so wide of the mark when an entire civilization was already on its way toward embracing Christianity.[61] The missionary endeavor took on new importance because the church was teamed with the nation in spreading the dual gospels of Christianity and American civilization.[62] Great indeed was the stature of a man participating in such work.

In his book *God's Missionary Plan for the World* James W. Bashford, missionary to China and later a bishop of the Methodist Episcopal church, outlined the opportunities for evangelization in China. Bashford was no fiery-eyed gospel preacher who spoke easily of converting the Chinese in one generation. He was quick to recognize the presumptuous nature of the title of his book and admitted freely to the difficulties which lay ahead for the church in China. At Foochow in 1904, where he was leader of a missionary conference, he emphasized that it had taken 1900 years to evangelize Europe with a great expenditure of time and energy and that the task in China would be no less difficult.[63]

The missionaries sometimes suffered from excessive optimism about their potential reception in China, at least until they had been in the field for a few months. But Bashford recognized fully the detrimental effects of linking the missionary effort to the commercial and military pressures exerted upon the Chinese and urged his colleagues not to rely on privileges won by force lest the objectives of the church be confused with those of commercial and national interests. Yet for all his reasonableness and his ability to understand the difficulties facing the church, he was convinced that this pagan people represented the greatest opportunity which had ever faced a Christian nation.[64] Though he was sensitive to Chinese customs and sympathetic toward their civilization, he was convinced nevertheless that the nation had the power as well as the responsibility to work in conjunction with the Christian church for the redemption of the Chinese people.

As the nation slowly digested the experiences which brought it into a closer relationship with the rest of the world, it savored the delights of its new prominence among other peoples. Power the nation had in ample quantity; it was the awareness of that power which it lacked. As the citizens of the greatest nation in the Western Hemisphere—and possibly, some argued, even in the world—began to understand the magnitude of their position, it was inevitable that they should develop a rationale. Surely it was God who had placed these blessings upon their shoulders, and it was therefore impossible to think of detouring from the path which seemed to lie open before them. The opening-up of China to the harbingers of progress from the West could not be understood as anything less than a God-given opportunity to fulfill the national destiny. Circumstances in China did not warrant such an interpretation, but because Americans never consulted with the Chinese, they were unaware of this. The awakening of China seemed to point only to an opportunity for the people of God in the United States to cross the water bearing the gift of a fullness of life heretofore unavailable to their lesser brethren.

To a few, however, the awakening of China presaged peril rather than opportunity. Although it was true, these people argued, that the undeveloped civilization of an ancient people offered exciting possibilities for commercial and spiritual enterprise, it also offered a threat to the security of the world. Perhaps it would be possible to convert a civilization so foreign to our own in language, custom, and religion, to make it over into a willing vessel into which we could pour the finest distillations of modern civilization. Yet suppose the Western world should fail in spite of the most energetic efforts and the opportunity became transformed into a threat which struck at the roots of the nation's very existence. Fanciful, perhaps, but real enough to a surprisingly large number of Americans who warned of the danger of an aroused Asiatic race bent upon conquering the world. The idea of a "yellow peril" was a minor but persistent note in American thought at the turn of the century, sounded by those who looked upon China as an awakening dragon.

A dominant theme during these years before and after the turn of the century was that of race. The followers of Mahan and the missionaries often saw their problems in terms of racial inferiority or superiority. A fundamental factor of America's relationship with China, whether in contact with the Chinese in the United States or in viewing their civilization from across an ocean, was race. In 1897 a sociologist suggested that races possessed inherent characteristics which made them either superior or inferior.[65] The Chinese possessed characteristics which made them inferior, and unless the superior white race defended itself, the Chinese race would drag it down to an inferior level. The conclusion drawn from this reasoning was that the Chinese, therefore, constituted a "yellow peril."

The racial characteristics of the Chinese were widely discussed, and many who could not have had more than the slightest acquaintance with individual Chinese—perhaps only once a week at the laundry, or even not at all—were willing to speak expertly on the subject. An exception was Edward A. Ross, sociologist and author of several books on China, who thought that the extraordinary power of the Chinese to accommodate to any circumstance was certainly "ominous."[66] From Siberia to Singapore the Chinese could outdo the native people at their own work. This aspect of their racial character made them an extremely dangerous people to the dwellers in every land because under normally competitive conditions the Chinese would always come out on top. The assistant commissioner of immigration in New York City summarized the characteristics which made them a threat.[67] They did not assimilate; they adapted to any circumstances; they degraded the community around them; and there were four hundred million of them. Because the Chinese were a colonizing race that did not mix with adjacent peoples but sought to control them, if given free rein they would eventually become populous in every region and thus establish themselves as the dominant race.

The person who did the most to popularize the concept of the "yellow peril" was probably Kaiser Wilhelm, whose plans for Germany seemed to include the notion of a far-reaching empire touching all parts of the globe and who was quick to take offense at the thought of any curtailment of the extension of German power. The idea of the "yellow peril" was not original with Wilhelm II; Joseph Chamberlain and some of the radical Japanese writers in 1894–95 who warned that China was a permanent disrupter of the peace in Asia elaborated upon the notion of an aroused China as a threat to the world.[68]

It was the German kaiser, however, who stirred up the most interest in the idea with an amateurish painting done in 1895 depicting the ominous danger to Europe posed by the presence of a foreign civilization to the east. The painting, entitled "Nations of Europe, Guard Your Most Precious Possessions," depicted in brilliant colors the archangel Gabriel standing on the edge of a promontory looking into the distance at the dark clouds with flashes of fire in them which had gathered over the valley below, where Europe's cities stood endangered.[69] Standing behind the archangel's spread wings and flaming sword were the powers of Europe represented by women adorned with their national ornaments and variously armed with spears, swords, and sticks. Over them glittered in faint outline the cross, and in the distance their adversary Confucius, the god of the Chinese as it was thought, sat astride a fire-breathing dragon. The picture needed no commentary; it was a sensational theme, and the notoriety of its author helped to increase its popularity.

Theodore Roosevelt, who was really quite fond of the German emperor, did not entirely accept his warning of perils in the East. He distinguished rather between the Japanese and the Chinese. The former, he felt, had accepted the ways of Western civilization, but the latter still stood in the barbarian tradition of their ancestors.[70] Arthur Brown, a good friend of Rockhill's and a Protestant clergyman, analyzed the problem of China and the so-called yellow peril in a series of lectures at Princeton Theological Seminary. Some people made light of the possibility, he warned; but when one considered the size of the population, it was "by no means impossible that some new Jenghiz Khan or Tamerlane" might arise.[71] "Making all due allowance for the exuberance of Emperor William's imagination, the fact remains that his picture represents the thought that is uppermost to-day in the minds of the world's thinkers."[72] The reaction to Wilhelm's idea was far from uniform, but there were many indications that his warning was not completely ignored.

The key idea of Kaiser Wilhelm's "yellow peril," the vision of a horde of Chinese descending upon Europe, was current before Wilhelm made his drawing. One traveler in 1890 said that Chinatown had left a sinister menacing impression, "a sense of this being the first gnawing yellow wave of an overwhelming flood—forced upward by the irresistible propulsion of an overpopulation behind."[73] The Chinese in California were driven to migrate by hunger, it was thought, and more would follow, resulting in the obliteration of civilization. The Chinese were likened to a plague or tide which was threatening to engulf the entire world.[74] European notions of the same sort were quoted in support of the alleged danger from the yellow race, as in the case of the secretary of the London Chamber of Mines who observed in 1900 that in his visits to China he had studied the question thoroughly and was convinced that the peril was a real one and comparatively near at hand.[75] Unless the "great white powers" acted quickly, he thought, the potential threat might develop into proportions which would paralyze the world.

The concept of a horde of Asiatics drew heavily upon the images of Attila and the Huns and of Genghis Khan and the

Mongols for its greatest impact.[76] Sir Robert Hart, an old China hand, in his analysis of the Chinese problem thought "that the future will have a 'yellow question,' perhaps a 'yellow peril,' to deal with, is as certain as that the sun will shine tomorrow."[77] People might laugh at such words as "imperil the world's future," he said, but "twenty million or more of Boxers, armed, drilled, disciplined and animated by patriotic—if mistaken—motives, . . . will carry the Chinese flag and Chinese arms into many a place that even fancy will not suggest today, thus preparing for the future upheavals and disorders never even dreamed of."[78] Hart was accused of writing his account while still under the influence of the ordeal at Peking. But others were also worried by the Boxer uprising and suggested that it was a sign of the future when the "yellow peril" would become a menace to the whole world.[79] Consul Fowler in Chefoo warned that if swift punishment was not forthcoming for the Boxer outrages, "then you can count on the most terrible revolution that this world has ever known, and that revolution is now being planned in Chicago, New York, San Francisco, Singapore, Honolulu, in fact wherever a chinaman can be found that has felt or longs for the benefits of the nineteenth century."[80]

Eight years earlier John H. Mitchell, senator from Oregon, admonished his colleagues to remember that "if those vast hordes of Chinese pagans, led on by the great Mongolian leader, Tamerlane, over five centuries ago, could, not by military prowess, but by the mere force of overpowering numbers, make a track of desolation through Russia and Turkey and Egypt and India which required for centuries the energies of all those nations to obliterate, they may do it again."[81] If the Chinese were capable of doing it with the most primitive weapons, how much more of a threat are they to the

United States now if they succeed in arming themselves with the weapons of modern warfare, he asked. During the same debate over the Scott Act, which was designed to strengthen the already severe restrictions against Chinese immigration, Senator Frank Hiscock of New York supported Mitchell's notion of an Asiatic horde poised on the edge of civilization awaiting an opportunity to engulf the world.[82] In fact, the image of the Chinese as a human mass about to overflow its borders much as water pours from an overfilled bowl was implicit in many of the arguments raised against the Chinese.

George Graham Vest told the Senate that in Kansas City the people were 100 percent opposed to Chinese immigration and completely in support of all restrictive legislation. He emphasized his voting record in favor of restriction and insisted that if the country were to avoid being overcome by a "Mongolian innundation on the Pacific slope or any other portion of the country," strong steps would have to be taken.[83] Vest had voted willingly to prevent the calamity of a Chinese invasion, and he was not alone. Opinion from all parts of the country echoed the same concern over the possibility that Chinese immigration was merely the first wave of a surging flood. In San Francisco the *Daily Evening Bulletin* warned that the Pacific Coast was fighting on the forefront of civilization and the rest of the country would do well to support this outpost, which was bearing the brunt of the fight.[84] From San Francisco to Kansas City, from Portland to Syracuse, the warning was the same: defend the country from the peril of the yellow horde.

With the rise of Japan as a power in the Far East the idea of an Asiatic horde was given additional impetus. Lafcadio Hearn, appreciative student of Chinese culture and author of books and poems on China, thought that if China was compelled to do what Japan had done voluntarily—that is, to accept Western progress—then "the increase of her population within one century will probably be a phenomenon without parallel in the past history of the world."[85] These millions of new members of an inferior race would pose a serious threat to the superior white race. The Russo-Japanese War prompted several writers to warn of the changed situation in Asia. Heretofore it was thought that the destiny of the Far East depended on the actions of Europe; but, noted Seth Low, president of Columbia University from 1890 to 1901, "the war between Japan and Russia has changed all that; at least in the sense that it is now apparent that Japan is a power which must be reckoned with in every movement relating to the Asiatic side of the Pacific Ocean."[86] The "yellow peril" was no longer a myth, concluded a major general in the army, now that the oriental race had a leader.[87]

The original "yellow peril" had been formulated upon the basis of a Chinese threat, but with the rise of Japan it became an "Asiatic peril." Wilhelm II was not all wrong, as many had thought; he was half right. If he had not depicted the menace as China alone, an anthropologist who was professor of prehistoric anthropology at the National University of Washington explained, he would have been entirely correct.[88] The real "yellow peril," thought an editor of the New York *Tribune,* lay in the possibility of the slogan "Asia for the Asiatics," a dream the possible realization of which had fired the imagination of every oriental mind.[89] The "yellow peril" of the Kaiser's imagination, thought another writer, will always remain a mere nightmare. But the threat of an aroused Japan capable of harnessing the vast political energy and natural resources of China was sufficiently real to promote the fear that the next Boxer uprising might be successful. China would become a "fearful menace to Christendom" if the work of the missionaries failed to alleviate the danger.[90]

The specific form which an Asiatic threat might take was thought by many to be industrial rather than military. A writer in *Atlantic Monthly,* author of books and essays on China, believed that "the future danger from China will be industrial, and will begin with the time that she passes under occidental domination."[91] In the early and mid-1890s, when antagonism toward the Chinese in America was still vocal, the threat of commercial competition from China tied in well with the charges against cheap labor. As more was learned about China, it was thought that China's resources in combination with Chinese labor and mechanical ability could prove to be a really serious threat in the world market. A longtime observer of the Chinese wrote in 1899 that an awakened Chinese population would not buy European goods but would instead produce them for themselves.[92] Consequently, China constituted a serious industrial threat for the future.

The phrase "yellow peril" never came into sufficiently wide usage so as to cause it to be written without quotation marks. The employment of such a term to describe the Chinese situation seemed a little strained to most people, if not completely misleading. A writer in *Forum* magazine, who had been legation secretary at Tokyo and later entered the Japanese foreign service where he was awarded the rare honor of the second class of the Order of the Rising Sun, explained the prevailing situation.[93] Those who advocated the theory that the awakening of China's millions would threaten the world as in the time of the Mongolian hordes were indulging in irresponsible speculation. Nor was China to be feared in combination with Japan because such a possibility was a "fanciful absurdity."[94] The peril of China was imaginary, and close cooperation between Japan and China was impossible. A professor of philosophy at Peking University thought that "the 'yellow danger' is a very catchy phrase, good to create a sensation and sell newspapers but there is nothing in it."[95] A missionary in China felt that "surely the Kaiser must be suffering from a severe attack of jaundice if he can detect symptoms of the 'yellow peril' emanating from calm, contemplative Buddha. . . ."[96]

The question remains, however, was there really a "yellow peril"? The answer must be phrased carefully because if it is asked whether the idea had some adherents at the turn of the century, the answer must be yes. But if the question is whether there was an actual threat of the kind envisioned by those who feared the approach to the nation's shores of an inundating mass of Asiatic peoples, then the answer is certainly no. The key idea behind the concept was that large numbers of Chinese were entering the United States yearly and that numerous though they were, they represented only a small portion of the number ready to embark when the opportunity arose. Estimates of the Chinese population in the country ranged as high as 400,000 and seldom less than 200,-000, but the census figures do not support these estimates. Only twice did the Chinese population top 100,000, the first time in 1880 with 105,465, and the second in 1890 with 107,488.[97] During other decades between 1860 and 1910 the population fell to about 70,000 or below, with the exception of 1900.[98] If we recall that the total population of the United States was about sixty-two million in 1890 and with the Chinese population in America at its peak, then it is apparent that even when most numerous the Chinese numbered less than two per thousand Americans.

An objection to this line of reasoning might have been raised at the time by those who suggested that it was not the total number of Chinese in the country which constituted the threat so much as it was the steady increase in the number arriving yearly from China. Yet here too the census records do not support the fears of the anti-Chinese advocates in the country. The number of immigrants arriving from China, principally from the area around Canton, increased substantially each decade between 1850 and 1880, from 41,397 in 1860 to 123,201 in 1880.[99] But in the following years the number of arrivals diminished by more than 50 percent during each of two ten-year periods until it reached a low of 12,792 in 1905.[100] By 1900 it would have been clear to any who wished to consult the record that the Chinese population was not only insignificant in relation to the total population but diminishing both relatively and absolutely. When one recalls all the trouble which arose over the presence of the Chinese, it seems ironic that the total number who came to this country between 1821 and 1905 reached the grand total of only 326,613.[101]

Perhaps the real nature of the concept of the "yellow peril" was not to be found in figures at all but in the attitudes of men. The notion of Asiatic barbarism was strengthened by the concept of a race which possessed the will to flood the world with its own members in an attempt to destroy a more advanced—at least in Western eyes—civilization. Kaiser Wilhelm's Asiatic horde was a useful device to whip up public sympathy for the cause of German imperialism and to justify the spoilation of the Chinese empire. When spokesmen for anti-Chinese sentiment in the United States needed to justify the harshness of the exclusion laws, it was convenient to raise the specter of the great danger which lurked in any assemblage of Chinese in this country. There is no question that some people remained convinced that the presence of the Chinese constituted a real and immediate threat to the security of the nation.[102] Yet other concerns such as the competition presented to the American workingman by the Chinese and the need to justify the notion of caucasian superiority were probably at the root of the matter.

The dragon which emerged from its lair at the end of the nineteenth century was greeted with a mixed response. Men gathered to discuss the meaning and consequences of the event and to plan a course of action. A division between two points of view was soon apparent. On one side were those who wanted to make friends with the beast to see if it could not be made to respond to the ministrations of the society into which it had emerged. On the other side were those who were afraid and who warned that though the creature was docile enough at the moment, it would one day consume the world if a defense were not raised against it. Thus it was that the awakening of the Chinese dragon focused American opinion more sharply than before on the problem of how to relate to China. Few indeed were those who sought an objective appraisal of a people who, although different in sharp degree from the West, were nevertheless quite human and possessed of an ancient and honorable civilization. Their voices were lost in the storm of fear and ridicule which resulted from contact with the Chinese and barely heard amidst the self-righteousness and egocentrism of spiritual and commercial apostles who were intent upon establishing the soundness of their cause. That the struggle of China to win nationhood for itself and self-respect for its people in a modern world was little different from the experiences of Western nations and could be understood in that light was a fact which was essentially lost upon the Americans of that generation.

1. Chester Holcombe, "Li Hung-Chang," *McClure's Magazine* VII (October, 1896), 427–36.

2. S. P. Butler, "A Modern Railroad System for China," *Harper's Weekly* XLI (November 27, 1897), 1175.

3. "Proposed Railroad in China," (editorial), *Scientific American Supplement* XXIX (January 11, 1890), 11687.

4. William B. Parsons, "Hunan: The Closed Province of China," *National Geographic Magazine* VII (October, 1900), 393–400.

5. "China" (editorial), *Missionary Review*, VII (November, 1898), 877.

6. Ibid.

7. John Goodnow to Senator C. K. Davis, March 17, 1899, *Despatches from United States Ministers in Shanghai*, National Archives (Washington: Government Printing Office, 1947).

8. Ibid.

9. "Chinese Boycott of American Trade" (editorial), *Literary Digest* XXX (May 27, 1905), 772.

10. "China and America" (editorial), *Outlook* XXXI (December 23, 1905), 952.

11. "China" (editorial), *Nation* LXV (December 23, 1897), 487.

12. "Our Legation in China" (editorial), *Harper's Weekly* XLIII April 1, 1899), 306.

13. Edwin Maxey, "The Far Eastern Situation," *Sewanee Review* XI (October, 1903), 490–96.

14. W. C. Jameson Reid, "The Asiatic Problem," *Political Science Quarterly* XVIII (June, 1903), 181.

15. William R. Thayer, *The Life and Letters of John Hay*, 2 vols. (Boston, 1915), II, 241.

16. Ibid., pp. 247–48.

17. John Hay, *Addresses of John Hay* (New York, 1906), p. 125.

18. Thayer, *The Life and Letters of John Hay*, II, 369.

19. William W. Rockhill "The United States and the Future of China," *Forum* XXIX (May, 1900), 324–31.

20. "The Week" (editorial), *Outlook* LVIII (January 8, 1898), 103.

21. "The Administration and China" (editorial), *Outlook* LXVI September 8, 1900), 97.

22. Mark B. Dunnell, "The Settlement with China," *Forum* XXXII (February, 1902) , 660.

23. Ibid., p. 661.

24. Albert Beveridge, "The War Cry of the German Empire in the East," *Saturday Evening Post* CLXXIV (March 15, 1902) , 18.

25. Edwin Maxey, "Our Policy toward China," *Arena* XXXIII (May, 1905) , 505–10.

26. William W. Rockhill to Alfred E. Hippisley, October 30, 1894, Rockhill Papers, Houghton Library, Harvard University.

27. William W. Rockhill, Lecture to the United States Naval War College, August 5, 1904, Rockhill Papers.

28. William W. Rockhill to Mrs. Henry Cabot Lodge, December 2, 1900, Lodge Papers.

29. Alfred Thayer Mahan to Bouverie F. Clark, December 19, 1900, Mahan Papers.

30. John Hay to Henry White, May 22, 1903, Hay Papers.

31. Charles Denby to The Tsungli Yamen, July 10, 1897, *Despatches from United States Ministers to China,* National Archives (Washington: Government Printing Office, 1946) .

32. John Fowler to William W. Rockhill, August 3, 1905, *Despatches from United States Consuls in Chefoo,* National Archives (Washington: Government Printing Office, 1947) .

33. Samuel L. Gracey to Assistant Secretary of State, William R. Day, March 7, 1898, *Despatches from United States Consuls in Foochow,* National Archives (Washington: Government Printing Office, 1947) .

34. Levi S. Wilcox to Assistant Secretary of State, David J. Hill, September 8, 1900, *Despatches from United States Consuls in Hankow,* National Archives (Washington: Government Printing Office, 1947) .

35. Edgar Mels, "The Women of China," *Harper's Bazaar* XXXIII (August 4, 1900) , 857.

36. Finley Peter Dunne, "Mr. Dooley: on the Future of China," *Harper's Weekly* XLVI (August 18, 1900) , 782.

37. Edwin Maxey, "The Far Eastern Situation," *Sewanee Review* XI (October, 1903) , 481.

38. Theodore Roosevelt to William W. Rockhill, August 22, 1905, Theodore Roosevelt Papers.

39. Theodore Roosevelt to Henry Cabot Lodge, May 15, 1900, Lodge Papers.

40. Theodore Roosevelt to John Hay, July 26, 1904, Theodore Roosevelt Papers.

41. Henry Cabot Lodge to Theodore Roosevelt, September 7, 1905, Lodge Papers.

42. William Byron Forbush, "America and the Far East," *Bibliotheca Sacra* LVI (October, 1899), 759–74.

43. Ibid.

44. Robert T. Hill, "The Commercial Relations of the United States with the Far East," *Annals* XIII (May, 1899), 131.

45. Reid, "The Asiatic Problem," p. 196.

46. "The Awakening of China" (editorial), *Outlook* LXV (August 1, 1900), 856.

47. D. Z. Sheffield, "Chinese Civilization: The Ideal and the Actual," *Forum* XXIX (July, 1900), 595.

48. Helen F. Clark, "The Chinese in New York," *Century* LIII (November, 1896), 104–13.

49. Ibid., p. 104.

50. C. K. Edmunds, "China's Renaissance," *Popular Science Monthly* LXVII (September, 1905), 393.

51. Paul S. Reinsch, "Governing the Orient on Western Principles," *Forum* XXX (June, 1901), 385.

52. Alfred Thayer Mahan, "The Problem of Asia," *Harper's New Monthly Magazine*, C (April, 1900), 747–59.

53. Robert Hart, "The Peking Legations," *Cosmopolitan* XXX (December, 1900), 121–39.

54. John Goodnow to Senator C. K. Davis, March 17, 1899, *Despatches from United States Consuls in Shanghai*.

55. Francis E. Clark, "The Empire of the Dead," *North American Review* CLXXXI (September, 1900), 387.

56. "Missionaries Vindicated" (editorial), *Outlook* LXVI (October 13, 1900), 383–384.

57. Ibid., p. 383.

58. Ibid.

59. Marshall Bromhall, *Martyred Missionaries of the China Inland Mission* (London, 1900).

60. D. Z. Sheffield, "The Influence of the Western World on China," *Century* LX (September, 1900), 791.

61. Alphonse Favier, *The Heart of Peking* (Boston, 1901).

62. W. A. P. Martin, *The Siege of Peking* (London, 1900).

63. James W. Bashford, *God's Missionary Plan for the World* (New York, 1907), p. 13.

64. Ibid., p. 139.

65. J. S. Stuart-Glennie, "The Conflict of Races: Reply to Criticisms," *Monist* VII (July, 1897), 608–11.

66. Edward A. Ross, "The Causes of Race Superiority," *Annals* XVIII (July, 1901), 69.

67. Z. F. McSweeny, "The Character of Our Immigration, Past and Present," *National Geographic Magazine* XVI (January, 1905), 10.

68. "The Ruling Dynasty of China" (editorial), *Public Opinion* XXIV (January 13, 1898), 43–44.

69. Fritz Cunliffe-Owen, "The Real Yellow Peril," *Munsey's Magazine* XXXI (June, 1904), 327.

70. Theodore Roosevelt to Cecil Spring Rice, June 13, 1903, Theodore Roosevelt Papers.

71. Arthur Judson Brown, *New Forces in Old China* (New York, 1904), p. 305.

72. Ibid., pp. 318–19.

73. Elizabeth Bisland, "A Flying Trip around the World," *Cosmopolitan* IX (May, 1890), 54.

74. William Arthur Cornaby, *China under the Searchlight* (London, 1901), p. 15.

75. Marcus L. Taft, "The 'Yellow Peril,'" *Missionary Review* XXIV (July, 1901), 518.

76. Ibid.

77. Hart, "The Peking Legations," p. 136.

78. Ibid., p. 137.

79. Gordon Casserly, *The Land of the Boxers* (New York, 1903), pp. 297–98.

80. John Fowler to William W. Rockhill, September 25, 1900, *Despatches from United States Consuls in Chefoo.*

81. *Congressional Record,* 52d Congress, 1st Session, 1892, 23, pt. 4:3620.

82. Ibid., p. 3561.

83. Ibid., p. 3626.

84. Editorial, San Francisco *Daily Evening Bulletin,* April 20, 1892.

85. Lafcadio Hearn, "China and the Western World," *Atlantic Monthly* LXXVII (April, 1896), 460.

86. Seth Low, "The Position of the United States among Nations," *Annals* XXVI (July, 1905), 5.

87. James H. Wilson, "The Settlement of Political Affairs in the Far East," *Annals* XXVI (July, 1905), 61–74.

88. Thomas B. Wilson, "The Asiatic Giant," *Overland Monthly* XLVI (July, 1905) , 39.

89. Cunliffe-Owen, "The Real Yellow Peril," p. 322.

90. Sydney Brooks, "Some Results of the War," *North American Review* LXXXI (October, 1905) , 595.

91. Hearn "China and the Western World," p. 454.

92. "China as an Industrial Menace" (editorial) , *Literary Digest* XIX (December 23, 1899) , 763–64.

93. D. W. Stevens, "Japan's Attitude toward China," *Forum* XXX (September, 1900) , 76–85.

94. Ibid.

95. Isaac T. Headland, "The Crisis in China," *Munsey's Magazine* XXXIV (October, 1900) , 15.

96. Taft, "The Yellow Peril," p. 221.

97. *Abstract of the Eleventh Census,* 2d ed. (Washington, 1896) , p. 42.

98. *United States Census, 1920* (Washington) .

99. *Statistical Abstract of the United States* (Washington, 1905) , p. 55.

100. Ibid.

101. Ibid.

102. Alfred Thayer Mahan to Bouverie F. Clark, March 12, 1912, Mahan Papers.

8

Conclusion

One of the most important ingredients in the American image of China was the hostile impression gained from contact with the Chinese in the United States. The Chinese had been encouraged to come to the West Coast by representatives of the Union Pacific Railroad and others who had described in glowing terms the opportunities for employment at high wages. When the demand for their services was sharply reduced in the 1870s by the decline in railroad construction, the collapse of the mining industry, and a general slackening of business activity, their presence tended to irritate the problem of unemployment. Largely because of the desires of California politicians and the added importance given to the far western states by the closeness of the presidential contests, the Chinese problem attained national prominence during the 1870s and 1880s. Anti-Chinese feeling was encouraged and exploited by politicians who sought to campaign on the issue of Chinese exclusion.

Those Americans who got their first impression of China from contact with Chinese laborers were the same workingmen on the West Coast who became antagonistic toward the Chinese because they felt that their jobs were being usurped by Chinese coolie laborers. Others who came into contact with the Chinese in their occupations as domestic servants and laundrymen had a slightly different experience. In these capacities the Chinese did not offer any threat to their employers nor did they particularly recommend themselves except for their reliability in the performance of what were considered to be menial tasks. Occasional visitors of high rank, diplomats, students, and some merchants also provided the possibilities for acquaintance with representatives of the Chinese people. On the whole, however, Americans saw little need to understand the Chinese and tolerated them only because of their usefulness.

The agitation for the exclusion of the Chinese resulted in their being generally condemned. The charges of cheap labor and of immoral behavior by California politicians and writers were repeated across the nation. The admitted weaknesses of the Chinese were magnified and their finer attributes either ignored or made into vices. Writers dwelt at length on the threat posed by the Chinese in the United States, who were described as the advance swell of a great following wave which would inundate the nation. The Chinese were characterized as a threat to American labor and prosperity because they would cause the lowering of wages. Innumerable articles pictured the "Chinaman" in his opium den, as a treacherous criminal, and as an enslaver of women. Because of his inherent immorality, it was thought he would degrade American civilization.

Americans who went to China formed their impressions under a different set of circumstances, although they tended to reach similar conclusions. Some men came as representatives of their government and lived in foreign compounds, where they utilized all the advantages which Western progress could provide in technologically backward surroundings and thrived on an atmosphere of Western superiority. Their attitudes ranged from contempt to paternalism. Businessmen in China were of small number and were allied with the diplomats by necessity as well as by preference; consequently, they reflected similar views. Missionaries saw quite a different side of Chinese life because many of them lived in the interior away from the Europeanized settlements in the port cities and entered far more deeply into Chinese life. Their viewpoint also needs qualification, but it largely reflects an experience which is closer to the heart of China. Travelers to China served as an important means of educating Americans at home. They were usually under no responsibility except to interpret their experiences as they saw fit, and consequently, the increasing volume of accounts of travels in China varied considerably in value and for the most part reflected as much about the traveler as they did about China.

The national attitude toward China was essentially a reflection of the anti-Chinese feeling in the United States. Travelers in China, diplomats, missionaries, and other observers, all emphasized the unfavorable aspects of Chinese civilization. Stories of cruelty, poverty, and debauchery were circulated widely and were believed by most Americans to represent the true picture of China. During the 1890s and early 1900s these impressions changed very little.

Another important ingredient in the American image of China was the attitude of Americans toward their own environment. By 1890 memories of past contacts with other nations were almost extinguished. Therefore, the decade of the 1890s was a period of increasing awareness of outside influences for many Americans. Interpretations of the state of American society, of where it had been and where it was going, were widely spread. Consequently, there were many perceptive observers who were sensitive to the changing role played by the United States in world affairs. They sought to analyze the significance of the changes for other Americans and to construct an image of the nation to fit these changes.

In seeking to reestablish their own identity in the midst of a changing environment, Americans were faced with the problem of China. China seemed threatening because of her vast and ancient civilization. As Americans struggled to interpret their own role in the world, China appeared as a roadblock to working out an interpretation of America's future greatness. Such men as Mahan, Strong, Roosevelt, and Lodge liked to picture America as a prophetic nation which, by capitalizing on its unique experience in creating a completely new government founded on principles of justice and freedom, would show the way to the rest of the world. An increasingly larger number of people responded enthusiastically to such a view during the 1890s.

China threatened this vision of America's destiny because of the uncertainty of her role in the development of the world as Americans knew it. If China was proved to have as great a civilization as that of the West, or perhaps even greater, then the claim of the United States to being the exponent of progress to the world would be threatened. Consequently, according to the American self-image, China had to appear as an inferior, backward, and uncivilized race. To a considerable degree the hostility toward the Chinese both at home and abroad was a result of this need.

As the details of the new image of America were worked

out by expansionists and others at the turn of the century, the characterization of China as uncivilized took on a new emphasis. It was not enough simply to remove the threat which China posed to America's expanding destiny in the world by describing China as inferior. A positive approach was required which would demonstrate the validity of America's claim as a superior race. China was certainly inferior, but she had not moved beyond the power of the United States to redeem her, reasoned the expansionists. With the tools of industrialization and the spiritual values of Christianity, many Americans felt sure that China could be brought to a higher level of achievement.

Two wars, a series of land grabs by European powers, and a revolution, all within the space of a dozen years, forced Americans to consider the prospect that developments in China could affect the future of the United States. The image of China which emerged after the mid-1890s was modified. The general lack of sympathy, ranging from dislike to tolerance, was present, but other attitudes were developing. The concept of an open door to China was firmed into the Open Door policy. There were few who did not hail this as the key to the China question, although probably there were an equal number who actually believed in the preservation of China's integrity.

Those who spoke most often on the subject of China seemed to say that China was important because it was an opportunity for American endeavor. Missionaries emphasized the need for converting the Chinese and thereby justified their efforts. Politicians referred to the need to protect China's integrity and thereby justified America's claim as the harbinger of democracy and freedom. Voices of caution were raised warning of the peril inherent in an aroused Asia.

Benevolence and contempt, sincere concern and opportunism, hope and fear—these were some of the attitudes which constituted the American image of China by 1905.

The most consistent aspect of the image, consequently, was its inconsistency. Americans viewed China in ways which were often conflicting, and the policy of the United States in the Far East reflects that divergence. Americans condemned the Chinese in the United States and in China as inferior barbarians on the one hand, while on the other they spoke of the greatness of Chinese civilization and the responsibility of America to preserve China's integrity. The Far Eastern policy of the United States was supposed to be based in part on the principle of the preservation of China's integrity, but Americans seemed just as willing to share in any benefits resulting from China's exploitation as were the European powers. The Open Door policy was predicated on the principles of integrity for China and equal rights in that country for foreigners, two concepts which were not compatible.

China was spoken of by the followers of Mahan and by such men as Albert Beveridge, senator from Indiana, and Charles Denby, United States minister to China, as the great opportunity for American trade. In 1898 figures could be cited which showed a rapid increase since 1890 in exports to China. On the basis of such evidence China was hailed as an unlimited market for American goods. After 1900, when exports to China showed a marked decrease, these prophets continued to speak of a Chinese market, though now primarily in terms of the unlimited future potential of such a market. Indeed, the figures were disappointing. American businessmen cared almost not at all for the China trade. American consuls in China complained about the apathy of American business. The consuls cited the failure to provide credit, the failure to establish warehouses, the failure to design goods to fit Chinese tastes, and the failure of business to establish a shipping line. In terms of total exports the trade with China was insignificant. The Open Door policy was designed to protect a trade which was practically non-existent.

Religious leaders spoke of the responsibility of Christian churches to minister to the Chinese. China was viewed as an example of the need for American religious leadership in the world. Spokesmen for Anglo-Saxon superiority pointed to China as proof that Americans were of a superior race and destined to play a leading role in elevating the backward areas of the world. Yet even in the face of such assurance China was feared. The Asiatic hordes of Kaiser Wilhelm's "yellow peril" were a phantom, but the fear of them was not, nor was the threat of an industrialized China. "Asia for the Asiatics" was a slogan which created fear in the hearts of many Americans.

Americans looked to China for justification of their new self-image; therefore, it mattered little if the policy of the United States in China was based on actual conditions. What did matter was that any policy had to be formulated in accord with the concept of America's new role in world affairs. The Far Eastern policy of the United States was inconsistent because the American image of China on which it was based was inconsistent. Americans thought they saw in China circumstances which justified their attitude toward the Orient. But in actual fact what Americans saw was only what they wanted to see.

The United States had only one real policy in China from 1890 to 1905: to protect the lives and property of American citizens. When the lives of missionaries and diplomats were threatened during the Boxer uprising, the government contributed troops to the Peking relief expedition. It was the only time that the United States actively intervened in China during these years. The highly touted Open Door policy of Hay and Rockhill was primarily a result of the nation's exaggerated notion of the importance of her role in the Far East. It was received enthusiastically in the United States because it fitted with the concept of the importance of the country's influence in world affairs.

The keystone of American policy in the Far East was the myth of Chinese inferiority. This myth was developed by Americans to shield themselves from the apparent threat to American superiority offered by Chinese civilization. The Far Eastern policy of the United States was designed to fit the American image of China, not the actual conditions existing in the Orient. It was formulated in an unreal atmosphere where visions of racial superiority and world leadership protected Americans from the harsher realities of the power struggle in the Far East. The policy which evolved from these circumstances satisfied the demands of the American image of China but not those of the Chinese problem. The policy was based on broad principles which were never elaborated and on inconsistencies which were never reconciled. Its essential ingredient was the mythical concept of Chinese inferiority and its chief characteristic was ambivalence.

A consistent, carefully thought-out attitude toward China did not exist in the 1890s and early 1900s. Because Americans never really examined the basis for their feelings toward the Chinese, the actual problems in China could not be dealt with. In the early 1890s strong language was often used to describe the Chinese. They were abused verbally and physically by Americans at home and abroad. Shortly, however, such behavior became somewhat inconsistent with the picture painted by expansionists and others imbued with the idea of Anglo-Saxon racial superiority. Open abuse of the Chinese diminished, and was replaced by descriptions of America's paternal responsibility toward China. The Chinese were still viewed with contempt, but now the superiority of America was expressed in more sophisticated ways which accorded better with the view of the United States as a nation with worldwide responsibilities.

The wellspring of these hidden feelings was probably a kind of national insecurity. The American environment was undergoing significant change, and traditional values were being subjected to the stress of a new emphasis on the acquisition of wealth in American society. Would the old way of life be changed so much that it would no longer be recognizable as characteristically American? The question was asked by many. America's position in the world was also changing, and although a growing realization of the nation's relationship to other nations and civilizations stimulated claims of the nation's destiny, it also raised questions as to the real significance and value of the American way of life. Because the myth of American uniqueness and individuality might not withstand scrutiny in the light of China's ancient civilization, Americans responded by emphasizing the bad aspects of that civilization.

The attitude toward China expressed at the turn of the century was formed out of the needs of American ethnocentrism rather than by the realities of the situation in the Far East. It was based upon the concept of unlimited economic opportunity but unsupported by the reality of profits. It was shaped by the fear of contamination through contact with a supposedly barbaric, heathenish people who in reality lived within a tradition of civilization more ancient than that of the West and from whose world the Christian God was partially derived. China was viewed as an unprecedented opportunity for evangelization with little willingness to face the difficulties caused by geographical distance and cultural difference which restricted any chance for success. Running through these conceptions of the China problem was the most important assumption of all; that China as a nation and as a people represented a unique opportunity to establish the American claim to cultural, economic, and moral leadership in the world.

The ideas about the Chinese which derived from these circumstances were as fanciful as they have been lasting, so that even today the nation's point of view has been heavily influenced by conceptions established more than three-quarters of a century ago. To understand these conceptions and the way in which they were formed constitutes the taking of a long step forward toward the establishment of conditions of mutual understanding and trust between the two nations, elements which appear to be essential now more than ever to the survival of the world as we know it.

Selected Bibliography

General

No attempt is made here to offer even a sampling of the many books pertaining to American relations with China. A few studies have been particularly helpful in developing specific topics. On the question of Chinese immigration to the United States, Mary R. Coolidge, *Chinese Immigration* (New York, 1909), Elmer C. Sandmeyer, *The Anti-Chinese Movement in California* (Urbana, Ill., 1939), R. D. McKenzie, *Oriental Exclusion* (1928), and David Te-Choo Cheng, *Acculturation of the Chinese in the United States* (Philadelphia, 1948) are older but still valuable. Gunther Barth, *Bitter Strength: A History of the Chinese in the United States, 1850–1870* (Cambridge, Mass., 1964), Rose Hum Lee, *The Chinese in the United States of America* (Hong Kong, 1960); and S. W. Kung, *Chinese in American Life* (Seattle, 1962) are later studies of value. Treatment of the Chinese by Congress is analyzed by three older and somewhat limited works: Roy L. Garis, *Immigration Restriction* (New York, 1927), Tien-Lu Li, *Congress' Policy of*

Chinese Immigration (Nashville, Tenn., 1916), and Wen Hwan Ma, *American Policy toward China As Revealed in the Debates of Congress* (Shanghai, 1934). For additional insight into American attitudes see Paul A. Varg, *Missionaries, Chinese, and Diplomats* (Princeton, N. J., 1958) and *The Making of a Myth: The United States and China, 1897–1912* (East Lansing, Mich., 1968).

For a general investigation into the problem of bias toward the East, see Harold R. Isaacs, *Scratches on Our Minds: American Images of China and India* (New York, 1958). Albert Feuerwerker, *China's Early Industrialization* (Cambridge, Mass., 1958) and W. P. Fenn, *Ah Sin and His Brethren in American Literature* (Peking, 1933) are helpful on their respective topics. Considerable insight into American prejudice can be gleaned from any dictionary, but Lester V. Berrey and Melvin Van Den Bark, *The American Thesaurus of Slang* (New York, 1942) and A. A. Roback, *A Dictionary of International Slurs* (Cambridge, Mass., 1944) are complete as well as thought-provoking. Jack Burton, *The Index of American Popular Music* (New York, 1957) and Albert F. McLean, Jr., *American Vaudeville as Ritual* (Lexington, Ky., 1965) are suggestive of the extent of the China myth in American culture. Frank L. Mott, *A History of American Magazines, 1885–1905* (Cambridge, Mass., 1957) is indispensable for analyzing periodical literature. William H. Jordy, *Henry Adams: Scientific Historian* (New York, 1952), Timothy Paul Donovan, *Henry Adams and Brooks Adams: The Education of Two American Historians* (Norman, Okla., 1961), Thorton Anderson, *Brooks Adams, Constructive Conservative* (Ithaca, N. Y., 1951), and Arthur F. Beringause, *Brooks Adams* (New York, 1955) were helpful in understanding these men as well as the era.

Manuscripts

The papers of William W. Rockhill on deposit at the Houghton Library at Harvard are extensive and contain considerable correspondence from other important people during this period.

Letters from Minister Charles Denby and consuls Goodnow and Conger are included in the papers as well as correspondence with Alfred Hippisley, whose friendship Rockhill valued highly. Taken altogether, the Rockhill papers provide valuable insights into the attitudes of key people in the area of Chinese-American relations. The letters of John Hay and of Alfred Thayer Mahan at the Library of Congress do not contain extensive references to the Chinese, but their attitudes are clearly visible in numerous instances. The Theodore Roosevelt papers at the Library of Congress and those of Henry Cabot Lodge at the Massachusetts Historical Society in Boston provide key insights into the attitudes of these men and corroborate their public statements on the Chinese. Charles Denby's correspondence is scattered, and there is nothing of particular value in the papers of his grandson Edwin Denby at the Detroit Public Library. The best sources are his diplomatic correspondence and State Department collections in addition to the Rockhill papers.

Government Publications

For an understanding of the point of view of American ministers, *Despatches from United States Ministers to China,* National Archives (Washington, D. C., 1946) is essential. Consular correspondence is contained in *Despatches from United States Consuls,* National Archives (Washington, D. C., 1947) and is organized by city. The reports from Singapore, Amoy, Canton, Chefoo, Foochow, Hankow, and Shanghai are very helpful in assessing the attitudes of the men who occupied these posts. Although most of the correspondence is confined to official topics and the language is guarded, it is possible to read between the lines. In addition to the *Congressional Record* for these years (51st Congress, 1st Session, April, 1890, to 59th Congress, 1st Session, January, 1906), the Lehlbach Report, 51st Congress, 2d Session, House Report No. 4048, March 2, 1891, *Public Documents,* Serial 2890, Vol. 6 (Washington, D. C., 1891), contains extensive testimony concerning the Chinese in the United States.

The pamphlet edited by labor leader Samuel Gompers, *Some*

Reasons for Chinese Exclusion (A.F. of L. Pamphlet [Washington, D. C., 1902]) , and a later one entitled "Arguments against the Passage of a Law to Prohibit Chinese Immigration," 57th Congress, 1st Session, 1902, Pamphlet, *Senate Documents,* Serial 4230, Vol. 12 (Washington, D. C., 1902) present two sides of the issue. The results of the Senate's investigation are contained in Senator Herman Stump's "Report on Chinese Immigration," 52d Congress, 1st Session, House Report No. 255, February 10, 1892, *Public Documents,* Serial 3042, Vol. 1 (Washington, D. C., 1892) . William W. Rockhill's report on his trip to China as special commissioner during and after the Boxer uprising is part of the record of the 57th Congress, 1st Session, *House Documents,* Serial 3042, Vol. 1 (Washington, D. C., 1892) . Wu Ting-Fang, "Letters Pertaining to Mistreatment of Chinese under Exclusion Laws," 57th Congress, 1st Session, *House Documents,* Serial 4268, Vol. 1 (Washington, D. C., 1902) , provides some accounts of experiences of Chinese who encountered American prejudice at firsthand.

Newspapers

The selection of newspapers was determined by the areas where the Chinese tended to congregate. On the West Coast the most important location was San Francisco, where the *Chronicle* and *Examiner* were two of the largest papers, both actively antagonistic toward the Chinese. The San Francisco *Daily Evening Bulletin, Call, Bulletin,* and *Argonaut,* all followed the same pattern concerning the Chinese and tended to be even more sensational than the *Chronicle.* In Los Angeles the *Times* began publication at the turn of the century and reflected the general California anti-Chinese attitude. The Seattle *Daily Times,* Seattle *Post Intelligencer,* and Walla Walla *Union* represented similar attitudes in the Washington and Oregon areas.

Away from the West Coast the *Rocky Mountain News* in Denver and the Great Falls *Tribune,* in Montana were spokesmen for the residents of typical small western towns. In Chicago it was the *Tribune,* in Atlanta the *Constitution,* and in Washington, D. C., the *Post* which expressed surprisingly similar points of view. None of these papers, including the New York *Times* and the Boston *Herald,* were able to refrain from the sensational and even the grotesque in describing the Chinese.

Periodicals

Among magazines published monthly, *Harper's New Monthly Magazine, Century Magazine,* and the *Atlantic Monthly* continued to occupy a leading place in the literary field, followed by *Scribner's Magazine,* which was started in 1887. Other monthly magazines such as *Lippincott's Magazine, Frank Leslie's Popular Monthly,* and *Drake's Magazine* were not as high in quality but had a wider circulation. Among the general monthlies the three most useful magazines, based on their broad appeal, high quality, and diversity of interests, were *McClure's, Munsey's Magazine,* and *Cosmopolitan.* These belonged to the ten-cent magazine phenomenon which played such a large part in boosting magazine circulation and influence in the 1890's. The *Saturday Evening Post* was a five-cent monthly which did not become important until it was taken over by Curtis in 1897.

The monthly review was a popular and widely circulated form of monthly magazine whch carried articles on a wide range of subjects. The most valuable of these were *North American Review, Forum, Arena,* and *Review of Reviews.* The latter tended to annoy readers because of its unwillingness to offer any opinion on the subjects reviewed. *Chautauquan, Bay View Magazine, Eclectic Magazine,* and *Our Day* were monthly review magazines which also carried articles pertaining to China.

Among weekly magazines the general illustrated weeklies were valuable for their responsiveness to matters of current interest. *Harper's Weekly, Illustrated American, Leslie's Weekly,* and *Collier's, the National Weekly* were well-illustrated publications with many short articles on current events. *Independent* and *Outlook* were weekly magazines which began as religious publications under the auspices of the Congregational church. The latter was published as *Christian Union* until 1893 when Lyman

Abbott became editor. They gradually lost their exclusively religious character and became sensitive and widely respected commentaries on American Life. The weekly reviews were lighter in weight than the monthlies, although the *Nation* often included perceptive comments. *Literary Digest, Public Opinion,* and *Living Age* presented summaries of weekly opinion.

The general quarterly magazines of special usefulness included *Current History* and two excellent reviews, *Yale Review* and *Sewanee Review.* Both of the reviews began publishing in 1892, and the former contained many articles on politics, history, and philosophy until 1897 when the advent of the *American Historical Review* caused it to drop its interest in history and concentrate primarily on the field of political science.

Special-interest magazines were useful for the insights which they gave into special areas of American life. The local and regional magazines were represented by such publications as *New England Magazine* and *Bostonian* (later *National Magazine*) in New England, and *Critic* in New York. Chicago was the home of *Dial,* and on the West Coast *Overland Monthly, Californian Illustrated, Out West, Lark,* and *Sunset Magazine* provided many insights into California attitudes toward China. The strongest of these was *Overland Monthly,* which gave Bret Harte a start as editor in 1870 and continued publication until 1923. *Out West,* which changed its name from *Land of Sunshine* in 1894, was published in Los Angeles and devoted to the prosperity of Southern California.

Journals of literary criticism and book reviewing were of limited value except for their editorial comment and occasional reviews of books on China. The best of these were *Bookman, Book Buyer, Current Literature, Literary World,* and *Publisher's Weekly.*

Scholarly journals, though publishing a limited number of articles on China, usually offered the most comprehensive analysis of a given subject. *Annals* contained several extensive articles on trade with the Orient and other subjects related to China. Other journals of this type which published occasional articles on China were *Political Science Quarterly, American Journal* of Sociology, Journal of American Folklore, and Journal of Social Science. The best scholarly journal on China was Royal Asiatic Society, North China Branch, which was published in Shanghai. National Geographic did not develop its present format until 1899, when in that year and the following ones it published many articles on China.

Religious magazines were numerous and of varying quality. Two of the best of these which started as religious periodicals have already been mentioned, Outlook and Independent. Andover Review was an excellent religious and theological monthly which discontinued publication in 1893. Methodist Review and Baptist Review were also of good quality and contained occasional articles on China as well as editorial comment. American Journal of Theology was published by the Divinity School of the University of Chicago, and Charities Review and Lend A Hand specialized in social problems. Catholic World and American Catholic Quarterly Review presented a different viewpoint on some subjects. Missionary Herald, American Missionary, and Missionary Review offered insights into the problems and attitudes of missionaries in China and in the United States.

Journals such as Philosophic Review, Internation Journal of Ethics, and Open Court carried occasional articles on Chinese philosophy and related subjects. The latter was edited by Paul Carus, as was a similar journal in Chicago, Monist. Several scientific journals contained miscellaneous items of interest on China. Science, Scientific American, Popular Science Monthly, and Scientific American Supplement were the best of these. Cassiers, Engineering Magazine, and American Architect published articles on housing and engineering in China. Outing and Nature occasionally described Chinese outdoor activities and other aspects of daily life in China.

The absence of comment on China in the Commercial and Financial Chronicle was consistent with a general lack of interest shown by other business magazines such as the Journal of Commerce and Commercial Bulletin. Women's magazines such as Ladies Home Journal, Woman's Home Companion, and Harper's Bazaar also largely ignored China.

Books

There were a large number of works concerning the Chinese published around the turn of the century. Many travelers to the Orient did not feel that their journey was finished until they had made available an account of their voyage. Most authors like Clive Bingham, *A Year in China, 1899–1900* (New York, 1901), Isabella L. Bird, *The Yangtze Valley and Beyond,* 2 vols. (New York, 1900), Archibald R. Colquhoun, *Overland to China* (New York, 1900), and *China in Transformation* (New York, 1912) emphasized the more disagreeable aspects of their experiences. Accounts like those of Eliza R. Scidmore, *China the Long-Lived Empire* (New York, 1900), William B. Parsons, *An American Engineer in China* (New York, 1900), Edward S. Morse, *Glimpses of China and Chinese Homes* (Boston, 1902) and William E. Geil, *A Yankee on the Yangtze* (New York, 1904) were representative of a cross-section of American attitudes. Somewhat more sympathetic were Edward H. Parker, *John Chinaman and a Few Others* (New York, 1909), Chester Holcombe, *The Real Chinaman* (New York, 1895) and *The Real Chinese Question* (New York, 1900), Herbert A. Giles, *China and the Chinese* (New York, 1902), and Ira M. Condit, *The Chinaman As We See Him* (Chicago, 1900).

Books by missionaries and other clergy connected with the China mission such as James W. Bashford, *God's Missionary Plan for the World* (New York, 1907), W. A. P. Martin, *The Lore of Cathay* (New York, 1901) and the *Awakening of China* (New York, 1907), Henry C. Potter, *The East of To-day and Tomorrow* (New York, 1902), and Arthur H. Smith, *China in Convulsion,* 2 vols. (New York, 1901) emphasized the theme that China's salvation could be achieved only through Christianity. Smith also wrote one of the most influential books on the Chinese, *Chinese Characteristics* (New York, 1894), which along with Charles W. Beresford, *The Break-Up of China* (New York, 1899) determined the attitudes of many toward China and the Chinese. One of the most sympathetic descriptions of the Chinese was by Goldsworthy L. Dickinson, *Letters from John China-*

man (New York, 1901), who described the problems of Chinese-American relations from the former's point of view.

After the Boxer uprising and the siege of Peking many books appeared about the events in China, including Alphonse Favier, *The Heart of Pekin* (Boston, 1901), Gordon Casserly, *The Land of the Boxers* (New York, 1903), W. A. P. Martin, *The Siege of Peking* (London, 1900), A. H. Mateer, *Siege Days* (New York, 1903), and James Ricalton, *China through the Stereoscope* (New York, 1901). Additional descriptions of the problem faced by missionaries were Marshall Bromhall, *Martyred Missionaries of the China Inland Mission* (London, 1900) and Sarah P. Conger, *Letters from China* (Chicago, 1909). William Arthur Cornaby, *China under the Searchlight* (London, 1901) and Arthur Judson Brown, *New Forces in Old China* (New York, 1904), the latter a series of lectures at Princeton and the former a much less scholarly description, were both attempts to analyze the Chinese. C. Campbell Brown, *China in Legend and Story* (New York, 1907) and James Dyer Ball, *Things Chinese* (London, 1900) suggested that Christian salvation was the only alternative for the Chinese heathen.

The Chinese appeared only occasionally in American fiction, but authors like Ambrose G. Bierce, *Collected Works,* 12 vols. (New York, 1909–12), Samuel L. Clemens, *The Writing of Mark Twain,* 22 vols. (New York, 1869–1909), Bret Harte, *The Luck of Roaring Camp and Other Sketches* (Chicago, 1899) and *The Writings of Bret Harte,* 20 vols. (Boston, 1899–1914) all presented Chinese characters and plots involving oriental themes. Frank Norris, *The Octopus* (New York, 1901), *Moran of the Lady Letty* (New York, 1898), and *Blix* (New York, 1902), as well as Rudyard Kipling, *From Sea to Sea: Letters of Travel* (New York, 1914) contained references to Chinese life. Other obscure authors like Atwell Whitney, *Almond-Eyed* (San Francisco, 1878), Claude A. Rees, *Chun Ti-Kung, His Life and Adventures* (New York, 1897), and Charles G. Leland, *Pidgin-English Sing Song* (London, 1876) caricatured the Chinese in uncomplimentary fashion. Two books on Chinatown, Helen F. Clark, *The Lady of the Lily Feet and Other Stories of China-*

town (Philadelphia, 1900) and Arnold Genthe, *Pictures of Old Chinatown* (New York, 1908), were typically unfavorable.

The writings of Brooks Adams, *The Law of Civilization and Decay* (New York, 1895), *America's Economic Supremacy* (New York, 1900), and *The New Empire* (New York, 1902), were influential at the time. In addition to his two major works Henry Adams, *Letters of Henry Adams*, ed. Worthington C. Ford, 2 vols. (Boston, 1930) is helpful, as is John Hay, *Addresses of John Hay* (New York, 1906) and William R. Thayer, *The Life and Letters of John Hay*, 2 vols. (Boston, 1915). Charles W. Stoddard, *In the Footprints of the Padres* (San Francisco, 1901) includes comments on the Chinese on the West Coast.

Index

Abbott, Lyman, 22, 127–28, 138, 180, 223, 225; on American policy in China, 217

Adams, Brooks, 63–66, 169, 208; *The Law of Civilization and Decay*, 164

Adams, Henry, 165–66, 216

Afro-Americans. *See* Chinese compared with other immigrants

Ah Fe. *See* Harte, Bret

Ah Sin. *See* Harte, Bret

Alger, Horatio, 180

American Architect 6, 91

American Asiatic Association, 197

American Asiatic Association of Japan, 197

American Association of China, 197

American China Development Company, 198

American Historical Review, 128

American Journal of Theology, 142

American Missionary, 114

American travelers in China, 246–47; contempt of, for Chinese, 88–91; ethnocentrism of, 104–05; and impact of point of view upon national attitudes, 72; sympathetic toward Chinese, 148–49

Anderson, George, 16

Anglo-Saxon race: future of, in China, 183–84. *See also* China and America

Anti-Chinese riots. *See* Chinese, violence against

Arena, 6, 15, 128

Associated Chambers of Commerce in England, 183

Atlanta *Constitution*, 77

Atlantic Monthly, 6, 171, 235

Attila. *See* "Yellow peril"

Awakening of China. *See* China: awakening of

Bakersfield, Calif. *See* Chinese, violence against

Ingersoll, Robert, 119

Irish. *See* Chinese, compared with other immigrants

Japanese: and immigration, 117; as inferior to Chinese, 117–18; as replacement for Chinese threat, 117–18; Theodore Roosevelt on, 221–22, 230; as weaker race than Chinese, 150–51. *See also* "Yellow peril"

"John Chinaman in New York." *See* Twain, Mark

"John Chinaman." *See* Chinese: stereotype of

Joss house. *See* Chinese: and joss house

Journal of American Folklore, 121, 128

Juneau, Alaska. *See* Chinese, violence against

K'ang Yu-wie, 212

Kearny, Dennis, 5, 8–9, 70

Kipling, Rudyard, 74, 207

Ku Cheng massacre, 86–87

Kuikiang, 212

Land of Sunshine, 121

Law of Civilization and Decay, The. *See* Adams, Brooks

Lawrence, William, 180

Lehlbach, Herman, 75

Lehlbach Report, 75–76

Leslie's Weekly, 81, 167

Li Hung Chang, 148, 211; visit of, to the U. S., 156–57

"Ling-chee." *See* Chinese: system of justice of

Lippincott's Magazine, 123

Literary Digest, 120, 126, 213

Lodge, Henry Cabot, 11, 159, 163, 166, 169, 199–200; on Chinese, 65, 69–70, 84, 98; supports Hay, 70

Los Angeles *Times,* 10

Lovering, William L., 191

Low, Seth, 234

McCreary bill. *See* Chinese, exclusion of

McKinley, William, 214

McLaughlin, Allen, 15

McLaurin, Senator, 198

Madeira, Calif. *See* Chinese, violence against

Magee, Thomas, 142, 157

Mahan, Alfred Thayer, 250; on American mission in China, 159, 163, 166, 184; attitude of, toward Chinese, 65, 219; on large policy, 219; on Philippines and sea power, 182, 208; opposed to "yellow immigration," 40–41; on race and the Chinese, 228; on responsibilities of missionaries in China, 224

Manchus: contrasted with Chinese, 148

Martin, W.A.P., 142, 154, 157, 175

Massacre of Chinese. *See* Chinese, violence against

Masters, Frederick J., 21, 158; "Can a Chinaman Become a Christian?", 153

Maxey, Edwin, 218

Medicine. *See* China: medicine in

Miller, Joaquin, 114–15, 128

Missionaries in China: and conversion of entire nation, 225–26; cooperation of, with political and commercial interests, 179–80, 227; and death of converts, 226; Mahan on special responsibilities of, 228; popular attitudes toward, 178–79, 224–27

—attitudes of, toward Chinese, 99–104, 249–50; evolution of, 134–36; as favorable, 142, 152–54; influence of, upon American attitudes, 134–